PRAISE FO ..ERE

'Heart aching and wonderful.'
– George Caulkin, The Times

'Recommended.'
– Oliver Holt, Daily Mirror

'Brilliantly written, thoroughly researched, warm, passionate and funny.'
– Harry Pearson

'Excellent.'
– David Conn, The Guardian

'An exhaustive and excellent new book about football in the North East.'
– Newcastle Chronicle

'Michael Walker explores [the] rich past, and the unavoidably depressed present, in Up There, an excellent and long-overdue social history of north-east football.'
– When Saturday Comes

'Michael Walker, author of Up There, a brilliant book about football in the North-East, considers the area's unique relationship with the game and asks why it's still strong despite the lack of trophies.'
– The Independent

'Carefully researched and thoughtfully structured, Up There is also very well-written. Walker is highly skilled at combining the best aspects of short-form journalism (anecdotal details, insightful interviews, concise scene-setting) with a more literary eloquence.'
– Of Pitch & Page

'Excellent.... You really need this book in your stocking by the esteemed and well known journalist of this parish, Michael Walker.'
– True Faith podcast

'A book about the boom and bust (and bonkers and barminess) of north-east football.'
– Daniel Taylor, The Observer

'The dislocation between Newcastle – the world's ninth biggest club in terms of income, who attracted an aggregate 100,000 to this season's first two home games – and its supporters is charted impeccably by journalist Michael Walker in a new book, Up There: The North-East Football Boom and Bust, which tells the Ashley takeover story and reveals the myriad ways in which the club has become a clothes horse.'
– Ian Herbert, The Independent

'If you care for the North East and you love football, then Michael Walker's 'Up There,' is a must read. Brilliant.'
– Martin Hardy, Sunday Times

'I can highly recommend Michael Walker's excellent book on North East football 'Up There'. Fascinating read.'
– Mark Carruthers, Non League Daily

UP THERE

THE NORTH-EAST FOOTBALL BOOM & BUST

MICHAEL WALKER

UP THERE

THE NORTH-EAST FOOTBALL BOOM & BUST

MICHAEL WALKER

deCoubertin BOOKS

First published by deCoubertin Books Ltd in 2014.
This revised second edition was published in 2016.

deCoubertin Books, Basecamp, Studio N, Baltic Creative Campus, Jamaica Street, Liverpool, L1 0AH
www.decoubertin.co.uk

ISBN 978-1-909245-34-1

A CIP catalogue record for this book is available from the British Library.
Cover design by MilkyOne Creative.

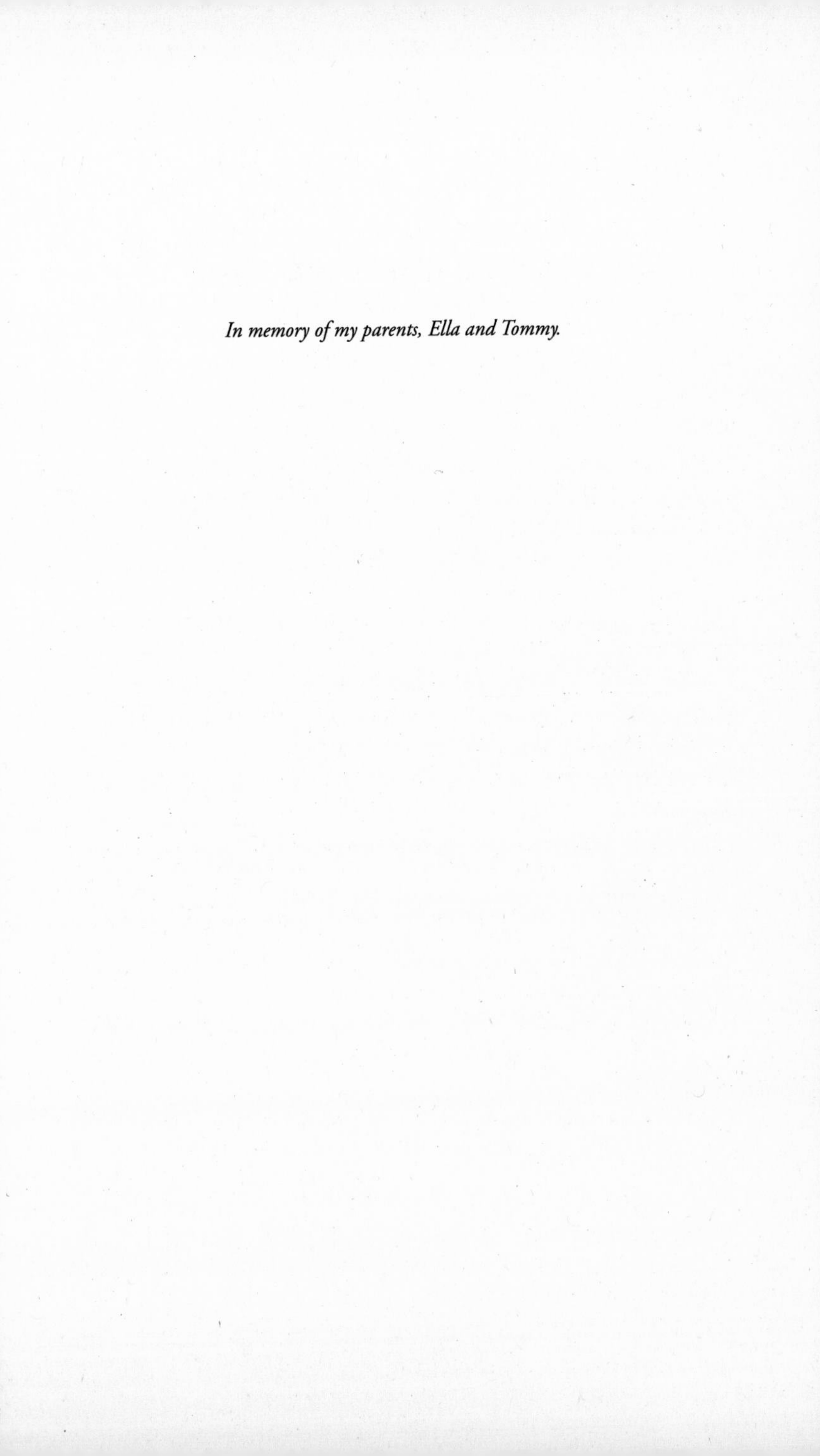

In memory of my parents, Ella and Tommy.

AUTHORS NOTE

THE FIRST EDITION OF THIS BOOK was completed in May 2014. All the book-specific interviews were conducted between December 2013 and May 2014.

As such the book is of a time and place. If there was an aim, it was to convey the importance of football to the north-east of England historically and today, to chart the attachment despite a formidable lack of recent success, and to look at the game in the wider context of north-east society. It also acts as a modern history of the major clubs in the area.

The new introduction to this paperback edition reviews what has happened to the clubs since 2014. This update was completed at the beginning of 2016.

There are some minor adjustments and additions to the original and some revisions. But one of the overriding themes – boom and bust – has definitely not changed.

For their help with this edition my thanks go to Sam Allardyce, Steve Gibson and Shay Given.

C O N T E N T S

INTRODUCTION TO NEW EDITION

BOOM. THERE WAS A BUZZ ON BRIDGE STREET EAST. It was the morning of 7 May 2016 and Middlesbrough had a skip in its step. This could be the day that the Boro go back to the Premier League after seven often drab and occasionally painful years in the Championship.

'It's been a slog,' chairman Steve Gibson would say. 'Getting out of this league was far, far harder than I expected it to be.'

As a sold-out attendance made its way from the town centre bars that had opened early to accommodate fans of both Boro and Brighton & Hove Albion, fans passed by the Ian Horn poem stencilled in white on the old red bricks of Bridge Street East.

Ironopolis
Where alchemists
Were born
Below Cleveland's hills
A giant blue dragonfly
Across the Tees
Reminds us every night
We built the world,
Every metropolis
Came from
Ironopolis

Teesside's industry had been integral to the club since its foundation – Ironopolis FC, Middlesbrough's early rivals, were formed by dockers and metalworkers – and, more than a century later, the relationship still mattered.

When Redcar steelworks closed in October 2015 with the loss of 2,200 jobs, it was the football club which became a symbol of support. At Old Trafford to face Manchester United in the League Cup, Boro fans used mobile phone spotlights to illustrate their point. There is light.

On this day that sense of loss was still in the air, but so was anticipation.

After a season spent almost entirely in the Championship top four, Middlesbrough required a point at home to Brighton to ensure promotion. The club could change Teesside's mood.

And it did. Cristhian Stuani, a 29-year-old Uruguayan, scored the Boro goal in a nervy 1–1 draw against Brighton's ten men. Eight minutes of injury-time did not help local anxiety but it was eight minutes at the end of seven years and when it was done the Riverside Stadium staged a pitch invasion and a party.

Mobile phones were again prominent, footage from some showing Boro captain Grant Leadbitter carried on supporters' shoulders singing the chant:

In '86, we nearly died
From Ayresome Park to the Riverside,
Europe twice, we won the Cup,
The mighty Boro, we're going up!

In the post-match press conference Middlesbrough's intense manager Aitor Karanka began by saying he would 'like to spend the next 24 hours crying'. He then dedicated promotion to, among others, chairman Gibson and 'the steelworkers – I know how hard it's been'.

There was a special mention, too, for 'our friend Ali'. Alastair Brownlee, a Boro fanatic, commentated for BBC Radio Tees and worked for the club's TV station. He died in February 2016. His loss was felt on Teesside, not least because on the April 2006 night when Middlesbrough came back from 3–0 down against Steaua Bucharest in the semi-final of the Uefa Cup to win 4–3, Brownlee delivered a soaring tribute to the club and community that took in '1876, the Infant Hercules, the foundries of Teesside' and the iron ore 'mined from the Eston Hills'.

Brownlee concluded: 'We're roaring all the way to Eindhoven in the Uefa Cup final. It's party, party, party – everybody round my house for a parmo. We're there!' A 'parmo' is not a drink but a breaded chicken dish particular to Teesside. In an area which attracts more detractors than advocates, Brownlee's local pride was appreciated.

After Brighton, the parmo was accompanied by something stronger. There was champagne in the boardroom, though Gibson was supping a pint.

'The football club gives the town its identity and a lot of pride,' Gibson says. 'We've got a population of 130,000 and we're punching above our weight by getting into the Premier League. But we're hungry for it, the town's hungry for it.

'We were all distraught about Ali Brownlee, it's a tragedy for his family. And we all know what happened with the steelworks. But Teesside is beginning to bounce back. There's a lot of good things happening and hopefully promotion and this club can be a catalyst for that. It's not doom and gloom on Teesside. Hopefully this is the start.'

In one sense it was an end. With £5m to spend on revamping the Riverside Stadium and new signings incoming, Middlesbrough are looking different to the club which left the Premier League in 2009 under Gareth Southgate and also to that which, 12 months before Brighton, had lost the play-off final 2–0 at Wembley against Norwich. Then the Boro team bus had turned up late and some said the team never turned up at all. Karanka's selection and tactics were questioned widely by fans for the first time.

Still, the players and management went to their hotel and held a party of sorts. From this came a collective determination not to be in the play-offs again; from Gibson came further investment. Stewart Downing came home from West Ham, dropping a division, David Nugent was bought from Leicester, Stuani from Espanyol.

It worked. Between November and January Boro kept nine successive clean sheets in the Championship. They had a grip on automatic promotion and in January Gibson spent again to make sure. For £9m Jordan Rhodes was signed from Blackburn.

Yet Teesside buzzed with rumours that Karanka would have preferred Fulham's Ross McCormack; Rhodes only made his debut from the bench and, when all had seemed serene, suddenly there was tension. It erupted spectacularly when Karanka missed training before the trip to Charlton Athletic in March.

The game was lost, Middlesbrough appeared in disarray and former player Neil Maddison used the words 'mutiny' and 'iron rod' to describe Karanka's relationship with his squad. It seemed inconceivable that the manager could return.

But he did, Boro won six in a row, and now Gibson says: 'If you speak to Aitor and you speak to me, we were really the two people who knew what was going on and there was no danger of Aitor leaving the club. We had a bump, the bump was because of all kinds of pressures, and we didn't just smooth it out, it was a catalyst and it galvanised us to move on. We've not lost since.'

True, after those six wins, Boro drew the last four to edge over the line behind Burnley, the team Karanka once said he wanted Middlesbrough to be.

Away from first-team drama, Boro's Academy continues to produce, the

Under-19s putting five past Dynamo Kiev to reach the last 16 of the Uefa Youth League. It was heartening to watch. A 1–0 defeat at Paris St-Germain followed, but in 18-year-old Harrison Chapman, the club have the 'Beardsleyesque' attacker mentioned anonymously – due to his age – in the original edition of this book.

And in Ajax's Viktor Fischer, Middlesbrough had their first signing for their return to the Premier League. As Gibson says of promotion: 'We've got to have a go. We're a sporting entity and if you're not going to be having a go you shouldn't be doing it.'

✦

FOUR DAYS LATER IN SUNDERLAND, it was again boom, the noise shaking the stadium's main West Stand. From the moment Patrick van Aanholt wrong-footed Everton's goalkeeper Joel Robles to put Sunderland a goal up, the Stadium of Light was reverberating to the sound of relief, delight and mockery. You could feel it. 'God, that's some noise,' said a passing Everton official.

Sunderland scored two more to ensure their Premier League status which, for the fifth consecutive season, had been in jeopardy.

That underplays it: bar one week in November, Sunderland spent from August to the end of April in the relegation zone – 237 days – before a run of one defeat in the last eleven games hoisted them to safety.

It was the second time in four seasons Sunderland had finished 17th. It was the fourth time in four seasons they had failed to reach 40 points. What it meant was enormous, a tenth consecutive season in the Premier League and the income surge that would come with the new £8.3 billion television deal; what it also meant was that Newcastle United were relegated, hence the mockery. 'Are you watching, Newcastle?' Wearside belted out.

On Tyneside they were watching through their fingers. But Sunderland as a club, as an entity, could hardly claim credit. Once again poised to drop, Sunderland's own identity now included off-field instability and dugout escapology.
During the course of the season, the manager had yet again changed. Sam Allardyce, a former Sunderland player and former Newcastle manager, was hired in October 2015.

'I'm the troubleshooter,' Allardyce said on arrival. He had plenty to aim at. Allardyce replaced Dick Advocaat, who had come from out of nowhere in March to replace Gus Poyet, who in turn had joined in October 2013. Paolo Di Canio had been sacked five games into season 2013/14 having been appointed with seven games left of the previous season. Di Canio came as Martin O'Neill went, O'Neill having replaced Steve Bruce mid-season, December 2011.

None of this was planned, Sunderland lurched from one appointment to the next. Even when things looked to be going right – under Poyet Sunderland reached the League Cup final of 2014 – they sagged. Poyet's remark, aimed upstairs – 'There's something wrong at the football club' – was made the month after that final.

Poyet had given Sunderland a new playing style, but the team lacked a cutting edge. Twenty-eight games into season 2014/15, Sunderland had won just four, one a 1–0 victory at Newcastle with a goal from Adam Johnson. Game 29 was a 4–0 home defeat to Aston Villa, when the home players' lethargy appeared conscious. Two days later Poyet was dismissed.

Advocaat, 67, had watched the Villa defeat on TV in Holland and said at his unveiling: 'I was very disappointed. When Villa scored their fourth, five players were standing still. I told them [Sunderland's players] I would have run on and grabbed them. Something is wrong.'

The word 'shock' was one Poyet had used for the squad. Advocaat's nine-game remit was of the short, sharp variety and it worked at first. Sunderland took 12 points from those nine games and when, at Arsenal, survival was confirmed, Advocaat was in tears.

The Dutchman was set to retire; Sunderland persuaded him not to. But when the new season began at Leicester City, Advocaat again felt like crying. Sunderland were 3–0 down after 25 minutes.

After the next match, lost 3–1 at home to Norwich City, former player Michael Gray accused owner Ellis Short of 'lying' to fans about transfer resources. Short delivered an emphatic response a week later, stating: 'I have never taken money out of the club. In fact, I have funded significant shortfalls each and every season. The amount that I fund, every season, exceeds the collective total amount funded by every owner the club has ever had since the club was formed in 1879.'

It did not help Sunderland win. They would not do so again under Advocaat, who departed saying the squad 'is not good enough'.

Advocaat's leaving was foreseen; what was not was that the club's sporting director, Lee Congerton, would hand in his notice. Sunderland looked chaotic and in the background was the forthcoming Adam Johnson court case.

This is what Allardyce met when he returned to the club he played for briefly in 1980. He was the Wearsiders' fifth manager in two and a half years. His first match was a 1–0 loss at West Brom but the second was a 3–0 win over Newcastle. Johnson scored the first goal.

It was an historical coincidence. Di Canio, Poyet, Advocaat and Allardyce all faced Newcastle in their second game as Sunderland manager and all won.

Yet on New Year's Day 2016, Sunderland were second-bottom of the Premier League with 12 points. Allardyce needed help and received it in the shape of four new players: Wahbi Khazri, Jan Kirchhoff, Lamine Kone and Dame N'Doye. They made a difference; so, too, did existing players such as Defoe.

By season's end Sunderland had rescued themselves again, though as Allardyce said: 'We want to move away from the fact we're all so happy at being heroes for surviving. We have to think much bigger.'

A week on from that Allardyce tells me: 'Looking at 2016 in isolation, it shows good progress – on and off the field – in a difficult season – on and off the field.' Johnson's goal at Liverpool on 6 February was his last act in a Sunderland jersey. Four days later at Bradford Crown Court, he went on trial accused of four counts of sexual activity with a child. When Johnson pleaded guilty to two, Sunderland sacked him. 'SHAMED' was the Sunderland Echo front-page headline.

The club remained under scrutiny. Johnson had been originally arrested in March 2015 and, though he denied the accusations, Durham Police were to say that they had given the club's chief executive Margaret Byrne details of Johnson's behaviour with the girl two months later – nine months before the trial began. After an initial two-week suspension, Johnson had been allowed to play on. When he was found guilty and sentenced to six years, Byrne resigned, citing a serious error of judgement.

It meant that, for all the noisy celebration of survival, Sunderland ended the season without a chief executive or a sporting director and with a player in prison.

Sam Allardyce had experienced strange and uncomfortable legal positions before. He was once wrongly arrested as a Bolton player when trying to buy a 69p adapter from B&Q; as manager of Blackpool, Allardyce was sacked by chairman Owen Oyston, who was in prison at the time.

It was that dismissal which led Peter Reid, then Sunderland manager, to offer Allardyce a job as head of the club's youth system. That was Big Sam's second time on Wearside, his first coming as a 25-year-old player in 1980 earning £300 a week. 'It was pretty basic,' Allardyce says of his playing career on Wearside. 'A football club then was a football club and not much else. It had a fanbase, match programmes, perimeter advertising, didn't yet have a shirt sponsor. There was some commercial activity but probably 80 per cent of income, maybe more, came via supporters.'

When asked to return in 1996, Allardyce found the club had not changed much, though it was Roker Park's final season.

'Sunderland had got promoted to the Premier League,' he says. 'There was a big push on Academy status. It was quite difficult, there was no Academy of Light then, there wasn't 10 per cent of what we have now.'

In 2015 Allardyce found a very different club in terms of infrastructure.

'The club now has everything, but stability,' he says. 'It's just finding that stability at the top end to enable us to grow and build on survival.

'Sunderland have consistently been in the Premier League – nine years now. Facility-wise, status-wise, fanbase-wise, it's there, it's just the football side of it hasn't quite married. But crucially the club hasn't suffered the devastation of relegation and now it has another chance to grow.'

At 61, Allardyce's experience has brought back hope and the club moved to replace Byrne with former Rangers director Martin Bain.

But is there the scope to go from troubleshooter to club-builder as Reid did? 'I said I'm a troubleshooter based on the idea that "Sam will keep you up",' Allardyce says. 'I'll still be perceived as that. It's a label. I accept it because you can't fight the label in football.

'I know how to build. It's how can we build? It depends on what we recruit, but that's not all, it doesn't just happen by buying good players. The football club infrastructure should be about building an environment for success. I know if I have an exceptionally good nucleus of staff then we can make strides to bring stability to the club.'

✦

BUST. NEWCASTLE UNITED HAD BEEN RELEGATED. For the second time in seven years in the era of Mike Ashley's divisive ownership of the 124-year-old club, an irregular collection of players proved less than the sum of their parts. It felt careless.

It's just that the noise St James' Park was making four days after relegation was confirmed by that Sunderland victory over Everton did not sound like relegation. It was not the sound of a club gone bust. It sounded like boom.

On the final afternoon of the 2015/16 season St James' marked Newcastle's exit from the Premier League with applause, smiles and songs. Even those who had been going for decades, and who have seen some queer events at the storied stadium, thought it was odd.

This positive atmosphere was not aimed at players who had performed halfheartedly at times, though; its target was a 56-year-old Spaniard in a waistcoat who had arrived at the club just 65 days earlier – Rafael Benítez.

Rafa Benítez had won the Champions League with Liverpool and had started the season as manager of Real Madrid.

In nine weeks at Newcastle he had been unable to prevent a potentially calamitous drop, but he had made his presence felt around the club and in the city. Benítez gave fans something to cling to amid the wreckage of a season that featured a 6–1 thrashing at Manchester City, 5–1 at Crystal Palace and 5–1 at Chelsea. There was also a 3–0 loss at Sunderland, Newcastle's sixth derby defeat in a row.
What the Spaniard gave the club, which had retreated into a shell, was a credible face. And here, on the season's finale, Newcastle United were beating Tottenham Hotspur 5–1.

A near sell-out, the crowd sang Benítez's name throughout. It had been the same since his introduction on 12 March, notably on 23 April when Newcastle travelled to Anfield.

Liverpool is the club most in England associate with Benítez. He has been a consistent supporting voice for the Hillsborough campaign and his home remains on the Wirral.

Now he was returning as the – temporary – leader of dysfunctional Newcastle United. Benítez is still a popular figure to many Liverpudlians but as his two daughters, Claudia and Agata, walked through the crowds to Anfield, they were struck by his popularity among the travelling support.

Back at home that night, Benítez's daughters told their father of what they had witnessed and said: 'You must stay.'

It would be naïve to think that when Benitez chose not to exercise the 'break clause' in his original contract ten days after the Tottenham game, it was solely because of his daughters, but the overall response from Tyneside had helped sway the Benítez family. Remarkably, he had agreed to go from the Champions League to the Championship in the space of six months.

Having asked for the correct English word to capture his feelings, rather than 'pleased' or 'delighted', Benítez said: 'I'm flattered.'

He then met owner Mike Ashley for contract negotiations. Ashley once won a bet at St James' with his chief executive Derek Llambias that ended with Llambias streaking across the pitch, but it was Ashley's Newcastle United naked in front of Benítez. When the club announced the Spaniard's signature on a deal lasting to 2019, it stated: 'Benítez will have day-to-day responsibility for all football-related matters at the club.'

Benítez was the 'manager', not the coach, which immediately made him more powerful within St James' than any of his predecessors under Ashley.

Supporters cheered again. It meant a curious optimism greeted the end of another wearisome season, when Newcastle had lost exactly half their league games. Benítez's immediate predecessor, Steve McClaren, came and went in eight months. Sacked by Derby County in May 2015 – the day after Newcastle had secured their 2015/16 Premier League status – McClaren was smuggled into St James' without a press conference, hoping he could change Ashley's Newcastle from within.

Belatedly, the club reinvested in the team but Newcastle did not win a league game until October and there were just two away wins all season, though it was a 3–1 home defeat in early March to Bournemouth that terminated McClaren.

The club handled his dismissal clumsily, the same way they conducted the transition from Alan Pardew to John Carver the previous January. After four frequently turbulent years at St James', Pardew chose to leave for Palace.

Pardew's departure was not lamented. His position in May 2014 looked untenable, so vociferous was the fanbase backlash against the club's ongoing, but profitable, mediocrity. Pardew was seen as complicit. When the next season began without a win until October, precursing McClaren, the mood slumped further. Yet a burst of victories followed and when Pardew left Newcastle were ninth in the table. The inevitable speculation came and McClaren was approached. He declined and the club turned to Pardew's assistant, Carver.

Carver was a Geordie, who had first joined the club as a teenager in 1980, but that did not make his appointment popular. The sense was Newcastle were treading water, happy in the new mid-table luxury of the Premier League. Accounts for the season would reveal a £32.4m profit, on top of the £8m the year before.

But, leading to the last day of the season, Newcastle lost nine of ten games. Ashley turned up for the final game, which was almost as big a surprise as his decision to give a first televised interview as the club's owner.

Ashley said he was 'a little bit shocked by where we find ourselves today', and that the responsibility for this lay at 'my door'. There was also defiance. The club was not for sale 'at any price', he said, and his ambition remained 'definitely to win something. By the way, I shall not be selling it until I do.'

Ashley is a difficult man to read. Ten months later he gave another interview at his Sports Direct HQ near Mansfield and sounded less gung-ho.

'Do I regret getting into football? The answer is yes,' he now said. 'I wanted to help Newcastle, I wanted to make it better, that's what I wanted to do. I haven't seemed to have had that effect.'

Ashley had just dismissed McClaren. The defeat to Bournemouth left Newcastle second-bottom and McClaren described the performance as 'going-down material'. Asked what disappointed him most, he replied: 'Our football.'

It had started brightly enough. Four players – Georginio Wijnaldum, Aleksandar Mitrovic, Florian Thauvin and Chancel Mbemba – had been signed for a total of £50m.

None of these players had been signed by McClaren though. His job was to mould, not buy. He had been placed on a new four-man board created by Ashley along with managing director Lee Charnley, chief scout Graham Carr and former captain Bob Moncur. But that was an illusion of influence.

'They want stability,' McClaren said, when he was allowed to speak.

When he pushed to sign QPR's experienced striker Charlie Austin, McClaren was given 20-year-old Mitrovic from Anderlecht. By September he was saying his new charges 'don't have an identity'; by early December, when asked if he and Newcastle were 'a good fit', he said: 'If it was, we would be winning.'

Behind the scenes, matters had soured. McClaren and his assistant Paul Simpson were staggered to receive a written warning after Simpson had given an innocent interview to local radio.

Nor did they consider themselves well-paid, or their staff, who were increasingly demoralised in a small, tired training ground they referred to as 'the squash club'. Privately they wondered why a club would spend £15m on a player such as Wijnaldum, then skimp on infrastructure.

They were not the only ones souring. The players rallied to beat Liverpool and Tottenham in December but they were soon out of the FA Cup at Watford and back in the relegation zone.

Four more players were signed in January, Andros Townsend and Jonjo Shelvey each costing £12m, plus Henri Saivet (£5m) from Bordeaux and Seydou Doumbia on loan from Roma. Saivet was given a 5½-year contract.

But at Goodison Park in February young defender Jamaal Lascelles was heard shouting, 'No one gives a fuck,' as he walked down the tunnel, sent off during a 3–0 capitulation. It was the day some inside the club thought it was over for McClaren. The players had stopped listening to him and initially refused to get off the bus for the traditional pre-match walkabout.

Bournemouth and a slow execution was a month away. Newcastle left McClaren hanging as they wooed Benítez, whose first decision was to request a louder whistle.

Everyone saw symbolism. Nine weeks later Newcastle United were relegated for the sixth time in their history.

And people smiled. As the St James' tannoy played the Smiths' 'There Is a Light That Never Goes Out', as punters filed past Sports Direct logo after Sports Direct logo, as players wore the famous shirt with the discredited Wonga name still plastered across it, as Ashley prepared to face Parliament to explain his business practices, people smiled.

The Rafa Benítez era had begun. Bust and boom.

IT WAS A SUNNY MID-DECEMBER MORNING IN 2014. At Victoria Park, Hartlepool, three men calling themselves TMH 2014 Limited were on the pitch discussing why they were taking over Hartlepool United 12 days after the club had been eliminated from the FA Cup by non-League neighbours Blyth Spartans.

The answers were not wholly convincing. TMH stood for The Monkey Hangers – a reference to Hartlepool's infamous monkey. They were buying from IOR, the club's owners of 17 years. IOR is Increased Oil Recovery and TMH's enthusiasm was fired by IOR's decision to write off the club's £13m debt.

It was the end of an era. Somewhat opaque owners based in Aberdeen and Norway, IOR had been good for Hartlepool United but the boom League One years were followed by relegation and Pools only stayed in the Football League by the skin of their teeth in May 2014. Colin Cooper was manager but when season 2014/15 began weakly, he resigned and was replaced by former player Paul Murray, who lasted just six weeks – long enough to lose against Spartans.

Now TMH were here, bringing the 1,000-game experience of Ronnie Moore with them. Hartlepool's chief executive Russ Green, who was staying on, stood on the Vic pitch that morning and told me: 'IOR have been here 17 years and they've invested heavily in the club for those 17 years. But the oil industry is not what it was, and – it sounds silly – we're affected by that. Oil prices have dropped, big-style. IOR have been brilliant and saved the club, but after 17 years we've come to a crossroads.' Six weeks later the sale was called off and when the team lost 1–0 at Portsmouth in February 2015, Hartlepool were bottom of League Two, nine points off safety. Bust and bust.

But then Moore, who remained in charge despite the failed takeover, staged one of the great rescue acts in English football and somehow Hartlepool were still in the Football League come May.

By June there was a real new owner – JPNG – a business fronted by Gary

Coxall, who backed Moore. But by February 2016 Pools were once again hovering above relegation and Moore was replaced by Craig Hignett, Aitor Karanka's assistant at Middlesbrough not long before. Hartlepool rallied under Hignett to finish 16th, their highest position since relegation from League One in 2013. In the summer of 2016 there are hints of optimism.

There are at Gateshead, too. Like Hartlepool, Gateshead have changed ownership and manager twice since the first edition of this book.

After their play-off final defeat in 2014, manager Gary Mills stayed another season, but it was less successful and at its end he left for Wrexham. In came former Sunderland manager Malcolm Crosby, appointed by club owner Graham Wood as he handed over to Richard and Julie Bennett. The Crosby appointment did not work and in November he departed. In came Neil Aspin.

Aspin, 50, was a former Leeds United defender, one born in Gateshead.

'Neil left Gateshead at the age of 16 to pursue a distinguished playing career,' said his new chairman Richard Bennett. 'His time has come to return to the north-east to manage his hometown club. This is the beginning of a new chapter in the history of Gateshead Football Club.'

Gateshead finished ninth in the newly titled English National League under Aspin. But the man who signed Jamie Vardy from Stocksbridge Steels while manager of Halifax was busy recruiting in the summer of 2016 and a new stadium is again on the agenda.

Darlington 1883, as they are known officially, have a new stadium on their mind also. When the club went bust in 2012, they were relegated five divisions by the Football Association and lost their ground, the white elephant 'Arena'. Darlington FC left their own town to play in Bishop Auckland and, though grateful for the hospitality, in August 2016 Darlington will return to Darlington. They will play at Blackwell Meadows, a 3,000-capacity rugby ground they will share.

Darlington do so as a National League North club, having just clinched a third promotion in four seasons. They pipped Spartans to the Evostik Northern Premier Division title even though Darlington had to play their last nine games in 22 days.

It has not been easy, and supporters have carried the club, but Darlington are two promotions away from being back in the Football League.

Martin Gray, Stockton-born and a former Sunderland and Darlington player, has overseen the rise. Gray first joined the club in 1999 and has said since then: 'There's been a lot of hardship. But we could not have asked for a better end to the season before going back to Darlington. The town will be buzzing.'

Blyth, who finished runners-up to Darlington, then lost in the play-offs. But the club has had good cup moments and on a memorable day at Croft Park in January 2015, Blyth reignited their famous FA Cup tradition by taking a 2–0 lead over Birmingham City in the third round. History beckoned barman Robbie Dale, who scored both goals. But magic gave way to realism when Championship Birmingham scored three times shortly into the second half.

Two north-east clubs who did make it to Wembley were North Shields and Morpeth, who have both won the FA Vase since the first edition of this book was published. Those two aspirational Northern League clubs suggest the grassroots are prospering, though there was less encouraging news in early 2016 when the famed Horden Colliery Welfare lost the keys to their ground of 108 years.

Horden CW produced three England internationals – Tommy Garrett, Stan Anderson and Colin Bell – between 1952 and 1968; when Roy Hodgson named his England squad for Euro 2016 there were just two north-eastern players in it, Wearsider Jordan Henderson and Hexham-born Fraser Forster.

These fluctuations fit a pattern, as does Steph Houghton captaining England's women's team at the 2015 World Cup and Sunderland's Beth Mead rising to prominence.

Another north-east trend saw a fibreglass horse called Herby, stationed outside a pizza restaurant in Newcastle, punched in the wake of a Newcastle-Sunderland derby.

Howard Kendall would have laughed at that. Sadly, the Tynesider, whose story gives Up There its title, died in October 2015, aged 69.

Kendall's death was not mourned in Newcastle as Pavel Srnicek's was two months later, in part because, tragically, Srnicek was only 47. 'Pavel is a Geordie', sang Newcastle fans of a man born in Czechoslovakia.

Srnicek came to Newcastle and was accepted sincerely as a local. Kendall was a local who departed and whose death was recorded with far greater depth in the north-west than in his native north-east. Up there, Kendall's relevance was, to use a word, overlooked.

INTRODUCTION

2 MARCH 2014. Down and down, grey concrete step after grey concrete step until the bowels of Wembley stadium are reached. The descent is all but silent and there will be no joy at the end of it. We have come to hear the losers speak.

In the steepling press room the Sunderland manager Gus Poyet answers questions in English and Spanish, speaking of his pride as well as his disappointment. It is brief. Sunderland have failed better, but they have failed again. Poyet can say only so much.

Manchester City 3 Sunderland 1 in the League Cup final meant another year is added. It will now be at least 42 years since Sunderland visited Wembley and took home the silverware. The veterans of the 1973 FA Cup win over Leeds United will be another year older, their memories will need dusting down again.

But the nature of Sunderland's performance, strong and coherent, also meant the 35,000-odd fans climbing on buses and trains, meeting at petrol stations and platforms, could take a sense of spirited defeat with them back to Wearside. The night before the game had seen a friendly red and white striped invasion of Covent Garden. Sunderland had enjoyed themselves, fans spoke of a renewal of belief in their club. There was something to cling to.

Yet they were returning up the M1 and east coast main line without the cup. Middlesbrough's victory in the same competition on the same weekend ten years earlier remained the last time the north-east was the home of a major trophy, meaning the north-east had still won one trophy in more than four decades.

This book is called Up There for a reason and it is not football's standard usage of up there, when a player or manager employs it to describe success: so-and-so is 'up there' with the best.

The reason is geographic. It reflects the sense of apartness and difference that the north-east feels internally, and to the rest of England, certainly historically. Part of that is distance, part of it was industry and part of it is political. Part of it is football.

The north-east's deep feeling for football is part of the region's character. It is riveted to the game. The same can be said of Merseyside, Manchester, areas of London and elsewhere in England, but if there is a difference, it is that the north-east's attachment has not been maintained by success.

In other places the month of May has frequently brought silverware and celebration; in the north-east May has often confirmed emptiness and a long wait until the next season. In that sense, it's not up there.

Middlesbrough did win that League Cup in 2004 and reached the Uefa Cup final two years later, while Newcastle United were Champions League group-stage participants three times between 1997 and 2004.

But Middlesbrough, Newcastle and Sunderland have each been relegated since Boro's League Cup and over a prolonged period of time stretching back to the 1950s and even before the Second World War, the three 'big' north-east clubs have been down as often as they have been middling, never mind up there.

Middlesbrough have never been champions of England or won the FA Cup. Sunderland have not been league winners since 1936, Newcastle since 1927, before the Tyne Bridge was completed. The year 2015 will mark the 60th anniversary of Newcastle's last domestic trophy, the 1955 FA Cup. Sixty years.

This could be a geographic quirk. An area of such supportive desire would be expected to have achieved more, much more. In recent times, as Premier League salaries have mushroomed and foreign players have spoken of wanting to go 'to London' as opposed to any particular club there, the north-east trio have had to work harder to get players up there. Working harder usually translates as higher wages and this has knock-on effects.

Historically this was not the case. The north-east had players on the doorstep. Issues then were competence and complacency rather than geography.

England's World Cup-winning brothers Jack and Bobby Charlton came from Ashington in Northumberland and both supported Newcastle United but Bobby joined Manchester United and Jack joined Leeds United. Their mother's cousin was 'uncle' Jackie Milburn, Newcastle hero, but the Milburn family had a dim view of how Newcastle treated young players.

That ranks as professional incompetence, as does Newcastle's opinion that they could do without a miner's son from Co. Durham called Colin Bell.

Between the World Cups of 1962 and 1990 England had, among many north-eastern others, this quartet of midfielders: Bobby Charlton, Colin Bell, Bryan Robson and Paul Gascoigne. Only Gascoigne joined a local club as a boy.

UP THERE

When Newcastle were in a two-way fight with Southampton for a sheet metal-worker's son from Gosforth, Alan Shearer moved down there.

Of course there are other factors - luck, timing. In September 2000, one year into his tenure at St. James' Park, Bobby Robson rang Jose Mourinho and asked him to be his assistant. Mourinho heard Robson say that he would step down in two seasons "and I would be the head coach and he the club manager [director of football]. But Bobby Robson had forgotten that I had worked with him for many years." Mourinho said it was "unthinkable" Robson would be satisfied watching training and games from a distance.

In 1938 Bob Paisley wanted to join Sunderland. His local club said no, so he joined Liverpool and won the league title as a player and then did a bit more at Anfield after that. In 1965 Sunderland had Brian Clough on their staff as youth team coach. They let him go to Hartlepool United.

Recognising the extraordinary talent in either man would have changed Sunderland's history.

As for Middlesbrough, in 1952 they had a managerial vacancy and interviewed a 39-year-old Scot. In its wisdom the board chose not to appoint Bill Shankly.

'Missing that job was a terrible disappointment,' Shankly said, 'because I was bubbling with ideas and Middlesbrough had a good ground and a lot of useful players. Before the war they'd had one of the best footballing teams in Britain. Ayresome Park represented potential, just as Liverpool did.'

Wilf Mannion is probably still weeping. Two years later Boro were relegated and did not return to the First Division until 1974.

Shankly was so eager for the job he had booked a room in Ripon overnight. That dramatic mistake had nothing to do with geography.

Yet as an example of fervour in the face of failure, over 200,000 people clicked through the turnstiles at St James' Park for four Newcastle United games from the end of November 2013 – an average of 50,572 to see Stoke City as well as Arsenal.

On Wearside, nearly 180,000 attended five Sunderland matches in that same pre and post-Christmas period. And on Teesside an average of 18,500 saw Middlesbrough play Bolton, Brighton, Burnley and Reading in the Championship.

That last figure may not be particularly impressive in the context of English football, but Middlesbrough were 18th in its second division and into their fifth season outside the Premier League.

One measure of the club's health was that local-hero manager Tony Mowbray had been sacked eight days earlier. Boro were in a slump.

Another measurement of Teesside health came in the same month Mowbray departed: Middlesbrough Football Club opened a food bank. A Save the Children survey revealed 34 per cent of Middlesbrough children living in poverty, 12 per cent higher than the national average. Middlesbrough Football Club, it could be said, were trying to sell tickets to a population they were helping to feed.

Sunderland also began December 2013 in the midst of managerial flux. Those thousands entering the Stadium of Light turned up to see the club bottom of the Premier League. Regulars knew a relegation battle when they saw one.

Sunderland had started 2013 with Martin O'Neill as their manager. There were then a torrid, florid few months with Paolo Di Canio in charge and as December dawned, Poyet was Sunderland's eighth manager in seven years.

Only Newcastle United could lay a claim on good form. A club of consistent unpredictability, Newcastle had retained Alan Pardew for three years and after winning four league games in November, Pardew was named Manager of the Month. The following week Newcastle won a league match at Old Trafford for the first time since 1972.

It was a moment for historic reflection. Between 1972 and 2013 Manchester United won 13 league titles, eight FA Cups, four League Cups, one European Cup Winners' Cup and, above all, two European Cups. Traditionally, that is how a club nurtures and sustains a fanbase.

Newcastle United's trophies of note in that period were for winning the second division, in 1993 and 2010.

But that 'Division One' trophy of 1993 is not insignificant. It shows where Newcastle had been when the Premier League was formed. Newcastle United were not in it and Sunderland were not in it. Middlesbrough were the north-east's sole representatives in the breakaway enterprise that would transform football. And in the Premier League's inaugural season, Middlesbrough were relegated. Ayresome Park's average attendance was 16,700.

Sunderland were almost relegated as well that season. It would have been to the third division. Rattling through three managers in a year once again – Malcolm Crosby, Terry Butcher and Mick Buxton – Sunderland finished one place above Brentford. Roker Park averaged 17,000.

At least at St James' Park, where nearly 30,000 were cramming in, there was some hope gathering. Much of this centred on Kevin Keegan, arguably the most important man in north-east football since the Second World War.

Keegan combined charisma, talent, experience and economics. Most importantly, he came.

Keegan brimmed with enthusiasm for an area where his great-grandfather is saluted in song as a coalmining hero. Frank Keegan was in the Stanley Pit Disaster of 1909 in which 168 men and boys lost their lives.

As Keegan wrote in his autobiography: 'Twenty-one who perished were under the age of 16. It is horrifying to consider there were kids of 12 and 13 down there.'

Frank Keegan had initially been rescued from the explosion but turned around, went back underground and helped bring others out. In a song written about the disaster by the Pitmatic chronicler Tommy Armstrong, Frank Keegan is referred to as 'bold Keegan'. Pitmatic is a strain of north-east dialect that emanated from the pits; Frank Keegan is part of Co. Durham mining history.

Kevin Keegan's father, Joe, was also a miner – 'a typical miner' as his son put it. 'He enjoyed a few pints, smoked his Woodbines and slept the sleep of an honest man. He left the north-east when work became scarce.'

Joe Keegan moved south to Yorkshire to work at Markham Main colliery on the edge of Doncaster. There son Kevin heard Geordie football stories, plus tales of his grandfather that he was unsure about.

'I thought it was just a story and there was no truth in it,' Keegan has recalled. 'When I was in Newcastle in the early 1980s, I was shown a picture of the survivors of the disaster at West Stanley. Looking back at me from the image was my grandfather, Frank.'

To Doncaster-born Keegan, his roots meant the north-east was up there somewhere in his imagination. He knew it as a football place in need of re-awakening and which would respond to attention. Keegan shook it once when the European Footballer of the Year of 1978 and 1979 joined second division Newcastle in 1982. When he returned as manager, he shook more than Tyneside.

Keegan understood the north-east the way he understood football. He understood it as his manager at Liverpool did. Bob Paisley once said: 'The north-east is a world of its own.'

Paisley came from the coalmining village of Hetton-le-Hole in Co. Durham, as did Frank Keegan.

For Paisley and Keegan, Up There would mean home, family, coal, football, roots. To Paisley, growing up in the 1920s and 1930s it was definitely a place apart – 'a little slice of England totally independent from the rest' – and if the region was better connected by the time Keegan arrived, the sense of difference resonated.

The difference, however, was not always warm to those outside, and sometimes inside. Even from the north-west the north-east can seem like a trek, even today.

That view has been expressed many times over the decades and once with force and consequences at Goodison Park in the early 1980s, at a time when Everton were managed by Howard Kendall.

Kendall is an essential figure at Goodison Park, as a title-winning midfielder and as a title-winning manager. He became as Evertonian as toffee. But Kendall was born and raised on Tyneside, in Crawcrook, on the southern bank of the river.

In 1981 Kendall signed the Welsh winger Mickey Thomas from Manchester United. Thomas sustained an injury not long after his move and as part of his recovery process, Kendall asked Thomas to play in the Everton reserves.

As Kendall said: 'The reserve game was at Newcastle, the longest journey of a reserve-team season. Mickey wasn't happy at all.'

Kendall says now he 'sort of understood. Mickey only wanted to play first-team football.'

But there was consternation because, to Kendall, St James' Park was football, it was opportunity. This was the ground Kendall first went to as a boy to watch Jackie Milburn's FA Cup-winning Newcastle team of the 1950s, where he fell in love watching graceful George Eastham, the history man. Newcastle United were the club Eastham took to court in 1963 to end the retention element of club contracts with players. It is arguably as important a decision as the change to the offside rule in 1925, again provoked by a Newcastle United player, Bill McCracken.

Kendall had a further personal connection to St James' as in 1952 his cousin, Harry Taylor, made the Newcastle United first team. These were giddy days in Kendall's childhood, a time of arm-tugging excitement as he travelled to St James' with his father Jack and his Uncle Billy, Harry Taylor's father.

Billy Taylor had been blinded in a mining accident and so could not see his son play. It was the Saturday job of Kendall's father to provide commentary.

Harry Taylor played for Newcastle but he warned Howard Kendall not to. One of the best midfielders England produced over two decades, Kendall shied away because Taylor was as unimpressed with Newcastle's handling of teenagers as Jackie Milburn. It is a recurring theme.

Instead Kendall joined Preston North End, whose scout Reg Keating had been on Newcastle's books in the 1920s, and Newcastle's loss was to be seen up close in May 1963, when, aged 16, Kendall made his Preston debut. It was an away game, one that would appeal to the young boy and his family: it was up there at St James' Park.

As Kendall puts it: 'In front of my own people.'

So it is clear that, even in 1981, St James' Park meant a good deal more to Howard Kendall than it did to Mickey Thomas.

As he considered Thomas, Kendall was self-aware. He knew managers could possess strange tics. Kendall, for instance, fretted about signing bald or blond-haired players - 'I thought they stood out, in a bad way' – and now he felt his own distrust of raven-haired wingers like Thomas.

It could have stemmed from Kendall's early days. He had gone to school with Bryan Ferry, later of Roxy Music, and played in the same school team. 'He was a winger, a wimp,' Kendall says.

'But then he had other talents, didn't he.'

Kendall wasn't so sure about the other talents of Mickey Thomas. And Thomas clearly had his doubts about Kendall. And Everton. And St James' Park.

Thomas ended his 11 game Everton career that afternoon by refusing to get on the bus to Tyneside.

'I'm not going,' he told Kendall, 'I'm not going *up there*.'

PART ONE

THE CULTURE

The foundation of an industrial culture: miner with apprentices, Ashington Colliery, 1981. (Mik Critchlow)

CHAPTER ONE

COALS & GOALS

THE BACK LANE, TENTH STREET, Horden, Co. Durham, some time in the 1940s, all the time in the 1940s. School has broken up for the day and children have returned home. They are playing in the lane, playing their favourite game. It is called 'Gates'. It is a football game in which the back gates of houses are used as the framework of goals. You play to protect your gate.

These are sprawling, unstructured matches with any number of children playing at any given time. There is freedom, there is competition, there is play.

But once a week, every week, play stops. The children are brought to a halt by the adult world. The reason they live in Horden returns home. Miners from Horden colliery – the children's fathers, uncles and brothers – interrupt 'Gates' to deliver a heap of coal outside each back yard. Then they go back to the pit. Then they go back underground.

The children stay in the bracing air rushing in from the North Sea, under which the miners are tunnelling. They go back to their game. Only now, these heaps of coal are part of it. The coal acts as an additional obstacle, makes the game harder. It means more dribbling, more weaving, in and around piles of coal. When Stan Anderson thinks back to his street days in Horden, this is one of the images that comes to him: coals and goals.

Stan Anderson came from No. 39 Tenth Street. In north-east coal towns it was commonplace for streets to be numbered rather than named. He was, and is, a miner's son.

Horden was a village like so many others in the north-east's coalmining area: it was both rural and industrialised. It was both cut off from, and central to, the society it energised.

From 39 Tenth Street, from games of Gates in the back lane, Stan Anderson played for England. He went to the 1962 World Cup in Chile. Jimmy Greaves called Anderson 'Boeing' because he cruised around the pitch like the engine ushering in something called 'the Jet Age'.

At club level Anderson played for Sunderland, Newcastle United and then became player-manager of Middlesbrough. In the course of the twentieth century only four men played for all three major north-east clubs; Anderson was the third. Billy Agnew and Tommy Urwin came before, Alan Foggon later.

Stan Anderson is unique. He is the only man in the 138-year history of professional football in the north-east to have captained all three of those clubs.

That says something of Anderson's status locally, and he did a lot more besides. While at his first club, Sunderland, Anderson played with both Brian Clough and Don Revie – as well as Len Shackleton – and, when he became manager of Middlesbrough, Anderson signed Graeme Souness from Tottenham Hotspur's reserves.

'He was a nice lad, Graeme,' Anderson says with a grimace. 'But a hard boy. He used to do things that would make me cringe, and I was his manager.'

Anderson was talking in the small back room of a bungalow in Doncaster, a pin-sharp 81-year-old, recollecting a life begun in Horden.

South of Sunderland, a mile from the North Sea, Horden was a late-starter when it came to coal. The mine was not sunk until 1904, but by the 1940s almost 15,000 people lived and worked in Horden. The colliery was huge and productive – seams were drilled six miles out from the coast, the North Sea roaring above this underground world. A simple piece of coal was the end product but this was a magnificent daily feat of engineering, architecture and bravery.

Horden's was a super-pit before the term was coined and it sustained a population. It filled a town with schools, shops, a football team – Horden Colliery Welfare – and purpose. It would do so for the next 50 years. Coal was Horden's reason.

'Where I grew up – Horden colliery, Blackhall colliery, Easington Village – everyone was a miner,' Anderson says. 'We used to go and pick coal off the beaches, you know where the waste would come up – sea-coal. It was the usual thing, you'd take sacks down and pick it up, sell it or use it yourself.

'Then, I can't remember which day of the week it was, but the miners used to tip loads of coal out in the street, outside your coal bunker. You'd then put it in. We used to play football around that tipped coal, oh aye. Someone would then say: "I'll give you sixpence to shift it".

'There's just nothing like that now.'

Anderson's imagery of coals and goals, of football intertwined with heavy industry, feels like the sort of north-east football folklore that has been trampled into untrustworthy cliché. Yet this is Anderson's memory of how it was and his concluding words are his reflection on how it is.

It is not myth. The line about being able to whistle down a north-east mineshaft and a centre-forward coming up is exaggeration, of course, and the not insignificant fact was that under the maximum wage a journeyman professional footballer would not be much better off than a miner. Frequently the player would be worse off. And a football career was shorter than a miner's.

But coalmining did more than supply sons of miners from the pits to the old First Division and the England team, it provided the economy and culture which helped establish and fund professional football in the region, and make it grow.

Stan Anderson's brother, Bob, was part of that culture. Bob was a Sunderland fanatic, but one who would go to see Newcastle United, Middlesbrough and Hartlepool too, who took Stan to Ayresome Park in 1946 to see Middlesbrough versus Newcastle in a post-war celebration friendly. Stan remembers they got the bus to Billingham and changed there.

Bob Anderson represented another vivid piece of north-east football, the fan. Bob was a miner and, as Stan says, 'it was typical that he was dead within a year of retiring. That's what happened.'

It was hard labour, mining. It was physically reducing, dangerous, sometimes fatal and Stan Anderson's father, like Bob Paisley's father and many other fathers, tried to find another way of life for their sons.

'When I was 14, 15, you'd go to the recreation ground on a Sunday morning and you'd have 30, 40 lads there,' Anderson says. 'You'd pick captains, play 20-a-side, it wasn't organised. The men used to come out of the Comrades Club at one o'clock and stand and watch.

'What surprises me now is that I played with three players in my school team in Horden and I looked in envy at these three. There was a lad called Frank Outon, a lovely player, outside right, he could beat anybody. I used to think: 'I wish I could do that.'

'Frank Outon went down the mine, never accomplished what he could have. I know why – that was what you did. But my father refused point blank to let me down the mine because he worked in it all his life. 'You're not going down the pub and you're not going down the mine,' he'd say. But that was the way of life. You left school and you went down the pit.'

The pit, the mine, coal, ensured employment. It ensured it for Bob Anderson and his father and, in the 1940s, 3,800 other men at Horden colliery. In 1985 there were still just over 2,000 working there, one year before its enforced closure.

Horden was one of 15 mines immediately south of Sunderland. Together they created an industrial culture, one that helped define a region, one that brought money, self-confidence and a sense of identity. Coal gave the area shape and character. That broad contribution can be forgotten.

It wasn't always. In 1937 George Orwell wrote: 'Our civilisation is founded on coal, more completely than one realises until one stops to think about it. The machines that keep us alive, and the machines that make machines, are all directly or indirectly dependent upon coal. In the metabolism of the Western world the coal-miner is second in importance only to the man who ploughs the soil.'

That analysis applied to the north-east specifically. If, in the beginning, there is always the word, then in the north-east that word is coal.

IT CAME TO BE KNOWN as the Great Northern Coalfield and in 1906 a man called James Tonge defined it in his book *The Principles and Practice of Coal Mining*:

> *Northumberland and Durham Coalfield. Area, 460 square miles; length from north to south, 50 miles; breadth, 23 miles at widest part. This old and important coalfield stretches over the greater portion of the counties of Northumberland and Durham. It extends from the River Coquet in the north to Staindrop (on the north of the Tees) in the south; and from Ponteland and Wolsingham in the west to the North Sea on the east.*

Those geographic boundaries have remained and, though coal is gone as an industry, this is still, roughly, the accepted definition of what we have come to understand as north-east England.

There are dissenters, those who say that Teesside is in Yorkshire, for example, and there are those who feel no kinship with their neighbours and have little sense of common identity. It finds an expression in the fresh, if not new, nasty rivalry between Newcastle United and Sunderland, the sort of aggressive posturing that saw a police horse punched outside St James' Park in 2013.

This opinion cannot be dismissed. There is a broader non-feeling behind it and the lack of a unified, official, north-east perspective was made clear in November 2004 when there was an historic opportunity to vote for a regional assembly, a measure of devolved government. When the votes came in less than half the electorate had bothered to take part. Of them only 22 per cent voted for the proposed assembly. So much for a north-east perspective.

Part of the issue was that the assembly lacked tangible power and, a decade on, the ongoing rise of London as a state within the state is felt more keenly. There is an increased sense, not just in the north-east but around the UK, that it is there to service London.

This is something of a full circle. Historically, the first role of north-east coal was to fuel London. This sparked much local invention, and gave rise to what academics call 'carboniferous capitalism'.

Once the tonnage of coalmining began to soar to feed the growing city of London, there was a need for better transport. It is not coincidence that the first railways in the world were designed and used in north-east England; they were created to move coal.

There was also a desire to transport coal by sea, which is why by the 1930s Sunderland was known as 'the biggest shipbuilding town in the world'. The club incorporated a ship on their crest until 1997, when they left Roker Park and shipbuilding on the Wear had become part of the town's 'heritage'.

Stan Anderson lived in Sunderland when he played for the club in the 1950s. By then shipbuilding's decline had started but he can remember 'launches were always special occasions'.

Stan and his wife Marjorie would push their daughter's pram to the banks of the River Wear to watch ships leave, just as half the town would. There was an air of self-celebration and though it seems like an image from a bygone world, it happened in Anderson's lifetime.

'There were three industries in Sunderland,' he says, 'coal, shipbuilding and football. Football has survived. Coal and the shipyards have gone.'

For more than a century Sunderland also had a glass industry. At its peak, one firm alone – Joblings – employed 3,500 people. The literal landscape has been transformed. Former pitheaps have been massaged into the contours of the countryside. Where it once teemed with daily business, the Wear is now becalmed.

It is either forgotten, under-appreciated or overlooked, but the north-east was a 'frontier economy' for two centuries. There is reportage from Middlesbrough in the late nineteenth and early twentieth centuries using Klondike terminology. In 1830 less than 100 people lived in Middlesbrough. In 1860, 20,000 lived in Middlesbrough.

Iron ore had been discovered in the Cleveland Hills and was superseding coal as the main employer. Middlesbrough was a place to go. In 1862 the Chancellor of the Exchequer and future prime minister, William Gladstone, arrived in town. He made a speech about Middlesbrough that became a source of civic pride: 'This remarkable place, the youngest child of England's enterprise, is an infant, but if an infant, an infant Hercules.'

By 1900, though coal remained a prominent industry, the Tees was known as 'the Steel River' and 90,000 people had rushed from across Britain and Ireland to a place that had not existed 70 years earlier.

It was also now a football town. There were initially two clubs, one of which was called Ironopolis. There is a banner proclaiming that name at Middlesbrough matches at the Riverside Stadium and on the night of the Middlesbrough-Doncaster Rovers game in October 2013, retired workers of the local steel and chemical industries were special guests. It was dubbed 'Spirit of Teesside' evening.

The roots of town and club were being reaffirmed. Boro defender George Friend, from agricultural Devon, was taken to see the 'gritty majesty' of Redcar steelworks. It once employed 20,000; today it's 1,800. It was once owned locally; today it is owned by a company headquartered in Bangkok.

George Friend was impressed: 'These people are proper men. ' But in October 2015, Redcar's coke ovens were closed, bringing anger and anxiety and more questions about Teesside's future.

Middlesbrough's dramatic population growth and industrialisation was happening all over the north-east in the nineteenth century, in pockets large and small. Newcastle's population in 1801 was 34,000; in 1901 it was 234,000.

If the region – and its footballers – now suffer from the effects of globalisation, the north-east was there at the beginning of global trading, instigating and benefiting from it.

Dr Bill Lancaster is Director of the Centre for Northern Studies at Northumbria University. 'In the seventeenth and eighteenth centuries the world economy shifts from one dependent on biological power to one dependent on mineral power,' he says. 'And that shift takes place up here.

'If you were to re-write a history of the Industrial Revolution you could start here and not with Cottonopolis, not with Lancashire. Factories and machinery are only part of the Industrial Revolution and you can't have them without power.'

Professor David Byrne from Durham University stressed the early prosperity. 'Coal,' he says, 'becomes the indigenous fuel of the Industrial Revolution, much of which is driven by the need to service coal-exporting – shipbuilding – then by the creation of technologies that require a lot of fuel – iron and steel, the railways.

'It was a frontier economy. There is this flow of people into the region, and it's a high-wage economy.'

The evidence of previous wealth and enterprise surrounded Bill Lancaster in the Mining Institute on Westgate Road in central Newcastle. It is one of those grand brownstone buildings obese hen parties stagger past in pink cowboy hats on their way from the railway station to the nightlife of the so-called party city.

'Newcastle in the nineteenth century controlled the world's most important commodity, which is coal,' Lancaster says, 'This is nineteenth century Dallas. Look at the architecture, Newcastle is the first city to pull itself down and rebuild itself. That's in the 1830s, 20 years before Paris.

'We're sat here in this magnificent library and next door the world's first light bulb was lit up [by Joseph Swan]; 25 yards over there, the world's first power station was built.

'Charles Parsons was a member here. Parsons was the man who invented the turbine engine, which generated electricity to power boats – also the basis of the jet engine. [George] Stephenson was a member, Stephenson needed to invent locomotives to move heavy coal. It all comes from where we are now. In a sense, the whole modern world in terms of power, energy, emanates from this building.

'I think at the time economic historians were writing their histories they focused on factories and overlooked other things that were important. People up here who have been involved in industry at a professional level really do feel quite miffed that the region has been overlooked.

'That feeds into a sense of regional difference. It's a part of the negative, this sense that the outside world doesn't see us as important but we really are. Our history really is something.'

In print, Lancaster's words can come across as evangelical but the delivery is methodical. However, beneath that academic understanding lies a frustration that is spreading and can be described in a word Lancaster used: Overlooked.

It is a sense that is historic and contemporary and if the legitimacy of the feeling is worth debate, it is there. Lancaster points around the room; to Sir George Elliot, son of a Gateshead miner whose company manufactured the first Transatlantic cables and to William Coulson, a Durham miner commissioned by the Prussian government in the 1840s to develop deep mining in the Ruhr.

In a relatively short period, such human invention, spirit and industry gave the north-east an economic purpose and from that a civic society and culture.

'Football comes at the end of that early period,' Lancaster says. 'Newcastle as a city still has a swagger. In the early 1900s you get the first great Newcastle United team, possibly their greatest-ever team, which has Colin Veitch as captain, an England captain and huge hero of the region. That gave Tyneside a particular sense of identity at a time when Newcastle still felt buoyant.

'But it takes a huge hit in the First World War. In August 1914 the North Sea closes down and the Great Northern Coalfield was based on export. A lot of pits close, a lot of pitmen join up. And they don't come back. In very large numbers. Horrendous.'

✦

EVEN THOUGH IT CAME more than 130 years after his birth, Lancaster's reference to Colin Veitch held meaning. It could be said Colin Veitch is Newcastle United's ultimate forgotten hero.

One detail alone makes Veitch interesting – he is the reason why George Bernard Shaw's last public speech was made in a theatre in Newcastle upon Tyne. But there were many aspects to a man who captained Newcastle United to their first league title, in 1905.

Veitch was captain again in 1907 and 1909, when Newcastle added two more league titles. In 1910 Veitch was captain at Goodison Park when Newcastle secured their first FA Cup.

Newcastle United were one of the clubs of the era and in a team with a Scottish secretary/manager, Frank Watt, and sometimes seven Scottish players, Veitch was its local emblem. In 1911 *The Times* stated: 'Veitch's personality is the soul of his team.'

Newcastle United had their foundation. A club formed after Middlesbrough and Sunderland, and in the shadow of Sunderland's triumphant title-winning 'Team of All the Talents', Newcastle moved from crowds of 4,000 on Gallowgate in 1895 to 50,000 on the enlarged St James' Park in 1905.

Previously regional and peripheral, Newcastle United were transformed into a national force and soon the new phenomenon – 'fans' – would start travelling to see them in their thousands. By 1908 Newcastle would take 8,000 from Tyneside to Anfield to see the FA Cup semi-final against Fulham. By 1911 there were 63,000 at St James' to see Derby County in the Cup.

Many attendance figures were estimates. However, train companies did provide details of numbers travelling and those sources are considered reliable. In 1905, for Newcastle's first FA Cup final at Crystal Palace, the Tyne-Tees Steam Shipping Company ran a 'sea special' to take fans from Tyneside to London by boat.

Veitch was essential to all of this. According to Herbert Chapman, no less: 'One of the best teams there has ever been was that claimed by Newcastle United for ten years or so before the War, and the part which so many of them have since played in the game indicates that they were intellectually above the average.'

The *Manchester Guardian* reporter Don Davies, who played cricket for Lancashire and died in the Munich air crash in 1958, wrote an appreciation of Veitch:

> *He gave unceasing thought to the game and soon gathered around him a group of footballers who had brains and could use them. In 1903, when the team was in a groove, the Chairman of the club told Veitch, Aitken and Carr to lock themselves in a room and pick what they considered to be the best team, a unique tribute surely to professional players' judgment. This was done, and from that point emerged one of the great teams of all time, champions three times and Cup finalists five times in seven years. According to Lawrence, their goalkeeper, it was during a post-mortem in a railway train that Veitch, McWilliam and McCracken first evolved the use of off-side as a tactical weapon. With players so willing to devote continual thought to the game's problems there is small wonder that their play had an intellectual quality and a cool, calm precision one can associate with no other club, not even Sunderland, the 'team of all the talents', the team which might have dominated the next decade but for the First World War and its aftermath.*

Yet despite being Newcastle United's leader-captain, and captain of England, Veitch's name has slid from Tyneside's vocabulary like other words such as 'netty' and 'trophy'.

This is peculiar, not just because of his playing achievements, but because of what else Veitch did. On the Coast Road that today's players use to reach Newcastle's training ground they pass the People's Theatre. Veitch was one of its founders. It was this that brought him into contact with George Bernard Shaw.

Chris Goulding, actor and author, sits inside opposite a bust of Shaw and explains: 'The People's Theatre was founded in 1911, it was a branch of the British Socialist Party, part of the Clarion Movement, which was more of a cultural movement. Their members were early "greens" – into cycling, vegetarianism, things like that, usually teetotal.

'They started off in the centre of Newcastle. It's about 100 yards from St James' Park and it was said people would see Colin Veitch running around on a Saturday afternoon at a match, then see him that same evening on stage. You can't imagine that happening now.'

In 1907 Veitch was a key figure in the foundation of the Players' Union – forerunner of the Professional Footballers' Association. He led a brief player strike over the issue of injury compensation in players' contracts – there was none – and missed the opening game of the 1909/10 season because he was in Birmingham negotiating with the FA.

The First World War ended Veitch's playing career. 'He volunteered and he became an officer in the Royal Garrison Artillery,' says Goulding. 'He was at the Western Front in France. There were sportsmen's battalions and footballers' battalions but Veitch doesn't seem to have gone into that. It's difficult [to know] because a lot of records have been destroyed.

'He came back in 1918 and re-joined the People's Theatre and did lots more Shaw. In 1921 when the People's Theatre had its tenth anniversary, they decided to put on *Man and Superman* and they asked Shaw to come up.' Shaw obliged.

Veitch also rejoined Newcastle United as a coach. He oversaw an early youth scheme – Newcastle Swifts – but that was disbanded in 1926 and he left to become manager of Bradford City.

That lasted two years; Veitch returned to the north-east where he became a reporter both in print and on the radio. This led him into conflict with Newcastle United, who were relegated for the first time in their history in 1934. Newcastle barred Veitch from travelling with the team.

More than 80 years later a reporter from the *Newcastle Evening Chronicle* – banned from St James' by owner Mike Ashley – was in the Heaton area of Newcastle where Veitch was born.

Around 30 people gathered in drizzling rain. With scant recognition at St James', Goulding had campaigned for the minimum, a plaque, to mark Veitch's life. Here it was, in September 2013, on the afternoon of the Newcastle-Leeds League Cup-tie at St James'.

It was 75 years after Veitch's death yet somehow it was timely. A debate had arisen around Newcastle United as to the value of history and of cups. The club of 2013 seemed uninterested in either. The black and white stripes first made famous by Veitch and his colleagues had 'Wonga' splashed across them. (Nine months later, money-lenders Wonga were fined £2.6m by the Financial Conduct Authority for pressurising clients by sending letters from fictitious law firms.)

One of Veitch's successors as Newcastle captain, Bob Moncur, represented the club. Moncur was captain the last time Newcastle won a major trophy, the Fairs Cup in 1969. In a captain's sense, this was first and last.

Later in the season Moncur would have to deal with accusations that he is an Ashley Yes-man, but he spoke sincerely of Veitch before unveiling a plaque that is not blue, but black and white.

'Colin played just about every position for Newcastle and was lauded as a master of his job,' Moncur said. 'He captained the team in 1905, 1907 and 1909, and he lifted the FA Cup in 1910. What the present-day fan or player would give for that record.'

✦

THE YEARS 1914-18 changed more than just the north-east but within 20 years the Jarrow March would offer defining images of an area in the grip of economic depression.

Jarrow had been a shipbuilding boom-town beside South Shields: from 1919 South Shields were in the Football League and in 1924 Shields finished five places above Manchester United in the Second Division. Ashington, Darlington, Durham City and Hartlepools United were all in the Third Division North.

As the economy worsened Shields were relegated in 1928 and folded two years later. A new club emerged in Gateshead. Durham and Ashington were soon relegated and today those clubs, and South Shields, are members of the amateur Northern League.

If economic self-confidence declined in the years after the end of the First World War, football was embedded in the social rhythm of the region. In Sunderland's Winter Gardens there is a video clip a 1930s sweaty shipyard worker saying: 'It's in our blood, football, like shipbuilding. You can't imagine Sunderland without football or shipbuilding.'

Football was, to use Arthur Hopcraft's phrase 'Inherent in the people', and Alex Ferguson would tell of a scene in Newcastle's Northumberland Street:

> *It's probably the only city in the world where this would happen: Archie Knox and I were once walking through the town centre and the newspaper seller was shouting out the story, 'Micky Quinn ankle injury - read all about it!' There were all these different stories in the world that day but they wanted to read about Micky Quinn's ankle. That sums up the city. I can relate to that. Manchester, Liverpool, Glasgow, Newcastle - they are all real working-class footballing cities. And that's because of the industrial*

> *nature of mining communities and ship-building communities. They seem to drift towards a passion for football as an outlet in life.*

As Professor Byrne says: 'It's the same as everywhere. Why did football embed itself in Glasgow or the big industrial cities of South America? It's a game which seems to fit very well with the working-class experience: it's cheap to set up, it's played relatively quickly – in an era of shift-work – and it was a game for all levels.

'In those days it was a consumer good. I don't think success mattered very much. What mattered was the industrial system – work – and this was an add-on, a very nice add-on.'

Success did no harm, though. The first Football League season, 1888/89, contained no north-east club, but that does not mean there was no north-east activity.

The Northern League was initiated at the Three Tuns Hotel, Durham in March 1889 and the first title was claimed by Darlington St Augustine's. Newcastle West End came second and Newcastle East End were fourth. Three years later an amalgamation of those two clubs led to Newcastle United.

The Football League is the oldest in the world. The Northern League is the second-oldest: 2014 marked its 125th anniversary.

Sunderland joined the Football League in 1890 and won the title five times before the First World War. After their first triumph the League held its AGM in the Queen's Hotel on Fawcett Street, Sunderland. They decided to create a Second Division. During Sunderland's yo-yo years, that always seemed an uncomfortable umbilical link.

In 1902, when Sunderland were champions for a fourth time, Newcastle finished third. Newcastle were coming – they won the league in 1905, 1907 and in 1909 when Sunderland were third. Middlesbrough came ninth that season – three north-east clubs in the top ten. Geography was not a problem.

In 1910 Newcastle became the first north-east club to win the FA Cup, though only after losing the finals of 1905, 1906 and 1908. They also lost in 1911.

These successes and final near-misses, this national prominence weekly and seasonal, nurtured a culture and gave definition to an area. Football became one of the characteristics associated with the north-east. It became established, a place where football mattered. Crowds boomed.

There were other indications of strength. In February 1904 Newcastle United paid the world-record fee of £700 to Sunderland for Scottish full-back Andy McCombie. McCombie was a title-winner and leader at Sunderland and his transfer was a sensation. As player and coach, he stayed at St James' Park for the next 40 years.

Sunderland invested £520 of that money in a striker born in their own town whom they had sold to Sheffield United: Alf Common. Common had scored in the 1902 FA Cup final for Sheffield United; now Sunderland wanted him back.

Yet he stayed only eight months because in February 1905 – the month England played at the recently constructed Ayresome Park – Middlesbrough made national headlines by signing Common for £1,000. He was, officially, the first player ever to be signed for a four-figure fee, which is why Alf Common, the son of a Wearmouth ship riveter from North Milburn Street, appears on lists today of world-record fees that includes Johan Cruyff, Alan Shearer and Gareth Bale.

Alf Common's transfer to Middlesbrough was another sensation, another sign of a contagious sporting culture. Or rather it was seen as the – unwelcome – commercialising of football, the subject of editorials and outrage that reached the floor of the House of Commons.

But this was also a sports story. The *Athletic News* said at the time: 'As a matter of commerce, ten young recruits at £100 apiece might have paid better, and as a matter of sport the Second Division would be more honourable than retention of place by purchase.'

At the time Middlesbrough signed Common, they were not near the top pushing for the title, they were second-bottom of the old, original First Division. They produced a world-record fee while second-bottom without an away win all season. In Common's first game Middlesbrough won away 1-0: scorer, Common.

Middlesbrough stayed up. Arthur Appleton, author of the incomparable *Hotbed of Soccer*, noted dryly: 'The First Division place was retained by purchase.'

Common, capped three times by England, stayed five years at Ayresome Park and then moved to Woolwich Arsenal. On retirement he returned to Darlington to run pubs. He died in the town in 1946.

The First World War interrupted football's rise but in the 1920s Sunderland were again quick to spend the money raised by huge attendances. In March 1922 they went on a spree, breaking the world-record fee by signing Warneford 'Warney' Creswell for £5,500 from South Shields and Michael Gilhooley for just £250 less from Hull City. The club spent more than £20,000 in under a month.

Warney Cresswell, whose younger brother Frank also played for Sunderland, was an England international already. In December 1925 Sunderland again broke the world record transfer fee when they signed Bob Kelly from Burnley for £6,550. All this activity stimulated ever more interest, and ever more players. Warney Cresswell would leave Sunderland for Everton where, with Dixie Dean, he won the league title in 1928 and 1932 and the FA Cup in 1933. He was elegant evidence of the spreading north-east influence, which, while by no means all one way, was rinsing south and west across England.

✦

In 1880 two men, one called Swan and one called Hunter, came together to form a shipyard on the River Tyne. In 1904 Swan Hunter decided to create an early form of youth club for the company's apprentices in the area, Wallsend. In time that developed into Wallsend Boys Club.

At the last count Wallsend Boys had produced 59 professionals from 1965 onward. In 1996, one of them, Alan Shearer, became captain of England.

Terms that came directly from industry, such as 'production line', are used about Wallsend Boys Club. Among many others, players of the quality and influence of Peter Beardsley and Steve Bruce also played for Wallsend. Shearer, Beardsley, Alan Thompson, Michael Carrick and Fraser Forster have all played for England.

There is a direct and traceable line that runs from a Tyneside shipyard to World Cup finals and it all started in a hut on Station Road, Wallsend, at the end of which was the Rising Sun colliery. In nineteenth century London, the domestic coal of choice was 'Wallsend Best'.

'It was, truthfully, a bit dilapidated, but it had a pull,' says Vince Carrick, father of Michael, and one of the many Wallsend BC volunteers. 'We were nomads, we didn't have our own outdoor pitches. Our indoor goalposts were made by welders from Swan's.'

It was one detail of many that reinforced the connection to industry. But Swan Hunter and the industries around it did more than supply welders and steel: they supplied a massive workforce with employment. The sons of those workers then played at the Boys Club.

'What you had were the sons of men who worked within the area,' Carrick says, 'in the yards, in the mines. There was Parsons, which employed 7,000 at one stage. There were 12,000 working at Swan's. Northeast Marine, next to Swan Hunter, that was heavy engineering. You couldn't move for heavy engineering. Visualise that – 7,000 at Parsons, 12,000 at Swan Hunter, thousands working at other places. Where have all these people moved to? Where have these families gone?'

Michael McGill is another who has spent years volunteering at the club. 'Wallsend was really thriving,' he says, 'you had thousands working down on the river and in the mines. It was a really busy town. But Swan Hunter's as we knew it shut in 1974. Families began to disappear. It made a big difference.

'The wife worked for Clelands Shipyards, only a small shipyard, but it was successful. A bloke called Graham Day came in from Canada – the Tory government brought him in – and his aim was to close shipyards. Which he did. A lot of miners moved down to the Mansfield, Nottingham area. There was definitely a conscious political decision to shut the mines. And the north-east, Durham in particular, suffered more than most.'

The River Tyne was once a hub of industry, the source of a city; it is now the subject of book titles such as *Lost Industries of the Tyne*. The removal of industry has had a knock-on effect on Wallsend.

'The culture of kids in the north-east has changed like everywhere else,' says McGill. 'The family structure, where the father worked, that's gone. Nowadays the father works, the mother works, the kids have got a key. Years ago you finished on a Friday at half-past four. Now you've got Saturday, Sunday work, weekend working is normal. Definitely social change is part of it, the way people live their lives now is different.'

McGill and Carrick have also seen a change in boys and their opportunities. In the late 1980s four lads from Wallsend Boys Club – Thompson, Lee Clark, Robbie Elliott and Steve Watson – all joined Newcastle United. They all made it into the first team and all had long, successful careers.

'You don't see three and four lads being picked up now,' Carrick says, 'it's the odd one. It must be a combination of things, but take those four who came from the Boys Club to Newcastle United, they were four mates. The four of them helped each other, spurred each other on. It gave them a competitive edge. The games I watch now, you don't see the outstanding players you used to see.

'We've been around football for years. The area hasn't changed in its love for football, it is a religion, but the standards have changed. The level is lower. Foreign players and managers are contributing factors. Newcastle have ten Frenchmen.' The globalisation of English football saw Newcastle United name the following starting XI for the opening home game of season 2013/14: Krul (born in Netherlands); Debuchy (b. France), Coloccini (b. Argentina), Yanga-Mbiwa (b. Central African Republic), Santon (b. Italy); Sissoko (b. France), Anita (b. Netherlands Antilles), Ben Arfa (b. France), Marveaux (b. France); Cissé (b. Senegal), Shola Ameobi (b. Nigeria).

Globalisation had clogged the old arterial route; it coincided with reduced local flow. As McGill says: 'Lads want to play football, just not as many. I would say it was more competitive in the old days, massively competitive. The production line hasn't been quite the same as it was.'

✦

BOB PAISLEY SAID OF HIS HOME AND UPBRINGING: 'Hetton-le-Hole is a typical Durham mining village, a close-knit community seven miles from Sunderland where coal was king and football was a religion.

'There are many similar villages dotted all around the north-east and working-class lads automatically turned to football, not just as a recreation, but as a way of life.'

There are times when Paisley's and others' comparison with religion do not seem overblown: faith, habit, rituals, difficult questions. And one act recognised as religious is that people have their ashes spread on pitches, perhaps most famously Jackie Milburn's at St James' Park.

On the darkening afternoon in January 2006 when Shearer drilled in the winner for Newcastle against Mansfield Town in an FA Cup tie at St James', the goal brought Shearer's Newcastle tally to 200, equal with Milburn. Shearer scored it at the Gallowgate End and peeled away, right arm raised, and ran to the main stand, the Milburn Stand. Shearer was aware of the symbolism.

'I was brought up being told how great Jackie Milburn was,' Shearer said after the game. 'I never had the pleasure of meeting him but I have met some of his family. From what I know, what impresses me most is that he was a man of the people and that is very, very important. I never dreamed of something like this when I signed, never in a million years did I think I would be sat up there with Jackie.'

Milburn died in 1988. He was 64. His funeral saw 30,000 on the streets of Ashington, his hometown, and Newcastle, where he won his success as a player.

On the 25th anniversary of his death, the *Newcastle Evening Chronicle* produced a special edition. Milburn's son – Jackie junior – was quoted: 'He was such a modest man and would never have expected so many to have turned out for him. He never realised what a legend he was.'

Jackie Milburn was notoriously modest and would have blushed at the notion that 25 years after his death the local papers would not just be marking the event, but that people would be buying those papers. Maybe he did not fully grasp what he added to the north-east's football reverie.

Born in 1924 into an Ashington mining and football dynasty, Jackie Milburn was lyrical, on the pitch and off it. His miner father – 'recognised as one of the best coal-cutters in the business' according to his son – sounds both heroic and hard.

Milburn's extended family included Jack, George and Jim who played for Leeds United and Stan who played for Leicester City. Before them Tanner Milburn played for Ashington in their Football League days. Jackie's cousin Cissie gave birth to Jack and Bobby Charlton.

From birth Jackie Milburn had two worlds, coal and football. He worked in both but if the former was a necessity, the latter was the dream: 'So keen was I to become a footballer I even kicked a stone to and from school – eight miles a day. I kept the same stone for three years.'

He revealed this Huckleberry Finn outlook again when writing of his grandparents' house on Sixth Row and boys on the street obsessed with football. Milburn depicted an area in thrall to a game and eight decades on it is one that speaks about modern childhood, too, about independence and unstructured play.

It was Christmas 1932 and eight-year-old Milburn had received a pair of football boots:

> *Like all youngsters I looked upon Christmas Eve as a night of magic. When I drifted into a half-sleep there was nothing by my bedside. When I awoke, at 3.30, there were a dozen gifts. I shall always recall opening my eyes, switching on my new flashlight and letting out a whoop of excitement when I spotlighted the football boots at the end of my bed. Hurriedly I slipped into my clothes, then the new football boots and, gliding like a thief from the house, I ran as fast as my legs would carry me to my granny's home. As it was only four o'clock in the morning, and several other young fellows I knew were going to have boots as presents, I meant to be first on the scene when the big get-together came about. But I was disappointed. When I arrived at Sixth Row – and remember it was only just after four o'clock on Christmas morning – most of my friends, wearing their new boots, were playing football by torchlight in the middle of the street. It nearly broke my heart. There were so many lads playing I had to wait nearly ten minutes before I could eventually get a game.*

MINING ENDURED. As David Byrne says: 'Coal employment peaks at the start of the First World War. In Britain there were 1.1m miners – one adult male in 13 of working age was a coalminer. This stays high after the War into the 1950s. The shipyards were similar. They boomed during the wars and after. But there was not a lot of re-investment in the yards. So they were run down.'

In 2014 the United Kingdom still relied upon coal power to generate 40 per cent of its electricity, but the coal, mainly, comes from abroad. British coal feels like the past and whenever it is mentioned today it is usually in association with the end of coal, the 1984/85 Miners' Strike.

The political drama of that strike has obscured much of what went before and there is reduced appreciation of what the coal industry meant to the UK and areas such as the north-east. The National Union of Mineworkers still exist. They have offices dotted around former heartlands. One is in Ashington – one of Ashington FC's sponsors is the NUM.

Denis Murphy spent almost 30 years in Ellington colliery, then became Labour MP for Wansbeck. Murphy was speaking from the NUM office in Ashington on what is now a business park.

'It was about more than just a pit,' Murphy says. 'It was about a town and what it supported. Ashington once had five cinemas, now it's got none. This was the original company coal town – 85-90 per cent of people in a town of 28,000 worked in the mine or in associated jobs. Ashington's existence is based on coal. It shaped the very people we are – the miners' church, the Holy Sepulchre, had no bell. The company didn't want miners' sleep interrupted.

'Miners built the town. They built a hospital, libraries, retirement homes and more, all by subscription from their pay packet. It was organised. Ashington miners in particular have a long history of football, cricket and rugby.

'The vast majority of benefits were provided by miners themselves. It was never a well-paid job, but it was reasonably paid. It was inclusive, there were people with university degrees working here and those who today would be said to have learning difficulties. They were all looked after. There was a spirit.

'At the beginning of 1984 there were 22,000 working in the north-east coalfield. It was generally accepted that each job there supported three more in the supply chain – distribution etcetera. Now there's 1,800 miners nationally, in Yorkshire and Nottinghamshire. We're up here in a cul-de-sac at the end of the industrial north-east. The whole mentality is about the south-east.'

Murphy pointed out that the HS2 rail project is due to halt at Leeds.

Bill Lancaster says of the 1984-85 strike: 'In the South there was a feeling that coal is a loser, they lost. Mrs Thatcher was bringing in a new world. Then there's the whole green agenda – coal is dirty, coal is causing all the problems, coal is the heroin of energy.

'The Great Northern Coalfield, which at one point was the world's largest, we've only ever taken one third of it out. If we do get clean technology we could boom again. It could be an asset for the future.'

Murphy's opinion of Northumberland is echoed on Teesside. That Teesside, much-maligned today, remained comparatively buoyant until 1970, and as recently as then had only London and oil-rich Aberdeen generating more of the UK's GDP, is not part of the 21st century depiction of the place. Rather, it is part of what *The Economist* newspaper dubbed 'Rustbelt Britain' in 2013. *The Economist* is written and edited in London.

'Steel and chemicals were still very big in the 1960s,' says David Byrne, 'engineering too. That's the stage in the UK's history when you had the highest proportion of the employed population in industrial work. Middlesbrough was probably the most industrial place there's ever been anywhere on the planet at that point.

'It drops like a stone from 1975 onwards. This happens in our lifetime.'

Bill Lancaster offers the contrast of how Middlesbrough was and how it is. 'Whereas Middlesbrough is now top of every bad statistic going, when I was growing up in the 1960s my posh relatives came from Teesside. Middlesbrough was a wonderful place, full employment, high wages, a combination of ICI and old shipbuilding, heavy engineering. It flows down the river. It was incredibly important.

'The reversal has been amazingly dramatic. The break-up of ICI, that took the confidence away from the whole area. Drive through Middlesbrough now and there's hardly any construction and the skilled labour has migrated. They talk about the petrochemical industries of the Middle East and Far East being dominated by the "Teesside mafia". What you have left behind are the unskilled, and they're having a terrible time.'

IT IS A DRAMATIC CHANGE. It is also part of a reality that stretches across the north-east and sparks fraught questions about what happens to an industrial society once industry withers.

Niall Quinn's hand rested on the door of a Sunderland pub with a hand-written scrawl on it: 'No cider warriors'.

Quinn pushed on. Inside he discovered a photograph of himself behind the bar, stuck up with Blu-tack and pride. It was late July 2007, a year after Quinn had led an Irish takeover of Sunderland by the Drumaville group, a year in which Sunderland were promoted back to the Premier League.

Quinn was the Irish chairman of a club with Roy Keane as manager and a boardroom predominantly Irish. When Sunderland won 5-0 at Luton Town to clinch the Championship, three of the four scorers were Irish. The club were dubbed 'Sundireland'. Quinn had reasons to be thinking and talking about identity.

Born in Dublin and having played football for Arsenal and Manchester City, Quinn had been in England 13 years before he joined Sunderland. He was the club's record £1.3m signing in August 1996. He scored two goals at Nottingham Forest on his full debut, but those were his only goals of that season. Quinn suffered a cruciate ligament injury one month after Forest and Sunderland were relegated from the Premier League.

The next season, Quinn was still carrying the injury, and considering retirement, when he played against Norwich City in the second home game. He missed a sitter, Sunderland lost 1-0. Afterwards, as he made his way to his car outside Roker Park, a Sunderland fan approached Quinn and spat at him. That was an indication of Quinn's status on Wearside in August 1997. Quinn had his wife and daughter beside him. He froze.

A decade on, Quinn had an altogether different status. He had blossomed as a player after recovering from that injury, and the car park, and earned herograms for his partnership with Kevin Phillips. But, more than that, Quinn began to speak up for Sunderland, for Wearside. He fell into company with former miners and talked their language, 'the spirit of coal' as he said. Wearside, sneered at from without and sometimes from within, had a champion. It's not to be overstated. But it's not to be underestimated either.

In 2006 Quinn had returned in a suit, with financial backers and a boardroom obligation to speak. But when he looked around, he saw a population struggling. The club inhabited the Stadium of Light but it was on the site where Monkwearmouth colliery had stood. The colliery had been there since 1835. No more.

Mining had gone from Sunderland and so had shipbuilding. In 1977 there were 7,500 still working in shipyards on the Wear; in 1984 that number was 4,400. In 1988 the last shipyard closed. The twin industrial pillars for Sunderland's existence had gone.

'Increasingly,' Quinn said then, 'the football club is no longer part of Sunderland's identity, we are the identity.'

The football club was not immune to unemployment. When Sunderland had been relegated from the Premier League in 2006 with the record-low total of 15 points, humiliation was followed by job losses. Forty per cent of the non-playing staff were let go; Sunderland's debt was around £40m.

There were other statistics produced then: seven of the country's 25 most deprived council wards were within a five-mile radius of the stadium; 37 per cent of local families lived on the poverty line; one fifth of the surrounding population lacked basic literacy skills; school truancy was alarmingly high. The data came from the club.

'We know who we are and we know Sunderland,' Quinn said, 'this is not Knightsbridge. We are different, we have something else and the one big ingredient is the people and their noise. We are aware of our history, of days when men went from the pit to the club, and sometimes into the team. What we're trying to recreate is the passion and spirit of the terraces in a team.'

David Byrne said then: 'Sunderland's history is all about heavy industry, the Industrial Revolution. With the development of north-east coal you get carboniferous capitalism – and once you could get coal on a ship it became much more valuable. That's what Sunderland comes from.

'But then Sunderland's shipyards are closed and coal disappeared because of a decision to smash organised labour. It's since then that the football club has taken on a heightened sense of identity.'

Six years on, Byrne's view has not changed. 'In the past,' he says, 'I think people's attachment to football clubs was quite real, but it has become of greater importance. It's hyper because there's nothing else.

'What do you have as an identity? I've done a lot of oral history work and when the last mines closed in South Shields I interviewed a lot of miners. There was sense of pride in their job. Coal was the energy of the world, there was pride in that. Shipyard workers always turned out for a launch and they brought their families with them: "I made that."

'Football is hyper because it is the one thing around that still has some of that character. It differentiates you from someone else.'

Another change, over the past decade in particular, is the character of football clubs. Sunderland, Middlesbrough and Newcastle United all now have charity arms – Foundations. Sunderland's, the biggest in the country, employs 91 full-time staff and 87 part-time, Newcastle United's 44 and 16 and Middlesbrough's 30.

Not too long ago a football club selected a team to play for it on a Saturday afternoon and in doing so represent its area, town or city. The club was basically its starting XI and results. Now football clubs, via Foundations, are involved in education, health, welfare and, in Middlesbrough's case, a food bank.

Andy Clay, head of Middlesbrough's Foundation, which was set up by local owner-chairman Steve Gibson in 1996, explains: 'As a charity we need to be at the heart of social issues on Teesside. There are some really horrible stats about child poverty and family poverty. Our aim was to use the club to bring in food, which could then be used by the food banks on Teesside, but also to raise our profile and show people what we are about.

'The response was huge, people bringing food hampers in on matchdays. We had drop-off points at various places, some junior football clubs then offered to be a drop-off point, so did some companies. The established food banks then weigh what you give them, a great way of measuring how many families can be fed with that food. It's a way of measuring the difference you can make.'

Clay was speaking at a sports hall run by the club on Normanby Road in Eston. At the top of that road is a sign that proclaims: 'Born of Iron, Made of Steel'.

Gibson recognised the power of the club's identity two decades ago. Once Middlesbrough moved from Ayresome Park to the Riverside Stadium, classrooms were installed. The remit has broadened since and while the Foundation is a separate organisation, that is a semantic and financial separation.

'We run a football league for the homeless – in here,' Clay says, 'and you should see the pride and passion when we supply them with a Middlesbrough shirt. They maybe have a Middlesbrough tattoo on their leg but they've not been to a match because they can't afford to go. That's where football has a tremendous reach. The shocking thing is that the average age is under 30. That exists on Teesside.'

The following day Boro defender Ben Gibson – nephew of Steve – was in a school in Stockton as part of the club's literacy drive. As Clay says: 'I think people outside football would be surprised at the variety of the work we do.'

The state of England's education funding and infrastructure means that the football club, via its body of coaching staff, is also used to provide PE in schools across the area. Where a school has no dedicated PE teacher – and there are many in a place of rising obesity – it can 'buy' a coach from Middlesbrough Football Club for either a day, a week or a term. The Foundation has to be economically viable.

'We have three classrooms within the stadium itself, all equipped with IT,' Clay says. 'It's a fantastic resource, we can bring schools to us. We have a programme about 'digital inclusion' that is used in welfare reform. There is also adult education, we're doing a lot around men's health at the moment.'

No longer on Sunderland's board, Quinn looked at the changed role of clubs and says: 'It's huge now in a place like Sunderland. It's a bit of a dilemma - you're trying to be a focal point for the community but you're also trying to bring in revenue from it. It's a strange phenomenon. You have to give value; and you have to give hope. And in the end you know that it all still boils down to results.'

Some other health statistics provide an insight into post-industrial culture where unemployment is stubbornly high, often twice the national average. In 2012 it was revealed that the north-east had the highest number of obesity-related hospital admissions in the country – almost three times the national average. Sunderland Royal Hospital has a specialist ward for the morbidly obese.

Peter Small, a senior consultant surgeon at the hospital, told the *Sunderland Echo*: 'This used to be a heavy industry area, and if you look at the other obese areas in the country, they were also heavy industry.

'What have our jobs been replaced with? We've got a lot of call centres around here, mainly sedentary. If you're unemployed, what are you going to do for the day? I'm sure having nothing to do doesn't help matters. The only way we increase our calorie-burn these days is to actually exercise, and that used to be how you lived.'

Today around 10,000 are employed in call centres in Sunderland. They make a major contribution to the local economy. At the Nissan car plant there are now 7,000 employed. There is a supply chain from the plant estimated to help maintain 40,000 other jobs.

And in Newton Aycliffe, about a hundred yards away from where George Stephenson assembled *Locomotion* No.1 in 1825, Japanese firm Hitachi have started construction on a new train-building site. Full production is expected to begin in 2016 with 700 jobs initially. The north-east will be making trains again and if the livery is black and yellow like the *Locomotion*'s it will be noted in Gus Poyet's home-town, Montevideo. Penarol, Uruguay's premier club, formed by English railway workers, play in those colours in honour of Stephenson's creation.

✦

THE DOLPHIN CENTRE, DARLINGTON, early March 2014. The television in the first-floor café is re-running pictures of Newcastle United manager Alan Pardew jutting his head into the face of Hull City player David Meyler. The news is that Pardew had accepted an FA charge of misconduct.

Upstairs in the Central Hall there are no television cameras but the life president of Newcastle United, Sir John Hall, is on his feet giving a speech about the state of the north-east's economy at the invitation of the Lord Mayor of Darlington. About 30 people have paid a fiver to hear this. They were entertained, possibly surprised. Few expect to hear Hall praising Clement Attlee.

Hall is another north-east figure connecting coal and football. Plain John Hall became known nationally in the 1980s for turning a derelict site in Gateshead into the Metro Centre, Europe's biggest shopping mall at the time. He became 'Margaret Thatcher's favourite businessman', then led a takeover of Newcastle United, brought

Kevin Keegan back as manager, re-ignited a club and a city and talked loudly of the 'Geordie nation'.

But long before all that, Hall was underground surveying coalmines in Northumberland, for 12 years. Here he was in Darlington speaking glowingly about the 1945 Labour government and its 'liberating' effects on the north-east and the British working-class. Hall has covered different terrain.

A fortnight later on his Wynyard Hall estate near Hartlepool, once owned by coal owner Lord Londonderry, Hall, 81, expanded on that theme.

'I worked on the coast,' he says. 'There were a group of pits, Lynemouth, Newbiggin, Ellington and Woodhorn. Three of them, apart from Newbiggin, belonged to the Ashington Coal Company.

'I was a surveyor at the coalface. I used to watch these men lying on their side digging, thinking: "What a job."

'The great thing was the camaraderie, the working-class spirit. The "Big Society"? All the mining villages had the big society long before anyone thought about that. You lived with each other. There were 34 houses on my street and you knew everyone on it. We lived as one.

'But a coal-village life was structured, your life was set out for you and ruled by the colliery manager, the headmaster and doctor, they controlled your life. I always feel that before the war I was fodder for the coal mines, working-class fodder.

'It was expected of me to go down the pit – it would have affected my father if I hadn't, he might have lost his house.

'Then Attlee came in and there was a social and political revolution. The Labour Party had fought hard for change and got in with a massive majority in 1945. I was a strong left-winger. I could never understand why my father and other miners didn't vote Communist. He was a Labour man, he wasn't left-wing. The miners were never extreme.

'I was a strong supporter of Attlee. There was one road in and out of our village and I remember holding a tin of paint, white paint, while my father and his friends painted on the road: "Vote for Labour, do it well, let the Tories go to hell."

'There was change. It was a tremendous liberation. It gave us free health, free education and nationalized industries. They nationalized the pits, and that was the pinnacle of my father's life. I can still see it, the day they pulled back a little curtain to say: 'This colliery is now managed by the National Coal Board on behalf of The People.' That was liberation.

'They also got more money. And money liberates you. You feel cowed when you don't have money. I'm a product of that Attlee government.'

Hall recalls the sense of power miners must have felt on hearing post-war Foreign Secretary Ernest Bevin saying: 'Give me a million tons of coal and I'll give you a foreign policy.'

But by the mid-1980s Hall was a face of the Thatcherite model of private enterprise. He is unapologetic about that but when he looks around the north-east he worries about a low-wage economy and a lack of political influence. Of nearby Hartlepool being described as rust-belt, Hall says: 'Hartlepool is there because it had a *raison d'etre.* The north-east had a *raison d'etre.* What is it now? Nobody knows.

'We were at the forefront of the Industrial Revolution before anybody else and we came to the end of it before anybody else. We've probably reached the bottom of a curve but we haven't found what is next. When China got organised, their labour was so cheap, it hit us. In shipbuilding we reacted to change too late, we didn't re-invest and look ahead. We had short-term capitalism.

'There's a negative feeling about the north-east. Labour brought us great change socially and economically. But it didn't change us culturally.

'This is a Labour fiefdom and it has kept us culturally static.'

Considering that Tony Blair was MP for Sedgefield, Peter Mandelson was MP for Hartlepool, Alan Milburn was MP for Darlington, and Durham-born Jack Cunningham was in the cabinet, the north-east had potential clout under New Labour. In 2007 Nick Brown was made minister for the north-east, a new office.

That influence, however, departed with the arrival of the Conservative/Liberal Coalition government. There is no one from the north-east in the cabinet either in terms of constituency or origin. Lord Howell, father-in-law of George Osborne, described the north-east as desolate and ripe for fracking. He apologised but it was felt.

It added to the complaint within the north-east of being overlooked. When prime minister David Cameron led a trade mission to China in 2013, he took 131 business leaders: 92 were from the south-east, two were from the north-east. It was noticed. It was on the front page of the *Northern Echo.*

In October 2013 a charity called the International Foundation surveyed government policy on the young. A report into its findings began: 'The north-east of England is the worst place in the UK to be young because of its high levels of youth unemployment and low levels of engagement with national politics.'

A report into Arts Council England found it spent £20 per head of population in London against £3.60 in the rest of the country. In 2014/15 the grant to the Royal Opera House (London) was to be £26.4m; the grant to the Sage (Gateshead) was to be £3.6m.

Even within 'the North' it can feel like the north-east is a far corner. Tom Bloxham is a Manchester-based entrepreneur. Interviewed in the *Sunday Times Magazine* about plans for Leeds-Manchester-Liverpool forming a new kind of northern corridor metropolis to rival London, Bloxham was asked about Newcastle upon Tyne.

'We'll have to think about that one,' he replied. 'They can't go back to coal and shipbuilding, but don't underestimate the talent and fresh thinking there.'

In January 2014 the Centre for Cities think-tank reported on the north-east's 'brain drain' to London. It said that between 2009 and 2012, 6,000 mainly 18–30 year-olds left the north-east for London, 4,500 from Newcastle alone.

'London is frightening,' Hall said that night in Darlington.

He was a mix of reluctant accountant and bullish native: 'Our wage structure is too low; there are three million people in the region, not enough. But we don't want companies coming here for cheap labour. Tell them to go to hell.'

'OVERLOOKED': a football application could be called the Stan Mortensen Syndrome.

On 2 May 1953 Stan Mortensen did something that no one else had done to that point of the twentieth century, or since – he scored a hat-trick in an FA Cup final.

Wembley Stadium had never seen anything like it. Mortensen's team, Blackpool, won that final 4-3 against Bolton Wanderers thanks to their centre-forward's three goals and it is regarded as the greatest ever FA Cup final.

It is known as: 'The Matthews Final'.

Stan Mortensen came from South Shields. 'Had it not been for this best of all games,' he said, 'I might have spent my life more or less glued to the docks of the north-east coast.'

Modern football is overwhelmed by dull statistics but Mortensen's merit accolades. There were many for Blackpool and England but the deeds of May 1953 defined him to the extent that when Mortensen died, in 1991, it was said: 'They'll probably call it "The Matthews Funeral."'

Given what teammates said about Mortensen, he might have laughed.

Mortensen described himself as 'one ordinary South Shields lad'. Clearly he was not. The grandson of a Norwegian sailor, which explains the surname, Mortensen's father died when he was five. His mother had two sons to bring up alone on Lord Nelson Street. He left school at 14 to work on the Tyne – 'sometimes I helped unload the ships bringing timber from Russia'.

Mortensen's gratitude at the escape route provided by football extended to a teacher, John Young, who ran the school team, four of whom, including Mortensen, would become professionals. So good were they that Young maintained the team after they left school and placed an advert in the *North Mail* asking for all-comers nationally.

One of the responses came from Blackpool FC. After that game, held at Bloomfield Road, Blackpool offered the 16-year-old Mortensen a contract. He said Yes. He was a Sunderland fan but as Mr. Young said years later: 'Both Newcastle United and Sunderland had opportunities to sign him but the management of both were adamant that he was far too small.'

So Stan Mortensen joined the ranks of the emigrant, overlooked by his own, part of the rich, regrettable pattern of departure.

Blackpool signed two boys that day: Mortensen and his pal Dick Withington. It was 1937 and the Second World War was about to intervene. Mortensen signed up for the RAF and received his papers in February 1941. Some months later, stationed at Lossiemouth, his crew were sent out for practice. Mortensen recalled:

'We were on operational training; the Wellington caught fire, and down we went in a dive. We finished in a fir plantation, the pilot and bomb-aimer were killed, the navigator lost a leg and I got out alive with various injuries of which the worst was a head wound which called for a dozen stitches.'

These 55 words are taken from Mortensen's autobiography. It's about all there is on the day he almost lost his life and saw two colleagues lose theirs.

It took others to talk about it. In 1967 Mortensen had become Blackpool's manager and was visited by Arthur Hopcraft, who wrote of the Lossiemouth incident:

> *The crash left him [Mortensen] with insomnia, which he has lived with ever since, and a scar which supports his assertion that he is one of the luckiest men alive. It is a curved line across the back of his neck, on a level with the top of his ear lobes and a good four inches long. He keeps his hair long enough at the back to cover it but will show it on request, bending his head low and palming his hair back up. 'Eh?' he says, and looks at the ceiling, astonished still.*

Another who discussed it was Stanley Matthews. It was Matthews who revealed that 'Morty' had to be discharged from the RAF. His head injuries meant Mortensen 'couldn't cope with Morse Code any more'.

Matthews' understanding would have been appreciated. Although Mortensen offered only 55 words on the crash that almost killed him in his autobiography he devoted 13 pages to Matthews.

It was written in 1949. The pair already had a deep, real friendship. In 1948 Matthews had been named the first-ever Footballer of the Year. Mortensen was runner-up. They roomed together for Blackpool and England and when they set off on the train in 1953, they sat beside each other.

Matthews loved Mortensen's attitude, thought it was shaped by Lossiemouth and, again, contained gratitude: 'Perhaps this had an effect on how he played the game. When decisions went against him, he simply shrugged his shoulders. If he blazed over from a good position, which he rarely did, he'd stand motionless and stare, his eyes focused on the trajectory the ball had taken. Then he'd smile to himself at the absurdity of the effort. Although a formidable battler, he would never retaliate when scythed down. He had everything in perspective.'

Others confirmed this. Frank O'Farrell has recounted an FA Cup tie between West Ham and Blackpool when O'Farrell put West Ham 2-0 ahead: 'As I ran back for the kick-off Blackpool's Stan Mortensen said to me: "Well done Frank, you'll feel better now as two is better than one."'

Jackie Milburn said much the same. After scoring his second against Blackpool at Wembley in the 1951 final, Mortensen shook Milburn's hand and said: 'Well played, Jackie, that goal deserved to win any game.'

Stan Anderson knew Mortensen, from afar and near. Anderson went to the 1953 Cup final as a fan, a neutral, 'though I went thinking "I hope Stan Mortensen scores."'

Anderson also knew Ernie Taylor. In Blackpool's team, Taylor was the player who gave the ball to Matthews who gave it to Mortensen. Ernie Taylor was born in Sunderland and started out with Hylton Colliery juniors.

Playing for Newcastle United in the 1951 final, it was Taylor's back-heel that set up Milburn. It was after this performance, it is said, that Matthews told Blackpool to buy Taylor. Six months later, they did. Taylor stayed seven years at Blackpool and won an England cap. It came in the infamous 6-3 defeat by Hungary, also at Wembley, also in 1953. Stan Mortensen scored in that game.

After Blackpool, Taylor joined Manchester United after the Munich air disaster and played in a third FA Cup final in seven years, for a third club.

'Ernie Taylor was brilliant tactically,' Anderson says. 'He had pictures of the game in his head. If Ernie could have demonstrated or talked, he'd have been a top-class manager. But he couldn't, or he didn't.'

Instead Taylor worked in the Vauxhall car plant on Merseyside. He died in 1985 aged 59.

Stanley Matthews admired Taylor and revered Mortensen. He overlooked neither. When it came to Mortensen, nor did Blackpool. They erected a statue of him outside Bloomfield Road.

Matthews said the 'paramount' aim of his own autobiography was to correct the accepted version of 1953. He called the relevant chapter: 'The Mortensen Final'.

On hearing the words 'The Matthews Final', he said: 'I cringe with embarrassment'.

And of his great mate Mortensen, Matthews added:

> *To this day I miss him dearly. He scored 225 goals in 395 league games and averaged more than a goal a game in FA Cup matches. He's the only man to score a hat-trick in a Wembley FA Cup final. In 25 games for England between 1947 and 1953 he scored 23 goals including four on his England debut in that memorable game against Portugal. I don't know if the good Lord has football teams in heaven but if He does I am sure Morty will have been handed a number nine shirt as he passed through the pearly gates and I know exactly where he will be now – waiting for me at the near post.*

Miner's son from Durham, miner's son from Northumberland: Colin Bell and Bobby Charlton take tea with England manager Alf Ramsey. (Getty Images)

CHAPTER TWO

MANAGERS, PLAYERS, INFLUENCE, DIGGING

'In this great north-eastern nursery of football the game seems as important as the industries which provide the daily bread' – Stan Mortensen

SHORTLY AFTER INFORMING Howard Kendall that he would not be travelling up there to Tyneside, Mickey Thomas left Everton. He joined Brighton.

Kendall did not blame Thomas and without him Kendall did what good managers do, he managed. It took him three years to turn the Blues around but in 1984 Everton won the FA Cup and reached the final of the League Cup. This was a team gathering momentum under a manager in his stride.

The following season Everton won the league for the first time since 1970, when Kendall had been a key player. They reached the FA Cup final again, and lost, but Everton won their first and only European trophy, the Cup Winners' Cup. Howard Kendall was named Manager of the Year.

The next season, 1985/86, Everton came second in the league and again lost an FA Cup final. But in 1986/87 Everton won back the league title. Kendall was again Manager of the Year. Between 1984 and 1987 Everton won the league title twice, the FA Cup and European Cup Winners' Cup.

The 1987 title meant that as a player and manager Kendall had his third league title with Everton. Unsurprisingly he was in demand and the post-Heysel ban on English clubs in Europe changed thought processes and opportunities. After Barcelona had verbally offered him the job at Camp Nou, only for Terry Venables to stay there, Kendall left for another La Liga club, Athletic Bilbao.

Bilbao were thrilled with their new man. The season before he arrived, they finished fifteenth in La Liga and avoided relegation for the first time only by winning a play-off. In Kendall's first season Bilbao jumped to fourth, two places above Barcelona, and an example of Bilbao's gratitude and hospitality, saw them present Kendall with a specially commissioned oil painting.

'They had sent a famous painter over from Bilbao to Newcastle,' Kendall says. 'It was the Tyne Bridge.' The gesture endeared Bilbao to Kendall.

Coming fourth in La Liga took Bilbao into the Uefa Cup. They drew Juventus and that was on Kendall's mind when, at the end of October 1988, after Willie McFaul had been sacked as manager at Newcastle United, the club's chairman Gordon McKeag landed in the Basque country. Kendall was offered the job at St James' Park, his hometown club. He told them the timing was wrong.

'I was enjoying it at Bilbao, enjoying being successful – we were about to play Juventus in Europe. I just felt it wasn't the right time. I still felt the pull of Newcastle, it was just the wrong time.'

Newcastle United appointed Jim Smith instead but he could not prevent their relegation six months later.

'Anyway, Jimmy Husband used to joke, say I wasn't a proper Geordie,' Kendall says. "You're from Crawcrook, if you can't hear the hootin' 'n' tootin' of the Tyne then you're not a Geordie." I knew I was, though. I had that culture, we all had that football culture. We didn't talk about it, we just understood it. Cricket too. There wasn't anything else.'

When a part of the famed Everton midfield alongside Alan Ball and Colin Harvey, Kendall had been managed by Harry Catterick. Catterick had been a young striker when he first joined Everton in 1937. He found first Dixie Dean then Tommy Lawton in front of him, but Catterick scored 23 goals in 59 appearances for Everton after the Second World War. Harry Catterick was born in Darlington.

In 1951 Catterick left Everton to become player-manager of Crewe. He continued his managerial education at Rochdale, then joined Sheffield Wednesday in 1958. Wednesday were in the Second Division.

At the end of Catterick's first season Wednesday were promoted as champions and in his second season they finished fifth in the First Division and reached the FA Cup semi-final.

Catterick was constructing a reputation, one enhanced when in his third season Sheffield Wednesday, who had not been champions of England since 1930, were runners-up to Tottenham Hotspur's double-winners. Catterick was 41 and on his way. Everton were watching and went for him.

Catterick arrived at Goodison Park as Johnny Carey's successor. In Catterick's first season, 1961/62, Everton came fourth. In his second season Everton were champions. It was their first title since 1939.

The following season Liverpool claimed that title from their neighbours. While the Reds had the charismatic zest of Bill Shankly in their dugout, the Blues had the brilliant restraint of Harry Catterick and when it comes to the mythologising of football managers, that restraint is a contributory factor in Catterick's decreased recognition.

Catterick's manner was another factor. Kendall described Catterick as 'a cold man' and if there was warmth in the genes of Catterick's miner father, it seems it was not passed on.

Harry Catterick senior worked in mining, steel and on the railways in and around Darlington. He played football locally, to a standard good enough for Stockport County to sign him in 1926 when they were a Second Division club. The Catterick family relocated to Cheshire, which is why Harry Catterick had no trace of a north-east accent when he was in charge at Goodison Park.

Kendall quickly understood Catterick's character. There would be no canny-lad banter, no discussion of their shared geography. 'Harry Catterick wouldn't admit he came from that background, from Darlington,' says Kendall.

It sounds a harsh assessment and it might be. When Newcastle were promoted back to the First Division in 1965, Catterick told the short-lived magazine *Northern Football*: 'Everybody at Goodison Park is pleased to see Newcastle back in the First Division. It is their rightful place, and as a native of Darlington I am doubly pleased at their promotion. Football in the North-East is just as keen as on Merseyside.'

But it was the north-west where Catterick grew up and it was Merseyside that Catterick called 'unique' saying: 'There is a different atmosphere in Liverpool to anywhere else in the country.

'The intensity of feeling, the personal involvement is unique. Working as I do amid all this emotion, it would be fatal for me to become part of it.'

So he stood apart and the aloofness extended to his team. There are numerous examples of ex-Catterick players referring to his inability, or refusal, to display the human factor someone like Shankly simply could not suppress even if he had wanted to, which he didn't.

'Harry's nature is to be withdrawn and cagey,' Shankly said. 'He was just as intense as me and hell-bent on winning, but he did things in a different way. I used to call him "Happy Harry" and he called me "Rob Roy".'

Kendall recalled that Catterick would sit in his Rover and watch Everton's players do vomit-inducing sand-dune runs in pre-season. At the training ground, Catterick was invisible, but he was there: 'You'd see the blinds twitching in his office.'

Catterick did little coaching, and according to Kendall his team-talks were 'not good'. But what Catterick could do was recognise talent and promote it, as in Harvey, or buy it, as in Kendall and Ball. In as competitive an era as there has been in English football Everton were champions twice, FA Cup winners once and beaten finalists once.

When Everton won the FA Cup in 1966 against his former club Wednesday, it was the first time Everton had won the Cup since 1933. Catterick's opposite number was Alan Brown. Brown came from Northumberland.

Fear and respect – as opposed to fear, respect and affection – was the Everton squad's feeling about Catterick.

'He wasn't someone you'd warm to,' Kendall says. 'Even his own staff didn't like him. They loathed him, or at best disliked him. But he knew what he was doing: you don't win two League Championships if you don't know what you're doing.'

WHEN EVERTON WON that 1962/63 title under Catterick, Burnley came third. The previous two seasons Burnley finished second and fourth. And the season before that – 1959/60 – Burnley won the league. Burnley were a force in the land. From 1960 their league sequence was 1,4,2,3.

From the Lancashire heart of the English game, Burnley were Football League founder members. From our perspective it seems faintly astonishing that a small-town club could already have been FA Cup winners once and League champions in 1921. That was a decade before Arsenal's first title, three decades before Tottenham's first.

It is a reminder that early English football was a northern game. Before Arsenal became the first London club, and first southern club, to win that title in 1931, the most southerly champions had been Aston Villa.

A small northern club, Burnley would spend from 1947 to 1971 in the First Division. And in 1958 they appointed a former player who had once shared an Everton dressing room with Harry Catterick. This was another Harry – Harry Potts.

When Potts moved to Goodison Park in October 1950 for £20,000, it was Everton's record transfer, even though Potts was a week away from turning 30.

Potts was a winger – with blond hair – who had made his name at Burnley. He was Turf Moor's golden vision, leading Burnley to promotion from the old Second Division in 1946/47, and to the FA Cup final against Charlton the same season. He hit the crossbar with the score at 0-0. This was a highly regarded number 10, yet what Potts did as a manager when he returned to Burnley outshone even this.

Harry Potts came from Hetton-le-Hole, the same small Durham coalmining town as Bob Paisley, Keegan's grandfather Frank and many other football men. One was Ralph Coates, another was Bobby Cram, who captained Colchester United when they beat Leeds in the fifth round of the FA Cup in 1971, one of the greatest shocks in the Cup's history. Bobby Cram was uncle of Olympic athlete Steve.

Another was Jack Hill, who played for Burnley in the 1920s. Hill was made England captain in 1927 – Dixie Dean's captain – and joined Newcastle United a year later for a club record £8,100.

Sunderland still hold their reserve games in Hetton-le-Hole, but the pit and pit life is long gone. Paisley's wife Jessie described modern Hetton as 'unrecognisable' from the place she knew through her husband.

Potts and Paisley were pals. They were separated by 18 months – Paisley the elder – but they went to the same Eppleton school, played in the same streets and absorbed the same culture. And they both left.

Jessie Paisley came to know Margaret Potts well and they had a nickname for their husbands – 'The Likely Lads'.

Margaret Potts wrote a poignant memoir before her death in which she recorded the Hetton she experienced: 'Though they weren't miners, they lived in a tiny terraced house typical of the area; the front door opening out onto the street; front step immaculately clean, a small back yard with an outdoor toilet and a tin bath hung on a peg on the wall. Outside the back yard was an unmade dirt road and alongside that one of the colliery railway lines. Gaslights lit the streets at night. Smoke from the engines billowed over the houses throughout the day.'

Harry's father – Harry Potts senior – 'was a Co-op salesman and he rode around the area with his horse and cart selling groceries. His stock phrase was "Why worry? Worry gets you nowhere at all." It was a trait that Harry junior would not inherit.'

Today, outside Burnley, Harry Potts is like buried treasure. He was 16 in 1937 when he swapped the north-east for the north-west, part of a migration that would eventually see Burnley FC transformed into a north-east colony.

By the mid-1950s Potts' Everton career had petered out amid injuries. Released in 1956, he was 35 and, as Margaret said, a worried man. But Potts had started preparing for the future, going on early FA coaching courses at Lilleshall and doing summer coaching at Butlin's camps at Filey and Pwllheli. On the Wirral, he coached the Stork Margarine factory team. Then Stan Cullis, a giant figure at the time and manager of Wolves, invited Potts to join the staff at Molineux. It was a measure of esteem.

Potts did not last long at Molineux. Within a year Shrewsbury Town offered him the manager's job, which he took, and six months later Burnley, with omnipotent director Bob Lord in charge, brought Potts back to Turf Moor.

Some have downplayed Potts' tactical ability. Stan Ternent, from Gateshead, and part of the north-east procession to Burnley, was signed by Potts. According to Ternent, 'Potts was a curious character . . . who more resembled a dapper middle-aged geography teacher than one of Britain's top soccer bosses.'

Then again, Potts sold Ternent after five appearances. It could be that Potts shared Paisley's placid ruthlessness as well as his Hetton genius of common sense.

Potts, for example, retained the man he replaced – Billy Dougall – a shrewd Scot admired by Matt Busby. Dougall had been at Burnley since 1932. So had Welshman Ray Bennion. Potts, Dougall and Bennion would meet where the apprentices cleaned their boots. As Margaret said: 'Harry, Billy and Ray had a boot-room of their own long before Bill Shankly ever thought of it.'

The combination inspired Burnley, they inspired camaraderie within the squad, they created a happy workplace. There was a Potts' phrase: 'Play with a chuckle in your boots.'

In just his second season as Burnley manager, on its last day, Burnley had to win at Manchester City to be crowned champions. In front of 66,000 at Maine Road, Burnley won 2-1.

'It was a feeling I can hardly describe,' Margaret wrote. 'For a small town and a small club that people from the south thought was in the back of beyond, this was just an incredible achievement. Burnley gained an identity and pride that night which lifted it out of the doldrums. It was a town of hardship and job losses with its rows and rows of old industrial housing and ancient mills, which had been closing one by one for three decades. It was a place full of neglect. I was just so proud of Harry. He had done something magical for this tiny place . . [brought] glory and distinction for our little town of cotton and coal.'

Burnley's league title led, in January 1961, to the first leg of a European Cup quarter-final against Hamburg at Turf Moor. After 72 minutes, Burnley were 3-0 up. Unfortunately Hamburg got one back and then won the second leg 4-1. It was Uwe Seeler and his teammates who met Barcelona in the semi-final.

The next season, 1961/62, one year after Tottenham had become the century's first Double winners, Potts had Burnley on course to repeat the feat. They fell just short, coming second to Alf Ramsey's Ipswich in the league and losing the FA Cup final to Spurs.

At Wembley Burnley had eight Englishmen in their team, five of whom were from the north-east. Jimmy Adamson was their captain; he was named Footballer of the Year in 1962.

Adamson came from Ashington. Between 1962 and 1967 there were five Englishmen named Footballer of the Year. Three of them came from Ashington.

The Charlton brothers are recalled rather more often than Adamson but he was a man of talent and influence. Aged 33, he was part of England's 1962 World Cup squad in Chile and acted as assistant manager to Walter Winterbottom. When Winterbottom resigned after that tournament, the FA offered Adamson the job: England manager. Adamson said no, and told reporters he planned to leave football and open a newsagents. The job was then offered to Alf Ramsey.

'He [Adamson] was a potentially brilliant choice,' said the man who sat beside him on the long flight home from Chile, Bobby Charlton. 'While I tended to bubble on a little about potential, Adamson kept bringing me back to the reality of performance.'

Adamson made nearly 500 appearances for Burnley over 17 years as a player. He was ever-present in 1959/60 when the league was won. Having declined England, he became Potts' assistant and then, in 1970, his successor. Burnley were relegated and promoted on Adamson's watch and he subsequently managed Sunderland after Bob Stokoe and Leeds United after Jock Stein.

Those were less successful experiences than Adamson's three decades at Turf Moor. There he was part of a north-east invasion. Burnley's prowess in the First Division was supplemented by a reserve team which won the Central League in 1962 and 1963, at a time when the Central League mattered. In 1963 Burnley travelled to meet Newcastle United and named a starting XI all born in the north-east.

Many of those players were sent to Burnley on the recommendation of a man who worked as a railway clerk at Newcastle Central station, Jack Hixon, who would later see the ability within Alan Shearer.

Burnley's success in scouting boys in the north-east led others to follow. Writing in 1969, in the *Park Drive Book of Football*, Jimmy Adamson reflected on his Burnley side which had just won the FA Youth Cup and said: 'Whereas seven or eight years ago 70 per cent of Burnley's youthful talent came from England's north-eastern corner, we now find it saturated with "scouts" from other clubs.'

Only Dave Thomas, later of QPR, Everton and England, played in Burnley's Youth Cup team in 1969. Thomas went to school in Bishop Auckland. His family's roots were in mining, and glory.

✦

BURNLEY'S 1969 YOUTH CUP TRIUMPH does not count in the following statistic even though it was overseen by a manager from the north-east, Jimmy Adamson. But Harry Potts' feat in 1960 is included.

Between 1960 and 1987 there were 15 League Championships won by managers from the north-east of England.

Potts (1960) and Catterick (1963 & 1970) came first. They were followed by Middlesbrough-born Don Revie in 1969 and 1974 and by Middlesbrough-born Brian Clough in 1972 and 1978.

Revie's two championships came with Leeds United, Clough's with Derby County, then Nottingham Forest.

At Liverpool Bob Paisley won his first league title in 1976. He did the same in 1977, 1979, 1980, 1982 and 1983. After Paisley came Kendall, who won those two titles with Everton in 1985 and 1987.

Six men from within a 19-mile radius won 15 league titles, and a few other trophies besides.

While 15 of 28 league titles from 1960 were won by six managers from the north-east, seven titles were won by clubs managed by Scotsmen – Shankly, Busby, Dave Mackay and Kenny Dalglish. As a collective, however, the template of the Scottish manager, the idea of the Scottish manager has been much more prominent in British football, particularly with the rise of Alex Ferguson.

It is a curiosity. It could be, in part, because those north-east managers all left the area in which they were born. The titles claimed were won in Lancashire, Liverpool, Yorkshire and the Midlands. But then the Scottish managers left, too. It could be, in part, that there was no north-east collective.

'No, we didn't talk about it,' says John Barnwell, 'because we just thought of it as natural. It's not something I'd really considered. It was never brought up: "Look, here's another manager from the north-east. Why is this happening?"'

Barnwell falls into a north-east sub-group of managers in that era. In 1980 Barnwell was Wolves manager when they won the League Cup against Clough's Forest at Wembley. Clough and Forest had won that competition the previous two years.

The phenomenon known as Bob Paisley then won the League Cup in 1981, 1982 and 1983. Clough added two more League Cups in 1989 and 1990 and when added to Jimmy Hagan's triumph in 1966 with West Bromwich Albion and Revie's with Leeds in 1968, there were ten League Cups won by north-east managers between 1966 and 1990.

Barnwell came from Newcastle and Hagan from Washington.

Bob Stokoe was brought up in Gateshead, in High Spen. Stokoe won the FA Cup in 1973 with Sunderland, a year after Revie had won it with Leeds. In 1976 Lawrie McMenemy, from Gateshead, won that Cup with Southampton and in 1978 Ipswich Town, managed by Bobby Robson from Durham, won it.

Add Catterick's 1966 win and Kendall's in 1984, both with Everton, and six FA Cups were won by six different north-east managers in 18 years.

Between 1960 and 1990 a total of 31 domestic trophies were won by north-east managers. It does not take into account beaten finalists or second-place finishes – Revie's Leeds had 11 of these alone.

Add the not insignificant five European Cups overseen by Paisley at Liverpool and Clough at Forest, the Fairs Cup and Uefa Cup victories for Revie's Leeds, Paisley's Uefa Cup in 1976 and Ipswich's 1981 triumph under Robson, plus Everton's Cup Winners' Cup win in 1985 and the trophy total rises to 41.

It is a torrent of achievement from 11 managers who were born within a tiny radius of the north-east. (This does not include the hat-trick of Portuguese titles won by Hagan when he became Eusebio's manager at Benfica in 1970.)

Was this not noticed, discussed, not even by the men themselves?

'No,' Barnwell repeats, 'whenever we met all we talked about was football, not north-east football. It never struck me to ask because, as I say, it just felt like the natural order. Think of the sheer numbers of players who came from the north-east, and their quality. It's no surprise you then get a lot of managers. It was taken for granted that you'd have this north-east presence in English football.'

Not any more. Since 1990 there has been one domestic trophy won by a north-east manager. In 1996 Brian Little, from Horden, was manager of Villa when they won the League Cup.

Bobby Robson, it must be said, moved abroad and won trophies with PSV Eindhoven, Porto and Barcelona.

But in terms of north-east managers at English clubs, between 1960 and 1990 there were 41 leagues and cups won. Between 1990 and 2014, there has been one.

The decline of influence, corresponding to a general decline in English influence, can be seen in today's Premier League. There is one north-east manager, Steve Bruce at Hull City. Bruce came close to interrupting the slide when Hull led Arsenal 2-0 in the 2014 FA Cup final, but Arsenal came back to win 3-2.

Bruce's proximity to silverware came at Hull, not his previous club Sunderland. An unmissable aspect of the managerial glory period is that 40 of the 41 trophies were won outside the managers' native region.

As Barnwell says: 'What's sad is that apart from Bob Stokoe, none of these managers won trophies for north-east clubs.'

✦

INFLUENCE WENT FAR BEYOND the collecting of medals in May. John Barnwell was an exceptional teenage footballer, who was wooed on a regular basis by his hometown club, Newcastle United.

'I had 15 clubs to choose from and the chief scout of Newcastle United, Temple Lisle, lived on my street in High Heaton,' Barnwell recalls. 'I've a photo of me and the chief scout in his front garden with the FA Cup. It must have been after the 1955 final. But I didn't sign for Newcastle United. I played for England U-17s and Newcastle Boys, but not Newcastle United Boys.

'I played for Whitley Bay and Bishop Auckland and when [Newcastle United manager] Stan Seymour came to my parents' house, and offered quite a lot of money, my Dad said: "Listen, wor lad, you'll go to the club that looks after you off the pitch, not just on the pitch."

'So I went to Arsenal.'

Arsenal's manager when Barnwell arrived at Highbury was Tom Whittaker. Whittaker came from Byker in Newcastle, about a mile and a half from Barnwell in High Heaton.

This was 1955. Barnwell was 16, Whittaker was 57 and had been at Highbury since 1919. He was first player, then coach – Herbert Chapman's coach – and then assistant to Chapman's successor George Allison. Allison came from Teesside.

'Tom Whittaker was the manager of Arsenal when I signed, and I've still got a hand-written letter from him to my father,' Barnwell says. 'He was one of the great managers of Arsenal. He passed away soon after I joined. I knew there was a north-east connection with him, but it was never pushed at me.'

Had Whittaker chosen to, he could have told Barnwell of his Byker childhood: 'I grew up a Geordie … my early games were of 'clouty baall' . . . boys are great dreamers and when our rag ball went scuttering over the rough ground, I was Colin Veitch running in to shoot.'

Instead Barnwell recalls: 'There was a strong line of discipline at Arsenal. Tom Whittaker would say: "Remember who you are, what you are and what club you're playing for." George Allison and Tom Whittaker were part of that line of discipline, that culture. That's the way I'd been brought up in Newcastle.

'I was signed on an amateur form. My parents refused to let Arsenal sign me on a pro contract because they wanted to see if a 16-year-old Geordie could settle in London. Arsenal gave me a debut very quickly. It was at Roker Park against Sunderland and I was marked by Billy Elliott. This was a very clear introduction to professional football.'

Arsenal's north-east connection, which saw the club managed by Allison and Whittaker from 1934 to 1956, is evidence of influence. During Whittaker's era as coach and manager, Arsenal won the league title seven times.

But then the club's second-ever manager, George Elcoat, had gone south from Stockton and the first Arsenal goalscorer at the newly built Highbury stadium in 1913 was George Jobey, from Heddon on the northern fringe of Newcastle. Arsenal's marble had north-east veins running through it.

Whittaker was not even 30 when Chapman made him Arsenal's first-team trainer. Chapman will have recognised Whittaker's dialect because when Chapman built the historic Huddersfield Town team that would win three league titles in a row from 1924, it was on north-east talent.

Chapman's captain was Clem Stephenson, from Seaton Delaval. Stephenson was in dispute with Aston Villa when Chapman signed him over the fact that Stephenson would not move from his home in Northumberland.

Huddersfield being closer than Birmingham, Stephenson joined Chapman, who promptly went back to the north-east for a 17-year-old playing for Mickley's colliery team, George Brown. Both Stephenson and Brown won a hat-trick of titles with Huddersfield. Both played for England.

After their first league title in 1924, Huddersfield's opening game of the next season was at St James' Park. Perhaps not wanting to rub it in, Chapman fielded only four north-east locals in his Town team. They won 3-1, Stephenson and Brown scoring. 'Ex-Novocastrians' was the newspaper term used in match reports then.

In total, Chapman had nine north-east players on Huddersfield's books in that 1923-24 season and added Sid Binks from Bishop Auckland, Norman Smith – later Charlie Mitten's successor as Newcastle manager – and Bon Spence from Ferryhill the following year. Before departing for Arsenal in 1925, one of Chapman's last Huddersfield acts was to sign Harry Raw from Tow Law.

As early as the 1920s the *North Mail* had a column titled 'The Football Nursery' and when Barnwell arrived at Highbury he found familiar accents in Arsenal's squad.

Geoff Strong grew up on Newcastle's Scotswood Road, Bill Dodgin jnr came from Gateshead and George Armstrong from Hebburn. When Arsenal secured the

'Double' at White Hart Lane in 1971, Armstrong's cross was met by the imperious Ray Kennedy. Kennedy came from Seaton Delaval.

In 1961 Laurie Brown arrived. When he returned to Shildon after playing, Brown drove a milk van.

Nor are Burnley or Arsenal exceptions. Travel across London to Charlton and standing in bronze outside The Valley is Sam Bartram. Bartram only ever played for one club – Charlton Athletic, 623 times. He was born and raised in South Shields.

Bartram joined Charlton in 1934, one year after the club had appointed Jimmy Seed as manager. Seed was born in Blackhill, Consett, and grew up in Whitburn, north of Sunderland. He was on Sunderland's books but the First World War intervened, Seed volunteered and when he returned in 1918, he was let go, one of many bad decisions made at Roker Park.

Three years later Seed was the inspiration behind Tottenham winning the FA Cup. He was capped by England that same year.

All the while monitored by Chapman, Seed left Tottenham for Sheffield Wednesday in a dispute over money and after an Arsenal-Wednesday game at Highbury in 1932 Seed recalled: 'He [Chapman] sent Tom Whittaker, then the Arsenal trainer, to see me as I left the dressing-room. It was arranged I should meet Mr. Chapman at the Great Northern Hotel at King's Cross the following Monday.'

Chapman had plans to buy Clapton Orient and turn it into a feeder club, and wanted Seed to run it. Seed agreed. The FA blocked Chapman's typically bold idea. So, instead, Seed became manager of Charlton, then in the Third Division. By 1936 Charlton were in the First Division, where they would stay until 1957.

Seed wanted Charlton to produce their own players, not buy them. He set up a scouting network. 'Although I arranged for most areas in Britain to be combed, I concentrated particularly on the north-east of England. With the help of my brother Antony who was the chief of the five scouts I appointed in this area, Charlton were to draw some of the club's most successful players at little or no cost at all. Sam Bartram and Jack Shreeve were two who did not cost a penny. In all, I secured some 30 players from this happy hunting ground.

'Apart from admiring Bartram for his ability as a goalkeeper, I always had a soft spot for him because in many ways he had followed a similar pathway to myself. He had been born in that north-eastern nursery so dear to me. Like myself he had worked in the coal-pits and possessed the same burning ambition to quit the mines and become a footballer . . . [and] Jimmy Seed and Sam Bartram both experienced the indignity of being rejected as not good enough.'

It was Reading, and Jarrow, who turned down Bartram. So he joined Seed as one of the departed and found his glory in south London.

In 1936, the first season after promotion, Seed's Charlton finished second in the First Division. The next season it was fourth, then third. On the resumption of football after the Second World War, Charlton made the first post-war FA Cup final. It was against Derby County, who won 4-1, but a noticeable trend was that of the 17 Englishmen on the Wembley pitch, five came from the north-east – Bartram, Shreeve and Bert Johnson for Charlton, Raich Carter and Jack Howe for Derby.

The following season, Charlton again reached the FA Cup final and this time won it, the only major trophy in their history. They now had five north-eastern voices in their team, as well as the manager. Tommy Dawson from Middlesbrough and Bill Robinson from Whitburn had joined Bartram, Shreeve and Johnson.

The opponents, Burnley, had Harry Potts, Alan Brown and George Strong, from Northumberland.

Of 20 Englishmen at Wembley in April 1947, eight were from the north-east. John Barnwell's comment about the sheer scale of the numbers and quality of north-east players was correct. And their influence continued after the whistle.

Of those eight players in 1947, five became managers. In the case of Bill Robinson at West Ham and Bert Johnson at Leicester City and Nottingham Forest, they became important youth coaches and assistant managers as well.

Johnson became Matt Gillies' assistant at Leicester during a time when they reached the FA Cup final twice and won the 1964 League Cup, Leicester's first-ever major trophy.

After Leicester, Johnson worked for Forest. When he died in 2009, the *Leicester Mercury* said: 'His coaching skills were regarded as being ahead of their time... Gillies left for Nottingham Forest in 1968 and Johnson was put in charge of the youth set-up, helping to find players such as Martin O'Neill, John Robertson and Tony Woodcock.'

The son of a Whitburn miner, who died when he was 12, Bill Robinson became a similar, perhaps greater influence at West Ham. They signed him from Charlton in 1949 for a club record fee, £7,000. He scored 61 goals in 105 games for the Hammers before moving onto the coaching staff.

West Ham historian Tim Crane wrote: 'Bill was appointed coach, trainer and administrator of the junior sides and as junior talent scout for the Greater London area. His first task was to organise trials for local lads. In effect, he was laying the foundation for a youth production system that would be the envy of the nation and which is recognised today as "The Academy". Class acts such as Bobby Moore, John Smith, Tony Scott, Andy Smilie, Derek Woodley, Joe Kirkup, Harry Obeney, Ken

Brown and Geoff Hurst are just a few who graduated through Bill's experienced hands and the structure he put in place.'

Geoff Hurst agreed: 'Bill was Ted Fenton's assistant and, with Wally [St Pier], was largely responsible for establishing West Ham's youth development programme. He came from Whitburn in the north-east and was as hard as nails. If he pushed his trilby to the back of his head, you knew you were in trouble with him. Few will remember today but he held West Ham's post-war scoring record – 26 in 40 games… Sadly, like Wally St Pier's, his contribution to West Ham's rise is largely forgotten. There is no doubt that they were significant figures in the creation of the team that won the FA Cup in 1964.'

Hurst and Bobby Moore both played in that Cup-winning team of '64. Hurst remembered Robinson as he said, but also because West Ham had reached the FA Youth Cup finals of 1957 and 1959. Hurst and Moore were in the 1959 team.

West Ham's connection to Whitburn reinforces the national perception of the area as a talent nursery. It went back to the 1920s and the Hammers' first FA Cup final in 1923. This was the first Wembley final, famous for an estimated 300,000 descending on the stadium and the lone white horse trying to clear the pitch.

The white horse was called Billy. Three West Ham players were also called Billy – Billy Henderson from Whitburn, Billy Brown from Hetton-le-Hole and Billy Moore from Newcastle.

Billy Moore, West Ham's original 'B. Moore', was still at Upton Park when Bill Robinson arrived in 1949 and stayed until retirement in 1960, by which time the other B. Moore was in the first team. Billy Moore won one England cap, and scored twice.

'Billy Moore? Jesus Christ, you don't hear his name often these days,' Vic Keeble says, stunned to hear the name all these years on. Keeble, born in Colchester, joined West Ham from Newcastle in 1957. He is the only survivor of the 1955 FA Cup-winning team, the last man alive to know what it is like to win a major domestic trophy wearing Newcastle United colours.

'God, Billy Moore. He was a real fella, always had a fag on, always. He was our trainer. Lovely man.'

HAVING 40 PER CENT OF THE ENGLISHMEN AT WEMBLEY in 1947 was a high point of north-eastern presence – until 1951.

In 1948 just three of the 18 English FA Cup finalists were from the region:

Allenby Chilton for Manchester United and Mortensen and Joe Robinson for Blackpool.

United won 4-2, Matt Busby's first trophy as manager. Busby had Welshman Jimmy Murphy as his assistant and behind Murphy was Tom Curry. Curry came from South Shields and had played for Newcastle. He arrived at Old Trafford as a coach in 1934, pre-Busby. Curry was a Manchester United man until his death in the Munich air crash.

Five years earlier Curry had been given a testimonial at Old Trafford. He had been Busby's assistant at the 1948 Olympics, when Busby managed the Great Britain team, and Busby said of him: 'Tom Curry was so fond of Old Trafford that he used to bring his open razor to the ground so that he would not waste time shaving at home. If the team played badly he would leave his open razor on the dressing room table and say: "Help yourself, lads."'

When in 1951 Curry's former club Newcastle reached Wembley, they had six locals in their team – Bob Cowell, Bobby Corbett, Charlie Crowe, Ernie Taylor, Tommy Walker and Jackie Milburn. Newcastle United were a representation of themselves then.

Blackpool were again the beaten finalists and again Mortensen was one of them. Tommy Garrett, also from South Shields, was another.

Eight of the 16 Englishmen on the pitch were from the north-east.

That, of course, involved Newcastle United, so there is no great surprise. But the pattern of north-east players appearing for other clubs continued. In 1968 for example, the West Brom and Everton teams at Wembley supplied 21 Englishmen of whom five were from the north-east. It was four of 15 in 1972 when Arsenal played Leeds and seven of 14 a year later when Sunderland played Leeds.

In fact, between 1946 and 1974, in 29 FA Cup finals, there was only one played without a north-east player on the pitch: Blackburn v Wolves in 1960.

But by the mid-1970s something was changing and by the end of the 1990s it had accelerated.

Although the change was not as dramatic as it would be at the turn of the 21st century, the 1975 FA Cup final provided an indication of what was to come. When West Ham took on Fulham at Wembley, the Hammers did so with an all-English XI, an English substitute, and an English manager, John Lyall. None of them originated in the north-east. Geographically this is logical but West Ham's north-east links were long and strong.

But Bill Robinson's youth system had begun to bear fruit: six of West Ham's starting XI came through the ranks via "The Academy".

Had Sunderland-born Bryan 'Pop' Robson timed his two claret periods differently, he would probably have appeared at Wembley in 1975. But he left for Sunderland in 1974 and rejoined West Ham in 1976. Fulham had no north-east players in that 1975 final either.

In 1978, 1979 and 1980 there was again no north-east presence on the pitch, although by 1989, when Liverpool and Everton met, three of the ten Englishmen to feature were from the region. There was a recovery as the next final saw Manchester United win with Steve Bruce, Gary Pallister and Bryan Robson a vigorous trio among United's nine Englishmen. Paul Gascoigne represented Spurs the following season and in 1992 Sunderland had five locals in their 13 who appeared against Liverpool. Sunderland's manager, Malcolm Crosby, came from South Shields.

Andy Linighan, from Hartlepool, scored the Wembley winner in 1993 for Arsenal to end their tedious games with Sheffield Wednesday and once Middlesbrough and Newcastle United had done something in the early 1990s about their mediocrity, they appeared in the finals of 1997, 1998 and 1999. Ben Roberts, Phil Stamp, Steve Vickers, Steve Harper, Steve Howey and Shearer all played at Wembley, and lost.

But in May 2000, four-and-a-half years after the Bosman ruling changed Europe's cross-border contract law, and football, Chelsea and Aston Villa started without a north-east voice on the pitch. Steve Stone (Gateshead) got 11 minutes as a Villa substitute, but not until 2007, when Michael Carrick appeared for Manchester United, did the north-east again have a representative on the pitch.

What was once considered natural, no longer applied. Even then, Carrick was a solitary voice and in 2008 and 2009, the north-east was again absent. In the first decade of the 21st century, the region known as England's hotbed of soccer, once its core nursery, provided one starter in ten FA Cup finals.

Since then Hartlepool's Michael Brown played for Portsmouth in 2010 and Adam Johnson was a Manchester City substitute in 2011. Jordan Henderson and Stewart Downing were in Liverpool's team in 2012 – and Andy Carroll was a scoring substitute. But neither Man City nor Wigan Athletic featured a north-east player in 2013.

In the 2014 final, Steve Bruce was Hull City's manager but in a match of 28 players, none were from the north-east of England.

The names of Downing, Johnson, Carroll and Henderson show that there are still north-east players operating in the Premier League but it only takes a dip in form or an injury to reduce percentages to the alarming level of New Year's Day 2014.

There was a full Premier League programme that Wednesday: ten fixtures, 20 teams, 220 starters. Of these just five came from the north-east – 2 per cent: Carrick, Henderson, Lee Cattermole and Jack Colback at Sunderland and Shola Ameobi at Newcastle United. Ameobi is included as although he was born in Nigeria and plays for Nigeria, he has lived in Newcastle since he was five and has had a local education.

Downing, Johnson and Danny Graham came on as substitutes for West Ham, Sunderland and Hull respectively that day but the torrent of talent that once coursed through English football has become a trickle.

✦

IN THE DUGOUT and on the pitch, this is a story of diminishing influence. When Jimmy Adamson and Bobby Charlton flew home from the 1962 World Cup, they were in the company of Stan Anderson, Alan Peacock and Bobby Robson. Five of the 21-man travelling England squad were from the north-east.

As recently as Italia 90, England's midfield in the opening group game against the Republic of Ireland contained Bryan Robson (captain) and Paul Gascoigne, Chris Waddle was on the wing and Peter Beardsley was up front.

England's manager was Bobby Robson. In the other dugout in Cagliari was a Geordie Robson knew well, Jack Charlton. This is high-level impact.

Along the way, Jack and Bobby Charlton had done a bit more and four years after 1966, when England were leading West Germany 2-1 in the Mexico World Cup quarter-final, and Alf Ramsey made the ill-fated decision to take off Bobby Charlton, the player sent on was Colin Bell. Bell's football origins are the same as Stan Anderson's – Horden Colliery.

Colin Bell came to be known as Nijinsky. He won 48 England caps and captained his country. In May 1968, less than five years after leaving Horden Colliery Welfare, Bell was a glorious feature of the Manchester City team that won the league. They did so on the last day of the season, at St James' Park.

Some people at Newcastle United knew what they were missing. Bell had been overlooked by them and the other north-east clubs. He signed for Bury, whose manager was Bob Stokoe.

Stan Anderson, for one, was unimpressed by the oversight. He had been asked to give his opinion of Bell by Newcastle manager Joe Harvey and remembers ringing Harvey to say: 'Leggy lad, sharp, nice touch on the ball, he's worth having a go.'

A short time later, Anderson asked Harvey if he had done anything about Bell. Harvey replied: "Aye, we've had another report and he's not very good."

'I said again that he was worth a chance. Super player, and what a lovely lad.

In fact, I spoke to Colin's father at the time who said that Colin would have signed for Newcastle.'

Bell had gone to Bury by then. 'That was a terrible decision,' says Anderson.

The other England substitute in that 1970 World Cup quarter-final was Norman Hunter. Hunter made his name at Leeds United. He came from Gateshead.

Barnwell remains unsurprised at the quality and quantity of those who left. 'The area had so many talented players,' he says.

'The local clubs abused that. The streets of Newcastle had football in them all the time, more than anywhere else in the country I imagine. The best place in England to go for young players was the north-east. We learned our football in the streets and in school, the environment was teaching us. We kept the ball because you knew that if you lost it you might not get it back for five minutes. You played with a smaller ball, you learned to dribble it and to keep it.

'Very few of us had TV and very, very few had cars. You went everywhere on foot. That environment was more conducive to the production of young players – we've lost that learning, that knowledge. We live in a more immediate society, everything's immediate – news, coffee, phones.

'We've lost our ability to develop things over time.

'And in football there's a difference between developmental coaches and results coaches – too often we've got that back to front. We're not playing in schools. My PE teacher was Bob Maddison – at Middle Street Commercial School in Walker. Dennis Tueart, Jimmy Husband, David Young and Derek Forster – who played in goal for Sunderland at 15-year-old – we were all at that school, and there were others. We were all looked after by Bobby Maddison, who'd been a good amateur player.'

WHEN ROY HODGSON named his original England squad for Euro 2012, north-eastern representation was down to Andy Carroll and Stewart Downing. When Frank Lampard was ruled out, Jordan Henderson stepped in. Henderson played 12 minutes against France and 26 minutes against Italy. Carroll played a full game against Sweden, eight minutes v Ukraine and an hour against Italy. Downing did not appear.

Two years later, when Hodgson named his preliminary squad for the World Cup in Brazil, neither Carroll nor Downing made the cut. Henderson did, and started England's opening two games, two defeats against Italy and Uruguay, after a prominent season with Liverpool. Celtic goalkeeper Fraser Forster was also on the plane. Forster, born in Northumberland, joined Newcastle as a teenager. Forster went to Brazil as England's third-choice keeper.

Shortly before Hodgson's announcement, John Topping gave a less-publicised address to a meeting of the Stockton & District Sunday League. The League has 33 teams in three divisions. There is a possibility some teams will fold at the end of the season. It is part of a pattern.

John Topping is the secretary of Durham County FA, a post he has held since 1996. He joined three years earlier as assistant secretary. Prior to that Topping spent 18 years in a Sunderland shipyard. He has played football all his life, ran the Sunderland & District League and runs a youth club with 22 teams in Jarrow.

Of the once-great north-east nursery, Topping says: 'We lost three adult leagues last season – the Spennymoor Sunday League, the Hartlepool Saturday afternoon league and the Hartlepool Sunday afternoon league. That's about 30 teams, boys from 17 through to whatever age. Hartlepool has a Sunday morning league, that's it.

'Twenty years ago each league would have had three or four divisions and 14 teams in each. I know of leagues that are worried about losing three or four teams at the end of this season. I went to see the Stockton & District Sunday League recently to speak to them about this. The League won't go, not this year.

'In Spennymoor six teams transferred across to the Wearside League but we still lost ten teams. There are still a couple of Hartlepool teams, they've joined the Wearside League.

'The big problem we have is Saturday. We have the Durham Alliance League, Crook and District League, Wearside Combination League – that's it. When I first started here in 1993 we had nine or ten Saturday leagues. Now we've three.'

It is not the only big problem Topping sees at grassroots level. In terms of boys' attitudes, parents' attitudes and volunteers: 'There's a massive change from 20 years ago.'

Within British football, there is recognition that retaining the interest of boys aged 16 to 19 has become a major difficulty over the past decade. Much of this is due to lifestyle changes – Steve McClaren held up his mobile phone when asked about it – but there have also been structural changes such as the FA's prioritising of small-sided football over 11-a-side.

There is collateral damage from clubs' academies, there are societal changes, the closure of pubs which once sponsored and hosted amateur clubs. And Topping is witnessing a new development: 'The drop-off was at 16, now we're seeing it at 14.

'We have lost a lot of adult teams and, when we lose one, I ask why. Some of it is sponsorship, some of the teams were attached to pubs which have closed, but what did surprise us was hearing from 18-year-olds saying: 'I want a break.' Then, when you think of it, they're playing football – organised football – from maybe four, five or six years old.

'I run my own youth club in Jarrow – Jarrow FC. We have 22 youth teams. We always started off with 'tots' – four or five year-old, so they would get involved in the club. Then organised football from under-seven. When they get to 17, 18, some of them have been playing for 13 years. I understand it, but it would never have happened before.

'One of the FA's focus points should be the decline of 11-a-side football. In the recent past the FA have put a lot of money into youth football, women's and girls' football, disability football, and it's great, all have grown. Now we need to be addressing the decline of the traditional base. I've said it to the FA, if we don't have a strong base, the rest struggles. It's logic.'

Topping makes a connection to his own industrial past and its degeneration from the mid-1980s: 'You can tie the decline in numbers to the decline in industry, definitely. In mining, you always had a Colliery Welfare team, always. I worked in the shipyard for 18 years, started at 16 in James Laing's in Sunderland, 1,000 to 1,500 worked there. We had our own inter-departmental games – welders v burners v shipwrights v caulkers. But they also played for outside teams. You had a lot of football going on.

'And in the shipyard, you could raise money to run your teams – the yards and the mines were the best places to raise money, you had working-class people who would give you a couple of shillings for domino cards or whatever, it all helped keep your club going, paid for referees and so on. When the pits and the shipyards went, teams started to struggle. You saw the effects within a few years.

'We've now got the public-sector cuts. Local authorities are selling off unused pitches. You've youth unemployment.'

Topping stresses the importance of organisation and volunteers, but he's noticed some asking: "How much?"

'Times are hard, they can get a little pocket money. Take away the volunteers and you take away football. About five of those teams in Stockton are one-man bands. One man does everything, pays everything, takes on the costs. He does it because he loves football.

'But those volunteers are ageing, that workforce is coming to an end. You don't find anybody under the age of 35 doing it now and if you lose one man who runs a team, you lose 19 players. We're losing a tradition. It's sad.'

Referring back to the Durham FA's 1983/84 Handbook, it listed 16 youth leagues under its jurisdiction. I read them to Topping:

Auckland Junior League: 'Gone'

Cleveland & Teesside Junior League: 'Gone'

Darlington Minor League: 'Gone'

Derwentside Youth League: 'Gone'

Gateshead YC League: 'Gone'

Hartlepool Church Junior League: 'Gone'

Hartlepool Sunday Friendly League: 'Gone'

Hetton & District Youth League: 'Gone'

Jarrow & District JOC League: 'Gone'

North West Durham Battalion Boys Brigade League: 'Gone'

Stanley YOC Sunday League: 'Gone'

Sunderland YAC League: 'Gone'

Teesside Junior Alliance: 'Still going'

TSB North Durham Youth League: 'Gone'

Tyne & Wear U13-U16 League: 'That's now part of the Russell Foster League and that's grown massively.'

Washington Youth League: 'Gone'

Many of these teams and clubs have been absorbed into other leagues; many have disappeared because of a withering structure. There is a broad theory in football that players, including English players, come from poverty. It is a theory deconstructed in the book *Soccernomics* and, looking at north-east England, it is equally valid to argue that players came from the industrialised working-class and the organised society built by it and around it. It was not rich but it had money, structure and an ethos, and if that class of society which naturally lent its support to football is either erased or eroded, then there is a knock-on effect. This could be what is being seen in the north-east. As is shown in wealthy countries such as Germany and the Netherlands, it is infrastructure and organisation which mattered – and matter – more than any one individual's economic background. These are countries with a municipal ethos and sustained municipal investment. That ethos and structure was once a direct product of England's working-class environment and had such a presence it went unremarked upon. Today, in England's de-regulated economy, that ethos and structure is frequently absent.

✦

JOHN TOPPING PROVIDES ONE PART OF THE PICTURE – and Topping running 22 teams in Jarrow is hardly a sign of disinterest.

Another is offered behind the old dairy in Cowgate, Newcastle. Keith Morris and Ian Coates accept that the traditional imagery of the north-east nursery has changed, but what they are seeing on a weekly basis is 'a mini-revival'.

Morris and Coates run the Pinpoint League under the jurisdiction of the Northumberland FA. Its geography encompasses Berwick-on-Tweed in the north to Haltwhistle in the west and down to Tyneside and into Durham in the south. It is the second-biggest boys league in the country after Sheffield and Hallamshire.

'We have 88 clubs who produce 728 teams,' says Coates. 'They are split into 76 divisions across the age range from under-7 to under-18. They are playing 5, 7, 9 and 11-a-side – over 13s and above play traditional 11 v 11. That equates to 12,500 players within the Northumberland FA borders. It's a vast area.

'In mini-soccer the numbers have increased in the last few years and the knock-on effect has been an increase in numbers in the 11-a-side game. I think the decline has been hyped within youth football to highlight the need for investment, and there's certainly a need for that. The Premier League told the government when they started they would donate 5 per cent to grassroots football. The government's done nothing about that.'

The Northumberland Association of Boys' Clubs was founded in 1945 and had its office on Newcastle's Pilgrim Street. The Pinpoint League is the modern, sponsored name and Morris has seen it develop from 1973 when he first became involved. He is one of those modest volunteers without whom, as Topping said, grassroots football withers.

'We pride ourselves on having a league for every ability,' Morris says. 'It's about getting out.'

Innovations such as 35 minutes each way and unlimited roll-on, roll-off substitutions have brought increased participation.

At the highest level, Morris has also seen boys being picked up by professional clubs, with Newcastle United renewing local activity. When speaking in mid-May 2014, Newcastle had just signed an under-18 player from Seaham Red Star, two under-16s from Richmond Town and a clutch of younger boys for the club Academy from youth clubs such as Newcastle City Juniors, Ponteland United and Boro Rangers.

'Newcastle United's recruitment policy has changed as of this year,' Coates says. 'They will not recruit any player under the age of 21 from overseas on a scholarship. The majority of their players are going to come from within a two-hour radius of Newcastle. They're going back to the old days.

'This is coming from the top. They believe there are technically gifted players within the north-east. Steve Nickson is head of their recruitment nationally up to 21, he is adamant about that, as is Lee Charnley, the new managing director.

'It disappoints us sometimes that everyone focuses on the foreign players coming in, how Spain play football, how the Dutch play football. But that's been driven by the Premier League, and by the FA, who sold the rights to English football.'

The recognisable names of clubs such as Wallsend Boys and Cramlington Juniors also provided players for Newcastle's intake but Morris says: 'Cramlington Juniors had the run of that side of town for many years, but now there are far more boys' clubs, it's far more competitive.

'Ponteland United Juniors didn't exist. Newcastle City Juniors didn't exist, it was only founded nine years ago and now it's one of the top teams – based at Benwell at the old Newcastle United training ground.'

Coates highlights other factors as to why concentration should not be solely on decline.

'Yes, the traditional adult Sunday morning football is dying in some areas,' he says. 'But things change. People don't like change. We're not living in 1970 or 1990. Working lives have changed. There is not the heavy industry where you worked Monday to Friday.

'A lot of young people who would have filled those Sunday league teams now work shift patterns and weekends, but it doesn't mean they don't want to play football. All the new 3G centres are packed every night – men, playing with their mates. A young man, a young parent, now has a role within a family, modern parents' lives aren't like they used to be. A young man's wife maybe has to work.

'There is a new generation – people don't want to sit in the pub every night and get blitzed, despite what some say. Kids don't turn up having had 20 pints the night before, huffing and puffing, playing long-ball football 15 minutes in. There's been a huge change in style. You go and watch Burradon & New Fordley – for the last five years they've won everything. The average age is 24, they're all Northern League or Northern Alliance players so they're playing a decent standard on a Saturday. Those lads don't turn up on a Sunday morning unprepared. They're prepared and their style of football shows that.'

Keith Morris once had Alan Shearer in his County representative team and with four decades' experience he has perspective.

'In 1985/86 the Northumberland County team won the national final at Villa

Park,' he says. 'We beat Devonshire in the final 2-0, Shearer scored both.

'I understand what's being said about producing players at the top, and in the early 1990s there probably was a dip. But football is much faster and more skilful – we've just held about 23 cup finals and the speed and fitness you see is a lot better than it used to be. The standard of coaching in this league today leaves me standing. I do think it's bottomed out, it's re-invigorated.'

Coates agrees: 'It's a mini-revival, that's what you're getting. And it will spike again because it's a World Cup year. In five years' time I think what you'll see are more local boys and better local boys playing for the big north-east clubs.'

✦

BACK IN HETTON-LE-HOLE, underneath the balcony of the Bob Paisley bar at the Eppleton Colliery Welfare ground, Sunderland had just taken the lead. They would hold on to it to maintain their unbeaten start to the new season. There is another change in the north-east's traditional role of supplying footballers: they are female.

When England women's senior team faced Ukraine in a World Cup qualifier in May 2014, four of the starting XI were from the north-east – captain Steph Houghton from Durham, Jill Scott from Sunderland, Demi Stokes from South Shields and Lucy Bronze from Berwick, though she joined Sunderland's academy before her teens.

Two others, Jordan Nobbs from Peterlee and Carly Telford from Newcastle, are regulars in the squad. But for an injury, Nobbs would probably have started against Ukraine.

But on this Sunday in Hetton, when Sunderland Ladies hammered London Bees – though won only 1-0 – in the FA Women's Super League, none of those six players were in Sunderland colours and Sunderland were in the new set-up's second division.

The format had only just begun. Season 2014 was the new FAWSL's first as a two-tier national structure with eight clubs in WSL1 and ten in WSL2. Sunderland Ladies and Durham Ladies, were both included in the second division and while at the top end, players such as Steph Houghton have been able to become professional, these young women aspire to that.

Sunderland – SAFC, the Premier League club – are helping considerably. The venue, the Eppleton ground, is where Sunderland (men) play their Premier League reserve games. If the players (women) are semi-professional, or not far off amateur, the structure is professional. The Eppleton pitch was perfect, the music of Prokofiev was imported from the Stadium of Light, there was a £4 entrance fee and a glossy match programme – 'SAFShe'. The following Saturday, there was an away game at Watford. Sunderland were travelling on Friday and staying overnight in a hotel at significant cost.

Sunderland won that, 4-2, and after five games of the season were joint top with promotion the ambition. Claire Robinson, head coach, sits in one of the seats in Hetton that had been occupied by a couple of hundred spectators and says: 'I think the WSL needed a team up here.

'We've shown we've got a calibre of player, but we've lost so many. I don't mean that disrespectfully, I know why they've gone, but now they can stay. Ultimately the aim is to give them a profession here at the club.'

Robinson teaches at Gateshead College, a sports hub. She has Uefa B and A coaching badges and is part of the development of the women's game over the past 15 years. Interest and organisation is growing.

'We've trials next month and 130 have registered already,' she says. 'That's just elite players, so you can think about the grassroots as well. It'll grow, having games here helps. You can come and see local girls. There's talent here.'

In 2010, Alysha Cook of Durham FA said, there were 35 ladies teams in the Durham area; by 2014 that number was 55. Co. Durham's long-established Russell Foster League has girls' leagues from under-13 to under-18 and is starting under-10s 7v7 and under-9s 5-a-side. 'There's greater quality, quantity and more opportunities than before,' says Cook.

On Teesside, Norton & Stockton Ancients, a long-established, traditional Northern League club, started a girls' section in 2000. There were 12 girls then, today there are girls' teams at Under-8, U-10, U-12 and U-16 levels and a women's senior team that last season won promotion to the FA Women's Premier League, one below where Sunderland and Durham Ladies are in the pyramid. There are around 80 girls and young women playing alongside the boys and men at the club.

'NASA' chairman Michael Mulligan says: 'We did it around 2000. We'd had a football team forever but we wanted to be more, to be a community club. We've now got 26 teams, male and female.

'In the beginning we put on some taster sessions and girls came out of the woodwork. What's nice is that those girls are now in their early twenties and some are coaching our Under-8s and U-10s.'

Norton's Northern League senior team is coached by former Middlesbrough and Cardiff striker Andy Campbell and from the male side of the club, Mulligan has seen 'growing respect – the women's game is much more athletic now and there are nights when the two train side by side. If a woman puts on a good coaching session, the men see it and respect it. There's never any silliness, there's a lot of interest, there's a club feeling.'

The club derives some of its income from a 3G pitch they laid. Norton have never had a sponsor for their women's team and the expense of travel and logistics could be testing should they win another promotion, but Mulligan said the players pay their subs in a way it used to be in boys' football, without complaint. Local girls have been inspired by the sight of Jordan Nobbs playing for Norton and where she has gone from there – Arsenal.

Mulligan is another of those low-key, grassroots folk who keep it all going. These are vital people, who work from the ground up in a football society that is increasingly top-down.

'We've got a good facility, pitches second to none and good changing rooms for female officials,' Mulligan says. 'We're geared up for further development over the next five years, we've a plan to create an elite youth team. One of our original girls has started calling it the Norton Female Football Factory.'

AND THE DIGGING GOES ON. It is a mossy January morning on Teesside. At Middlesbrough's lush training ground, Rockliffe Park, in the gentle village of Hurworth, the scene is leafy, green, serene.

The original Rockliffe Hall was a grand 18th century manor and is now a five-star hotel. It came with 160 acres. Middlesbrough FC have owned the land and buildings since 1997, when the club's ambition was unlimited.

The Prime Minister of the day, Tony Blair, opened the complex. It was a £7m investment, and it was a sharp one. Since 1997 Middlesbrough have generated home-grown player sales of £48m. The club have been in the Championship since 2009 but their Academy, under the new Elite Player Performance Plan (EPPP) rules, receive the top Category One status.

Boro know about producing players – for the Premier League, for the Championship, and further down the English football pyramid. Two wingers – Stewart Downing and Adam Johnson – have been capped by England, James Morrison by Scotland.

Morrison, born in Darlington, had represented England at Under-17, U-18, U-19 and U-20 level. Numerous others from Middlesbrough have reached those levels and on this January morning the current captain of England's U-17s, Callum Cooke, is playing for the club's U-18s versus Blackburn Rovers.

On the adjacent pitch, Blackburn's U-16s are facing Boro's. There are dozens of parents and relatives around the white perimeter fences but there is none of the angry touchline behaviour witnessed at local league level. Middlesbrough will not tolerate it.

A significant part of their brief, as the Academy sees it, is to produce rounded young men as well as footballers. It is another example of the expanded role of the football club. Above a room for parents is a sign: 'Humility, Respect, Honesty'.

It looks and feels a long, long way from when Middlesbrough's first team trained on local pitches and the man from Juventus, Fabrizio Ravanelli, moaned. And moaned. It looks and feels a long, long way from the days of collieries and coal.

Dave Parnaby knows about both. Parnaby has been head of Middlesbrough's Academy since 1998. Previously he had been a teacher, prior to that he had been manager of Gateshead and a player who almost made it at Stoke City. He was also, for seven years, assistant, then manager of England's youth team.

Parnaby, whose son Stuart, is one of the 45 to have made it from youth to first team since 1998, has a reputation to match his experience. Dave Parnaby understands the north-east from the ground up. In his modest office, the first thing he says is: 'I was a coalminer's son.'

Parnaby uses the past tense. He still is a coalminer's son, and will be always, but the use of the past tense reflects a reality that Parnaby was addressing – the difference between what there was and what there is. To him, these differences have consequences daily.

'I was born in a village called Kelloe,' he says. 'It's right next to Coxhoe. Coxhoe, Kelloe, Quarrington Hill, Cassop – all Co. Durham villages. The whole of the village, all these villages, thrived on . . . .'

Parnaby pauses, looking for the right word. He settles on: '*Employment*. The whole of the village thrived on employment.

'It was a real, tight community. My mam still lives in the same house. Sadly me dad passed away. He was a coalminer all his life.

'Also born and bred in Kelloe was Stan Seymour, who was known as "Mr Newcastle United". He lived across the street from me granddad, Billy, who was the village barber. Billy Bird was his name, good billiards player. We had a great childhood.

'Street football, as it was, that was part of the culture in Kelloe. It was about the mining industry, and along the road at Coxhoe, there was Raisby Quarry, at one time one of the largest quarry-faces in the world. So industry was thriving, employment was thriving.

'My mam's house looks across at the local working-men's club and whereas that was the focal point of the community, it's now open once or twice a week. Industry has gone, employment's gone.'

Parnaby is in a position to make connections about the consequences of the change from how it was to how it is. He can cross-reference jobs and football with culture and modern adolescence. On his wall are the names of around 150 boys whose age-range runs from seven to 21. On his door is a quotation from Paul Scholes that reads:

> *Kids are different nowadays, don't you think? Kids, particularly at big clubs, are mollycoddled. I was talking to Nicky Butt because we had the Under-19s this week in Leverkusen: there is nothing streetwise about them. They are almost trying to be manufactured into players whereas when we were growing up, we had to look after ourselves. We had to get three buses in the morning to get to Carrington, now they are dropped off, they are picked up in a minibus at the training ground, taken to school. They don't really have the tough part of life of trying to look after yourself. And sometimes it does show. Sometimes they are a little bit quiet when they play, or not as tough or streetwise as you need to be on the football field. I am not saying the players are weak. It is not the players' fault, it is just the way the world has gone. We had advantages without knowing it.*

Parnaby and Scholes are far from alone in recognising behavioural change over the past 25 years. Most football coaches see it every day. One of Parnaby's profound observations is succinct and concerns the meaning of play in modern childhood: 'Play,' he says, 'has gone from external to internal. 'In quite a short space of time, play has gone from being something we understood as happening outside to something that happens inside.

'Not that long ago everybody was able to play, everybody was out playing. Sadly those days of street football have gone. You don't see children on a scrap piece of land playing late at night below a lamp-post. That's gone.

'We'd play til' all hours. And we very rarely had this person called "the coach". The coach was the game. We just played the game.

'It's a saying we use now in coaching: 'Let the game be the teacher.'

'Because of the way society has gone – TV, technology, etcetera, the word "play" has changed. The concept of play has changed. What is play these days? It's probably sitting in front of a screen with controls.

'Playing in our day was outside. Football, throwing and catching; cricket with a bit of wood and a dustbin lid, that's how it was.

'Sadly the dangers that are out there are very much in the minds of parents: child protection issues, safeguarding of children. The advance of society has been exciting but the basic experience of outside play has disappeared. Now in football we are trying to re-create the old play environment. But to create that we have to provide a facility, a ball.'

Parnaby does not quite say that Middlesbrough have re-established an old street in their Academy, but in the games against Blackburn on this morning there was a fluency and free rhythm that contrasted with so much of youth and senior football, where over-coaching and rigid tactics can lead to manufactured players and sterile play. There was a 15-year-old Beardsley-esque attacker from Hartlepool who has been causing ripples locally. You could see why.

'I'm not saying what we have is un-structured but the art of communication, like everything else, has been affected by changes in society,' Parnaby says. 'You see that in Twitter and all that, but it affects communication on a pitch.

'I stuck that quote from Paul Scholes on my door. It's about personal responsibility. Yet we have two boys going away tomorrow with England, both Under-18, and a taxi will pick them up from their homes and take them from here to St George's Park [Derbyshire].

'Now that's not the fault of the FA, the parents or the boys, it's just an indication of how things have changed – safeguarding of children. Those rules we live under are very demanding and we live in a world of litigation. It's strict. We have to have a policy for transport, for housing.'

Two months earlier, three Boro Academy players – Luke Williams, Bradley Fewster and Bryn Morris – spent three weeks in Spain in a new link-up Middlesbrough have with Atlético Madrid. On the surface it looked an interesting – and straightforward – experiment, but Parnaby highlighted complications as well as benefits.

'We had three boys out there for three weeks recently for the experience,' he says. 'To cover our child protection issues, I had to send our head of Education and Welfare with them to make sure they bedded in. We nearly asked them to fly back by themselves but we thought it "best practice" not to.

'In Spain it's different, in England the rules seem a lot tighter than in France, Germany, Holland and Spain.

'We are now dealing with emotional issues, family issues, we have counsellors being brought in. It's a minefield. The changes are massive. Teesside was built on people coming in from other regions, it's not as old as Wearside or Tyneside. Sadly the chemical industry has taken a big hit. The changes I've seen in my village, that's what we've got on a bigger scale on Teesside. It's high unemployment.'

Sociologically, Parnaby has also noticed knock-on effects of long-term economic decline. The headline in this day's *Middlesbrough Evening Gazette* was: 'Gran Dealt Crack Cocaine' and concerned a court case, a 49 year-old grandmother from Ayresome Street and 'a wrap of crack'. She was supplying.

'Unemployment creates pressure,' Parnaby says, 'pressure within families, pressure to survive. So my mam would knit to provide extra income to my dad's wage from the pit. In poorer areas, when people are unemployed, where do they get extra income? A small percentage will go down the wrong track. It's all linked.

'A nice piece of land on a council estate, in my day, would simply have had kids playing on it and the parents would have been happy – 'make sure you're in at 9 o'clock'. Now those spaces, some of them, are surrounded by drugs. That was never the case.

'You always had the tough boys but the drug and alcohol influence is massive. Because of the way society has gone, those tough kids don't play football now. They get dragged in to all kinds – drugs, alcohol, causing bother.

'We don't have any toe-rags here. We will, if they're talented, and we've had one or two from the most needy backgrounds. But there's very few from that background because there's been a massive cultural change – those boys don't go and play for the local clubs any more.

'They don't get involved. There is a horrible, underlying problem for them – there's no play. That's the thing that's missing, you see. That thing called play is so vital.'

Asked how that can be changed, Parnaby replies: 'Education.

'But the school environment has changed, school sports has changed. When I began teaching it was accepted that teachers were involved in some extra-curricular activity. Now what you see are the demands on teachers and society have changed. Children's approach to teachers and adults has changed.

'So much has changed. Society, schools – schools are all about Premier League-style results tables now. I've been out of teaching 16 years and I hear it would be strange for me now.

'Perhaps what we do here is give them a little bit of freedom, the freedom of the street – 'just go out and play.''

ON THE SUNDAY MORNING OF 7 MAY 2006, Dave Parnaby received a telephone call telling him that that afternoon at Craven Cottage, Fulham, Middlesbrough would be fielding an all-English XI, ten of whom had come through the club's youth system. He got in the car and headed south.

It was the last day of the 2005/06 Premier League season and three days before Middlesbrough met Seville in the Uefa Cup final in Eindhoven. Steve McClaren was Boro's manager but he would be leaving to manage England after Eindhoven and here he was making a statement about young English, predominantly north-east talent.

Middlesbrough's starting XI at Fulham that afternoon was: Ross Turnbull (born Bishop Auckland); Andrew Davies (b. Stockton), Matthew Bates (b. Stockton), David Wheater (b. Redcar), Andrew Taylor (b. Hartlepool); James Morrison (b. Darlington), Lee Cattermole (b. Stockton); Jason Kennedy (b. Stockton), Adam Johnson (b. Sunderland); Danny Graham (b. Gateshead), Malcolm Christie (b. Peterborough, signed from Derby County).

The three used substitutes were Colin Cooper (b. Sedgefield), Tom Craddock (b. Durham) and Josh Walker (b. Newcastle). The two unused substitutes were David Knight (b. Sunderland) and Tony McMahon (b. Bishop Auckland).

'Everyone talks about the McClaren era and the XI at Fulham,' Parnaby says. 'It was wonderful, nearly all of that group have gone on and had really solid careers.

'That day came about because of the success of the first team. We were safe in the Premier League and we had a Uefa Cup final three days later. Steve McClaren knew he had a talented group of kids he could trust. And his job wasn't at risk.'

Bearing in mind that Uefa Cup final, it is tempting to dismiss this as a look-at-me gesture from McClaren, but that ignores the team he selected in Eindhoven. Stewart Parnaby (b. Durham), Stewart Downing (b. Middlesbrough) and James Morrison started against Seville. Lee Cattermole came off the bench. Four boys local to Middlesbrough appeared in the 2006 Uefa Cup final.

McClaren explains. 'I was resting players before a European final, I was making a statement about young English talent, about young Teesside talent – it was a bit of all of that. [Chairman] Steve Gibson stressed at the beginning he wanted a trophy, play in Europe, fill the stadium and a team of local kids. We were able to do that. What pleased me that day at Fulham was that the team competed and lost by a late goal. That was great for the future. I was as proud of that as anything else I did there.'

Less than eight years later, four north-easterners started in the Premier League's full fixture list on New Year's Day.

'The game has changed dramatically, everything outside the pitch,' Parnaby says. 'Because of the world changes and the emergence of the Premier League, people ask about home-produced players. If the people who govern the game really wanted it to be about England and the England team, then something has to be done about the Premier League. Which is not going to happen.

'So those numbers, they're normal now.'

And the north-east? The hotbed of soccer?

'The old saying was that you'd be able to shout down a pit and find a centre-forward. On Teesside we have one of the biggest junior football leagues in Europe. Hundreds in it from five, six upwards to 18. Teesside's grassroots are OK.

'I'll say there's talent here. But while all that is happening here, at the other end of the spectrum clubs are going global. There is talent – it's about the pathway, the opportunity. And are the boys committed?'

Parnaby ran through the U-18 team facing Blackburn: five from Teesside, five from Co. Durham, one from Northumberland. But there is no complacency.

'The U-18 environment is diminishing. Why are boys not continuing to play the game after 16? There must be something more attractive to them. That's why we ask questions about our environment here.

'We're not producing, we're educating. It's holistic. We put a high value on manners. What I say to the staff is that all we can do is what we do, and with an open mind. You hope that at the other end something called a player comes out.'

Massed rivals: Roker Park, 1980. Eight thousand Newcastle United fans (left) are separated from Sunderland fans. (Mirrorpix)

CHAPTER THREE

13 MILES & 116 YEARS

THE MORNING WAS NEW but this day was old. It had been here before and whatever the atmosphere was once – sporting, benign, fraternal even – now it was raw. It was as raw as the cold sniping around the corners at the foot of Barrack Road.

The wind was harsh; the taxi radio forecast warned of storms. As Sunday sermon bells began an ominous peal from St Andrew's church on Gallowgate and nervy yellow pints began to bubble in The Strawberry pub across the road from St James' Park, the 149th Tyne and Wear derby was under way.

It was not yet 10am and kick-off was not for another three-and-a-half hours, but these are games that start well before the players walk onto the pitch. On Wearside and Tyneside they begin with newspaper supplements seven days before a whistle is blown.

Particularly if the week before a derby game is blank – as it was in late October 2013 – the days before the game march to the drumbeat of derby talk, derby history, derby whispers. The Northumberland FA cancels all its boys' fixtures if the derby is on a Sunday. There is only one game in town.

To many, this north-east derby is the essence of north-east football. To others it is a menace.

Even though it has all been said before and will all be said again, the old, recognisable rare energy has a new coat, and it's always the biggest derby since the last one.

As Alan Candlish, author of a history of this derby, wrote: 'This game was arguably the most important Tyne-Wear derby ever.'

Candlish was referring to 25 April 1903. It was the last game of that season and Sunderland needed to win at St James' Park to secure the league title. They lost 1-0 and finished third. More than a century on, there will be people on Tyneside happy about that.

This was Colin Veitch's first derby experience at St James'. It's always someone's first time.

It was again in October 2013. This was the first Sunderland-Newcastle United derby since the Wearsiders arrived at St James' in the April of the previous season, doomed by relegation angst, and won 3-0.

That was the Paolo Di Canio derby. He would like it to be named after him. The Italian manager of Sunderland, not known for reticence, slid down the touch-line when Adam Johnson scored Sunderland's second goal. 'We want dirty knees too' sang Sunderland fans, quickly forgetting the many reservations they held when Di Canio had been appointed a fortnight before.

Newcastle's followers couldn't cope that Di Canio day, at least some of them couldn't. They wailed out of St James' and they wailed out of the pubs of the city centre. There was a hot mix of anger and alcohol and 3,000 Sunderland fans who had to get home through an angry sea of resentful Geordies.

This was the day a police horse was punched on Barrack Road with television cameras present to record it. The horse was called Bud. Bud was from West Yorkshire Police's mounted section. The 45-year-old man who threw the punch was called Barry Rogerson. He came from Bedlington in Northumberland. He was 'stupid', he would later say. He had never punched a horse before.

Rogerson was arrested and received a 12-month prison sentence. He was banned from football grounds for six years. Six other Newcastle 'fans' involved in the incident outside St James' were also jailed. At the last count, a total of 90 people faced a range of charges.

Tyneside looked through its fingers at this. The mini-riot, the horse, the defeat, it was all broadcast nationally. It was as bad as it gets.

Wearside laughed. It had been another long season at the Stadium of Light and this was their one moment of real jubilation. What a postcode in which to both deliver and receive.

And now, on this cold morning six months on, and at just the spot where Rogerson lunged at Bud, black and whites were assembling again. It was sedate this time. There were seven luminous yellow buses parked on Barrack Road about to make the trip down to the Redheugh Bridge, across into Gateshead and join dozens of other coaches and mini-buses in a circuitous convoy around Wearside and finally up into Sunderland towards the Stadium of Light. This was the long way round.

As a senior commander from Northumbria Police explains, the fans' convoy will not take the most direct route as it has passages where the convoy would be slowed and vulnerable.

'We have four routes we can utilise,' he says. 'We use roving traffic cars, they are out ahead scoping these routes looking for potential traffic hazards or trouble-makers who would stop the convoy from being free-flowing. I'll select the route into the stadium at the last possible minute so there's an element of surprise.'

As soon as the fixtures and derby dates are published, the police begin speaking to the Highways Agency and utilities companies to see if they have any planned works on possible routes. Local authorities, ambulance and fire services are also consulted.

'It's multi-agency,' the commander says, 'it's a military-type operation for what is ostensibly a football match.'

Military. Ostensibly. These are 90 minutes that have changed from a football match requiring policing into a police operation involving helicopters, horses and a codename – 'Jerrettspass' (from Irish history). There is assistance from other police forces.

'The derby now involves 1,000 officers working from morning until into the night,' he says. 'It is more than just policing a match. For example, on derby nights reports of domestic violence go up as much as 80 per cent.

'It begins in the morning when we "take out" a number of people we believe to be key individuals. We put "spotters" on them, we don't arrest them. We just make sure they know we know where they are, though we have lifted some. It sends out a message to those actively seeking to cause trouble.

'In 2000, before kick-off, we had a group of Sunderland fans about to enter Northumberland Street in Newcastle. We swept in and we locked them all up, about 50 of them. Now we're seeing a willingness to engage in trouble three to four hours after the match. That's another challenge.'

Is it getting worse?

'It's cyclical. It isn't easy at the moment because youth unemployment is high, people are leading more austere lives and that's a breeding ground for trouble.'

The taxpayer picks up much of the bill. Although clubs pay for policing on their stadium 'footprint', at St James' Park that does not extend to Barrack Road or Strawberry Place, the roads encircling the ground where the April 2013 trouble took place.

It is why police hope there can be a new debate about the state of the derby. A lot of fans agree. Before the February 2014 match at St James', the police – with the support of the clubs – planned to turn the fixture into a 'bubble match'.

This is what happens at Cardiff-Swansea and other tense fixtures. Essentially it entails curtailing freedom of movement among travelling fans. They must meet at a designated place and be moved from there to the match, then back again without ever leaving police control. Sunderland fans objected, Newcastle United fans supported them and the clubs backed down. So did the police.

Together with the Football Supporters' Federation, they lined up behind a 'Pride in the Derby' campaign. It worked in as much as there was no bubble and there was little trouble (comparatively). But it was still tense, still hostile.

And there was still the horse. A favourite chant on Wearside since Bud was struck had been: 'Lock up your horses, there's gonna be hell.'

At Wembley in February 2014, ten minutes before the start of Sunderland's League Cup final against Manchester City, a giant screen picked out a Sunderland fan wearing a large horse's head. Wembley roared. And on this morning the theme was being mined. On Keir Hardie Way leading to the Stadium of Light two Sunderland fans were waiting for the opposition wearing a brown pantomime horse outfit.

Bud was back on duty, too. A police spokesman was quoted on the morning of the game: 'Bud is due to attend the derby with other horses. He's fit and well.'

There had been horse issues before in the fixture, more serious and on Wearside.

That final game of 1903, which Candlish refers to, was Sunderland's second visit to St James' that season as the FA had banned Sunderland from using Roker Park for one game after Sheffield Wednesday's bus had been stoned there. Sunderland were offered St James' Park as an alternative venue and the fixture they had to fulfil was against Middlesbrough.

Sunderland and Middlesbrough staged a Wear-Tees derby on Tyneside.

The disturbances surrounding the Sheffield Wednesday game showed crowd trouble was not specific to Sunderland-Newcastle but there was near chaos at the derby of September 1909, in front of a record then of 40,000 at Roker.

The *North Mail*'s Monday morning account contained the following:

> *The first half was about two-thirds over when the crowd broke onto the field at the Fulwell End of the ground. Play had to be suspended, and for nearly a quarter of an hour the players had to be kept idle. The referee (Mr. J. Mason), the Sunderland secretary (Mr R.H. Kyle) and the police endeavoured to get the people back and they were subsequently assisted by the directors and two mounted police. Eventually, play was resumed. This was the signal for one of the horses to start a game of its own, prancing about the field to the inconvenience of the players and the amusement of the spectators. The horses did not go quite scot free,*

> *one being hit by the ball. It afterwards transpired one had been stabbed, and the Chief Constable is offering £5 reward to anyone giving information leading to the detection of the offender.*

✦

THERE IS AN ONGOING DEBATE within the 13 miles that separate the clubs as to the true nature of the rivalry. Some trace it back to the English Civil War, when the two cities were on opposite sides; some like Dr Bill Lancaster rubbish this as 'nonsensical'.

Lancaster argues that until the mid-1960s and the first national stirrings of modern football hooliganism, the relationship between Tyneside and Wearside, and Newcastle United and Sunderland, was one of friendly rivalry, of common identity.

'Whenever I grew up here,' Lancaster says, 'there was a tremendous sense that Middlesbrough, Sunderland, Newcastle and Hartlepool were all part of our mental universe. There's been a big change.'

Part of that change can be seen in football, part in language. The title of Alan Candlish's history of the derby is *Ha'Way/Howay The Lads*. Candlish explains this is because on Wearside they use 'Ha'way' and on Tyneside it is 'Howay'.

The terms mean 'come on' and originate from the mines, when men were lowered in cages 'halfway' down.

This could be seen as small and parochial, a minor difference in dialect, which is all it is. But there is increased attention paid to language. Sunderland no longer observe the Tyne & Wear alphabetical order when the games are at the Stadium of Light and the word 'Geordie' has now come to mean exclusively Newcastle when a generation ago it encompassed broader geography and many more locals.

'The whole idea of Geordie culture being confined to Tyneside is very new,' Lancaster says. 'The origins of the word Geordie are rooted in coalmining, the word comes from the coalfield.

'We live in a region with an incredibly distinctive language. It's old English, often unintelligible to the rest of England – *Auf Wiedersehen Pet* had to have subtitles in America. We rarely came on the media. So there was a strong sense of who we were, and that what brought us here was under the ground. How we spoke to each other – you speak "Geordie" – it becomes part of you.

'When the "Pitmen's Derby" [Northumberland Plate] was moved from the Town Moor to Gosforth Park in 1882, the local press report the pitmen walking up the Great North Road to Gosforth and they talk of "the Geordies coming over from

Sunderland". What they meant were the Sunderland miners. Up to the 1950s the word Geordie referred to the coalfield. "Geordie" meant pitman until then.

'We forget that all this Sunderland-Newcastle rivalry is nonsense. It just wasn't there before the 1960s, it's false. Basically this is skinhead culture.

'But if you live in Sunderland now, you are maybe part of a family with two generations experiencing this. There are 40 years of lads who don't set foot in each other's town centre. If you are born after 1970 and you're coming to Newcastle, it's enemy territory. It wasn't like that before. All this stuff about the Civil War is nonsensical. All this nastiness is really very recent.'

The word 'Mackem' is also a modern invention. It stems from industry too, from shipworkers on Wearside referring to those on Tyneside – 'we mak'em and they tak'em'. That at least is one theory.

There is little evidence of the use of Mackem or mak'em before 1970, the *Oxford English Dictionary* finding nothing written before 1973. It was certainly not adopted widely on Wearside as a marker of difference until the 1990s. Football was fundamental to that and there are many on Wearside who refuse to adopt it because in the beginning it was a term of mockery, an insult.

In support of Lancaster's opinion is the song "The Blaydon Races". Re-watch the 1973 FA Cup final when Sunderland beat Leeds and a song being sung by the red and white supporters at Wembley is The Blaydon Races, which is about a horserace in Newcastle.

Go back further and here are some lines from 1961 from *The Times*' reporter covering the epic Sunderland-Manchester United FA Cup quarter-final replay:

> *'The scenes at Roker Park were alone enough to make the pulses race. The gates were closed, thousands were locked out and youths were allowed onto the apron running around the field. Ambulances and first-aid men were busy from the beginning. . . officials were uncertain as to the attendance figures long after the game had passed but the general guess was that the crowd was in the region of 70,000, of which, perhaps, 20,000 had entered unethically . . . at times the roar found a pitch rising to hysteria. . . this was a baptism by fire for a Manchester team that has not before tasted this inferno of the north-east where the battle hymn of 'Blaydon Races' swirled across the arena.'*

There are many supporters of both clubs, over 40 generally, who can testify to going to Roker Park one Saturday, St James' Park the next. Nine days after Sunderland's historic Cup win in 1973, Sunderland went to St James' to play in Newcastle's testimonial for Ollie Burton. A year later, at Jimmy Montgomery's testimonial at Roker Park, the guests were Newcastle.

When a fund-raising target of £73,000 was set for a Bob Stokoe statue outside the Stadium of Light, Newcastle United ex-players' association contributed. Stokoe, after all, played for Newcastle for a decade and won the FA Cup as a black-and-white player in 1955. He was not just a hero in 1973.

When Newcastle came to defend that 1955 Cup, they were drawn against Sunderland in the quarter-finals in 1956. Sunderland won 2-0 at St James' to knock out the holders.

While Newcastle felt the pain, in their next match programme Newcastle's 'United We Stand' editorial said: 'In dismissing the tie, do not let us forget to congratulate Sunderland. It is up to them to uphold the football tradition of the north-east and we wish them well, with a visit to Wembley and with a return with the trophy we have failed to retain.'

To some modern fans these are inconvenient truths.

Stan Anderson can remember others. He went to celebration derbies after the Second World War when 'there wasn't anything between people. There was a different spirit then. This was a lift for people, they just loved going to the match again.'

Anderson knew tension, too, and if there was no hooliganism then, there was some animosity. From a Sunderland-supporting family, Anderson was the club captain when he was transferred directly to Newcastle in 1963, and made their captain. His father did not speak to him for a fortnight. Three decades later the same aura of tension immediately settled upon Jack Colback when he left Sunderland for Newcastle, the first such direct transfer in 22 years. Sunderland said Colback's free transfer left 'a bitter taste'.

You could feel the mood, even out of season. Yet five weeks later, when two Newcastle United fans, John Alder and Liam Sweeney, were killed in the Malaysian plane shot down over Ukraine, Sunderland supporters' response was to raise £100 for a floral tribute. Alder and Sweeney were en route to Newcastle's pre-season tour of New Zealand. Sunderland fans recognized their commitment. Within four days, the £100 fund had attracted donations from fans across the country and had raised over £23,000. Wearside's counterparts on Tyneside were stunned and impressed. 'Can we now stop calling each other scum?' wrote one. The reaction to a tragedy could prove to be a turning point in a relationship that had become abusive.

Anderson was understandably nervous before his Newcastle debut. 'A surprise for me was that when I first walked out I got the biggest cheer of me life. We lost 4-0 at home – the first match.

'But there is this conflict between Newcastle and Sunderland. The north-east is very intense. Sunderland v Newcastle has got so intense now it becomes violent. That annoys me. We used to have similar intensity when we played but not violence – you might have a couple of blokes having a punch-up. There was tension rather than hatred. The difference between now and then is huge.'

Levels of fascination have not changed. When the two first met in the Second Division, in December 1961, the attendance at St James' was 54,000. The next season, still in the Second Division, saw 62,000 at St James' – with an estimated 10,000 locked outside – and 62,000 at Roker Park.

The rivalry was more innocent then. In 1966 Newcastle fans broke into Roker and painted the goalposts black and white. But as the 1960s ended there was hooliganism at Newcastle Central Station and by 1978 fear of violence meant a 47,000 capacity was ordered by the Tyne & Wear Council at Roker and only 35,000 turned up. There were 13 train carriages wrecked, 40 arrests and 60 ejections.

The derby continued to produce football stories: Gary Rowell's Sunderland hat-trick in 1979, Peter Beardsley's Newcastle hat-trick in 1985. But it was spite-filled. There was serious trouble at the Second Division play-offs in 1990 and by the mid-90s the relationship was so fractious two derbies were played without visiting fans.

While England bathed in the afterglow of Euro 96, on 4 September Roker Park staged what proved to be its last-ever derby – in front of home supporters only. Newcastle's attack that eerie night at Roker consisted of Beardsley, Shearer, Les Ferdinand and David Ginola – players worth travelling to see. In the return game, Sunderland fans were banned from St James'.

Sunderland were relegated that season, so there was a gap until 1999 before the clubs met again. This was no less dramatic but it was about football: this was the Ruud Gullit derby.

The Dutchman had caused consternation on the eve of the match by comparing it unfavourably to his derby experiences in Milan. He made the north-east seem irrelevant and to him it was. But it wasn't in the city where he worked.

Gullit had omitted Rob Lee from his squad, questioned Shearer's abilities and in their place selected Jamie McClen and Paul Robinson. Kieron Dyer put Newcastle ahead but in an atmospheric August monsoon Niall Quinn and Kevin Phillips scored for Sunderland and 48 hours on, Gullit was Newcastle's former manager.

Maybe it did not matter as it did in Milan, but Ruud Gullit's first Tyne & Wear derby was his last.

✦

WHEN THOSE YELLOW NEWCASTLE BUSES pulled up outside the Stadium of Light those disembarking were met with an onslaught of fierce verbal abuse that is considered routine.

The name of the Newcastle United centre-half Steven Taylor was the focus of much of this. Taylor comes from Whitley Bay and is not slow to play up to the Geordie hero of his imagination. Asked before the Sunderland-Newcastle match of October 2012 if he could ever envisage himself in a Sunderland jersey, Taylor replied: 'I would rather go and collect stamps than stick on that shirt.'

Because of opinions like this and his on-pitch demeanour, Taylor has become Sunderland's pantomime hate figure: 'We're having a party when Steven Taylor dies', they sang. 'Steven Taylor, we wish you were dead'.

Grown men from Sunderland, with children around them, were revelling in these and other chants outside the stadium as a posse of Newcastle fans were escorted from St Peter's metro station along Easington Street and to the far end of the ground where away fans are newly housed.

There is a 'ring of steel' that is meant to create a 'sterile area' but the two sets of supporters could still see and hear each other. The atmosphere is unpleasant – at best – and, even if in the words of the Newcastle United fanzine *True Faith*, a lot of these would-be scrappers are 'pavement dancers', were the police not around in such force and organisation, there would be mayhem.

In the midst of this foaming contempt and scattering nerves, there is something else, something forever, something out of keeping with all this hyped venom.

As the players leave the red Sunderland tunnel and file out together onto the Stadium of Light pitch, they pass over a piece of grass that might make everyone take a step back from their posturing if they remembered what lies beneath.

Grant Leadbitter will never forget. In October 2008, Leadbitter, then a 22-year-old midfielder playing for his hometown club, Sunderland, scored a late goal to put his team 1-0 up against Arsenal. As the stadium erupted in celebration and surprise, Leadbitter ran to the touchline, bent over and kissed the turf.

It was an untypically demonstrative act from a young man known for his unease with modern football celebrity. It was untypical, but Leadbitter had a reason to do something different: below the piece of grass he kissed lie the ashes of his father

Brian.

A couple of months earlier Brian Leadbitter, in his early fifties, had died suddenly. Brian was a Sunderland fanatic, had been to Wembley in 1973; you can imagine the pride at seeing his son play in red and white. Brian Leadbitter's ashes were buried where he wanted them to be.

Grant was devastated by his father's death and the fact it made the news locally. It was his family's sad news, not the public's. Grant, determined to be resilient, played on, head down. Now he had scored against Arsenal and was faced by microphones. Reluctantly, he spoke.

'People close to me know why I went down on the floor like I did and I just want to leave it at that,' he said. 'My dad's ashes are buried there. I don't want to go on about it, it just means a lot to me and my family.'

Within a year Leadbitter left Sunderland for Ipswich. Almost five years on he has been back to the Stadium of Light just once. In 2012 he joined Middlesbrough and three months in, Boro drew Sunderland in the League Cup. Leadbitter played 90 minutes on the pitch where his father's ashes remain.

But in a private capacity, Leadbitter has not been back. He can't. It is too painful.

It had seemed reasonable to speak to Leadbitter about the state of Sunderland-Newcastle and north-east relations. His experience is from the inside, plus he plays for Middlesbrough. But once he started speaking it was obvious that it was unreasonable. It is still too soon to discuss his father and what football can come to mean. Leadbitter tried, but each time he did so his eyes reddened, the words stopped.

After he had said: 'I've not been back,' there was a long silence. He looked out the window of a small office at Middlesbrough's training ground.

Another insensitive question followed: You've been back once as a player though, how was that?

'Fine. Just doing a job. Everything was OK. Fine. Good.'

Another silence.

Brian Leadbitter had once taken his son to the factory where he worked to show him real life. The room fell silent again until Grant managed to say: 'I still remember it now.'

But that was all he could say and Leadbitter was probably asking himself why he had agreed to this. But when the subject broadened, so did his answers. What does he make of today's rivalry?

This answer came fast: 'The best. It's the best rivalry in the country. It's the best feeling playing for Sunderland against Newcastle. The atmosphere. Unbelieveable. Hard to describe. I've played in a few.'

You don't think it's acquired an ugly edge?

'Can't lose its edge,' he replies, 'can't lose its edge. The moment it loses its edge the rivalry is over and you don't want that. North-east football doesn't need that. North-east football needs Sunderland-Newcastle.'

When you went to Ipswich Town, how did you describe the north-east to people?

'The best place, the best place in the country to play football because everybody knows, everybody lives and breathes football up here, from under-sixes all the way through. When I went to Ipswich I found it nowhere near as intense as the north-east. I'm not sure my character fitted in there. Day-to-day everyone breathes it in the north-east. Anywhere else I've been, it's not been as intense.

'Ipswich is a family club and it's a lovely area. And football does matter there – there's a big rivalry with Norwich. I enjoyed my time with Ipswich. A few people speak football there, it is in the language up here. It's life.'

After that, Leadbitter relaxed, a little. But he returned to intensity – personal and sporting – and industry.

'It'd be a lie to say I didn't come back for the intensity,' he says. 'Because of my character, the person I am needs that intensity in their life, needs that day-to-day, body on the line.

'In my opinion the northern people have been brought up that way. Pits, mining, industry, when you're brought up in that – and my family were – you have a work-hard attitude. My family were factory-workers, my dad, all their lives factory-workers. When you go back through the generations, mining.

'I come from a little village, Fencehouses, everybody scrimping and scraping. I think that's good. Fencehouses is losing that now. When I go back you don't see that, you don't see people around the street who you know. When I grew up you knew everyone.

'Industry goes, that's the key, factories shut down. Where my dad used to work, Clearex Plastics, at the top of Fencehouses, that's shut down, it's a building site now with houses on it.

'I was brought up in that industrial environment. It's deep within you and it's got to stay within you. If you go away from that, then you lose yourself. I think a lot of footballers forget what goes on around them, forget working people. Some players think they're better than working people. And they're not.

'That's my opinion. I might be wrong.'

Symbolically, there is an argument that industrial loss has brought even greater attention on football, made it more important, but Leadbitter disagrees.

'No. It's less,' he says. 'I look back to Roker Park, the early days at the Stadium of Light and the atmosphere, the crowds, now you don't get those loud crowds, you see empty seats at the stadium.

'I'm talking in general, week-to-week, football has lost some tenacity, maybe. You go back to jobs, environment, money – that affects football because you can't afford to go to games. There aren't enough jobs for local people and local people are the ones who go to the game.

'These are tough times, and I'm not so sure you'd get as many fans in other parts of the country in these times up here. Middlesbrough do well to get 16, 17, 18,000 in tough times. We took 4,000 away to Doncaster.

'I remember at Sunderland we took thousands and thousands to Barnsley, filled two stands. When you see Sunderland, Newcastle on the TV, the away end's sold out. You can guarantee the away end is sold out. I have friends who are big Newcastle fans and every week they're there. Their wages come in and they spend it on Newcastle United.

'Newcastle-Sunderland, that's massive. Hopefully it will always be massive.'

THIS WAS GUS POYET'S FIRST TIME. Parachuted into Sunderland after Paolo Di Canio had been dismissed following a plea from the players, Poyet's first Wear-Tyne derby was also his first game as manager at the Stadium of Light. Some welcome.

In the match programme, the club's American chairman, Ellis Short, had the sense and sensitivity to apologise for that. 'The club has been in turmoil as a result of the change of head coach so early in the season,' wrote Short. 'I have to take the blame for that. Clearly at least one of the decisions I made over the last several months was the wrong one.'

Short's angst was understandable. Sunderland had one point from eight games. They had conceded 20 goals in those eight games. They had lost the last six. Their last home win was in the previous season.

Poyet had already been in charge for one game. It was at Swansea where Sunderland lost 4-0. The *Daily Mirror* stirred Wearside with its repeated description of the players as 'gutless'.

Sunderland as a club, as a support, had to clutch at a straw and it came in the shape of their new manager's record against Newcastle United. As a player Poyet had scored six times against Newcastle and had become the player who most annoyed Bobby Robson. Poyet had kept a newspaper clipping of Robson saying: 'I hate that Poyet.'

This was revisited two days before Poyet's first north-east derby. 'I took it as a compliment, but it was an interesting statement.'

Then, as a manager, Poyet's Brighton had knocked Newcastle out of the FA Cup in the past two seasons. Poyet had reasons for a small amount of confidence.

'This could totally be the turning point for us,' he said of the game. 'I find the situation with these two clubs so strange. It's two cities that are so close together, two clubs in the Premier League. It's unique.'

He knew that Newcastle arrived on Wearside as favourites. Newcastle manager Alan Pardew could afford to say nice things about the neighbours such as: 'I want to win so badly, not just for the team but for our fans, who we know we owe from the last game. But in ten games' time, I would like to think Sunderland's position will improve.

'I want Sunderland to stay up. It's important for everyone involved. We want to be strong up here. If you have two Premier League clubs it encourages kids to play, and we want more kids coming through.'

Newcastle had their own local difficulties. Five days before kick-off the club had banned three newspapers written and printed in the city for coverage of an anti-Mike Ashley march the weekend before. On the pitch, a lack of local presence had also become an issue.

At the Stadium of Light Newcastle United took to the field with one player born in Newcastle – Paul Dummett – and six born in France. This had been an asset rather than a hindrance previously but the local politics of a derby match mean that it will always attract negative focus should things go wrong and, five minutes in, Newcastle were 1-0 down.

Sunderland's starting XI contained Lee Cattermole, Colback and Johnson, all local, but in total only four players of the 22 starters were from the north-east.

A Scot, Steven Fletcher, scored the first. Eleven minutes after half-time, one of Newcastle's Frenchmen, Mathieu Debuchy, equalised. Newcastle were now in the ascendancy.

Poyet made a substitution. Off came Johnson, on went Fabio Borini. It was Borini's first time. He made the most of it. A 22-year-old from Bologna, who was owned by Liverpool and only on loan at Sunderland, where he had not scored, Borini collected the ball about 25 yards out and lashed in the winner.

Sunderland were off the bottom of the Premier League, and it was the losers, not the victors, who moved into the spotlight. Pardew, the public face of a regime keen not to have a public face, bore the brunt of Tyneside anger.

'The first Newcastle manager to suffer back-to-back derby defeats since 1967 was how one report started. The *Journal*, one of the three newspapers banned by Newcastle, said: 'This is an unhappy club that needs results to prevent rebellion.'

Three days later Newcastle lost 2-0 to Manchester City in the League Cup.

But then Newcastle beat Chelsea at St James' and won the next three after that. After derby defeat, Newcastle won seven and drew one of their next nine league games. Derby fallout is not predictable. There was no rebellion.

Unlike Ruud Gullit, Pardew kept his job. Even after the next Tyne-Wear derby – the 150th – when Sunderland won 3-0 again at St James', Pardew kept his job. A Newcastle fan may have run onto the pitch and thrown his season ticket down in front of Pardew, but a tale that has been inflaming, teasing and entertaining two cities since 1898 expects this.

As the backpage headline of the local *Sunday Sun* newspaper on the morning of 149th said: 'Here We Go Again'.

PART TWO

THE CLUSTER

Trophy-laden: the extraordinary Bob Paisley returns to his home village of Hetton-le-Hole in Co. Durham with the 1977 European Cup and League championship. (Mirrorpix)

CHAPTER FOUR

BOB PAISLEY, THE BEATLES, THE KENNEDYS AN' THAT

THE REMAINS OF THE DAY were slipping away over the brown stone walls of the squat cold Liverpool graveyard where Eleanor Rigby lies buried. The happy screeching from Quarry Street playground had gone in for tea and across the road from St Peter's Church, in the fading white winter dusk-light, the verger was winding down the silent afternoon. It had been busy, lots of pre-Christmas parish work.

And for him there was the usual line of excited tourists bustling down to Woolton in the south of the city regardless of the season or the weather. They arrive at St Peter's in a state of religious expectation. It was here in July 1957 that John Lennon first met Paul McCartney. The very place.

Nine fabled years after the Quarrymen Skiffle Group appeared in this little landmark church, the Beatles penned 'Eleanor Rigby'. Although Paul McCartney has said that the song's title and its dismay did not originate from a greying headstone in the grounds of St Peter's, there is one here marking the life of a woman named Eleanor Rigby.

Maybe it is coincidence that the man who raised John Lennon, his uncle George Toogood Smith, is also buried here, though Beatlemaniacs will think not. They will feel it is magic or fate or whatever, and there is indeed something unusual, special, in the fact that the greatest-ever English football manager, Bob Paisley, is another who lies here close to Eleanor Rigby.

Paisley was the first of only two managers in history to win the European Cup three times. Carlo Ancelotti equalled his record in 2014.

Paisley said his finest hours were spent in the shadow of St Peter's, but it was

Rome's St Peter's he was talking about. As Gunner Paisley he helped liberate the Italian capital in the Second World War, and it was in Rome in 1977 that Paisley plotted Liverpool's first-ever victory in the European Cup. Paisley became the first English manager to lift that Cup.

'My first glimpse of Rome in 1944 was through the dusty wind-screen of an army truck,' he said. 'My second visit was rather different.'

On the latter occasion it was Liverpool 3 Borussia Moenchengladbach 1 and Paisley joked it was the second time he'd beaten the Germans in Rome.

In Liverpool, St Peter's was also the name of the Paisleys' chosen church and if that were not enough coincidence – or magic – the verger who deals with the daily line of tourists has the surname Paisley. He is Graham Paisley, son of the father.

On this late afternoon, a matchday 17 years after Bob Paisley's death, there had been some football footfall in Woolton. Graham tidies some pastoral paperwork and says: 'At St Peter's we have a mix of the Beatles and my dad, a mix of music and football.

'My dad still attracts people here – today there was someone from Chicago and someone from Israel. The taxi drivers always like it when Liverpool are at home because people come here as well as Anfield. Liverpool have this worldwide following and I'd like to think a small part of that pays testimony to the success when my father was here. He helped make them a European and world name. So, sometimes he becomes part of the Beatles tour.'

The Beatles never declared which club, if any, they supported. McCartney's preference was for Everton – he attended the 1968 FA Cup final Everton lost to West Brom – but he was not an avid fan and the Beatles' most direct connections to football are red. Matt Busby is mentioned in the song 'Dig It' – Busby played for Liverpool. And on the cover of the album *Sergeant Pepper's Lonely Hearts Club Band*, there is one football face in the 61 crowding around The Beatles. That face belongs to Albert Stubbins. Stubbins, too, played for Liverpool.

Albert Stubbins came from Wallsend, Newcastle. He was Bobby Robson's early hero. As a teenager Stubbins joined Sunderland on the understanding that if his hometown club wanted him he could go there. Aged 18, in 1937 this happened. Stubbins played 30 times for Newcastle United before the Second World War and during it scored 244 goals in 'wartime football'.

This led Everton and Liverpool north across the Pennines in 1946. Newcastle were prepared to sell, for money and to accommodate a young player, Jackie Milburn. Stubbins was at a cinema in town when he was summoned to the boardroom at St James' to meet the Merseyside clubs. He did not know who to speak to first.

He tossed a coin, spoke to Liverpool and that was that.

Liverpool paid a club record fee of £13,000 and Stubbins joined a man back from the war, Bob Paisley, at Anfield. Together they helped Liverpool win the first post-war league title, Paisley at left-back, Stubbins at centre-forward. Stubbins scored 24 goals in 36 games and became a local hero.

Paul McCartney once sent Stubbins a telegram that read: 'Well done Albert for all those glorious years of football. Long may you bob and weave.'

John Lennon was seven when Liverpool claimed that title and presumably heard the playground rhyme: 'A-L-B! E-R-T' Albert Stubbins is the man for me.'

On the 1967 Beatles' album cover, Stubbins is adjacent to Lewis Carroll. Carroll was the inspiration behind another Lennon creation: 'I Am The Walrus'. Carroll spent a lot of time in the north-east near Sunderland, where today there is not a statue of Albert Stubbins, but there is one of a walrus.

'A SMALL PART' was Graham Paisley's reference to his father's contribution to Liverpool's global status.

The modesty must be genetic. Alan Hansen once said that Bob Paisley's autobiography would contain two references to Bob Paisley, and Graham offers further evidence. When Paisley was announced as Bill Shankly's successor in June 1974, news that shook the world, Graham heard it, not from his father, but 'on the radio'.

Paisley was football's definition of discreet genius. 'If I can walk down the street and nobody recognises me, I'm delighted,' he said.

His unease with publicity and his willingness to avoid the media was sufficient to deter him seeking the England job. As he said: 'It's a specialist job and you've got to be a bit more of a diplomat. If there's one thing I preach, it's knowing your strengths and weaknesses. I might have been caught out from a verbal point of view.'

Liverpool's players have countless tales of Paisley's idiosyncratic language, when every sentence contained 'doings' or 'an' that'. In the case of Newcastle's Stewart Barraclough, Kevin Keegan said Paisley would warn: 'Watch that fellow Wheelbarrow.'

Paisley probably knew the mirth he was creating – in his office he had a clock that went backwards – he just didn't shout about it.

Discretion was a trait Paisley traced back to his roots. He was humble in the days before humility became part of football's ostentatious parade of personal promotion. The son of Sam Paisley and Emily Bones, Bob Paisley was born in Hetton-le-Hole, Co. Durham in 1919, six months before Stubbins was born 12 miles away.

Paisley's father was a miner who worked at the Hetton Lyons colliery in the town and on the occasions when Paisley was prepared to look back on his life, he said of Hetton: 'The population was about 12,000 and it was just mad about football. When I was a youngster, about five years-old, when the New Year was coming in I kicked a ball on New Year's Eve, and in the north-east this was a sign: that if you kick a ball through New Year, you'd be kicking a ball through the rest of your life.'

There was the pit and there was the ball, or a pig's bladder from the butchers where Paisley's Uncle Alan worked. As a boy, Paisley witnessed the effects of the General Strike of 1926 and with his father he scoured coal tips to bring home crude fuel.

It gave him perspective, saying in 1978: 'The poverty was there to be seen but the people were happy, they accepted their lot. It grieves me now to hear people say what a state the country's in when you look back to those days. Yet you were happy, and you didn't have anything at all.'

And Hetton gave him something deeper: 'Character, to be modest, to be thankful for small mercies. This was the upbringing, what I was taught. The character, reluctant to be pushed down. Perseverance, reluctance to give in.'

In 1935 Paisley's father almost lost an arm in a pit accident and reacted by withdrawing his son, who had not yet gone underground.

'I was sorting coal from stone, what they call "on bank", on top of the pithead,' Paisley said. 'I'd little interest in this. It was either going down the pits or being a footballer. This is where the north-east was in pre-war days, and why there were so many footballers. It was such an incentive. I was at Hetton Lyons colliery for three months. The colliery closed down and my father had been badly injured. He wouldn't let me go to another colliery.'

Paisley got a bricklaying job 12 miles away in Blackhall, cycling there and back. But professional football would intervene. Paisley had been a prolific medal-winner at Eppleton school and was looked at by Wolves when he was 13. He was rejected, then by Sunderland, which hurt more.

'Sunderland was my team, the team I supported. These were the days of Jimmy Connor, Patsy Gallacher, Alec Hastings.'

Paisley joined Hetton Juniors, with Harry Potts, and then the great amateur club Bishop Auckland. The Bishops knew what they had uncovered, they would send a Rolls-Royce to Hetton to pick up their new youngster. Although amateur, there are numerous stories of how Bishops paid more than Football League clubs and the Paisley family needed it. Samuel had not worked since his accident.

But Bob Paisley always credited luck in his life and he had proof when one of his brothers, Hughie, got 14 of 15 predictions correct on his football pools coupon and won '£315, nine shillings and a penny', a fortune in the 1930s. Financially the Paisleys could relax and matters improved further when Liverpool manager George Kay went to see son Bob to offer him a contract at Anfield.

'Sunderland had turned me down because I was too small,' Paisley said. 'They came back again but I'd promised to come to Liverpool. We won the Championship in 1946/47. That had to be my highlight as a player.'

His last Bishop Auckland game was in the Durham County Cup final at Roker Park. Considering what Paisley was to achieve, just as a player, never mind coach and manager, Sunderland's error ranks as historic ineptitude.

It was 1939 and Paisley's time at Anfield was brief. He was soon in the Royal Artillery, serving in North Africa and Italy. Part of Montgomery's Desert Rats, Paisley's brother Hughie said that Bob temporarily lost his sight during the battle of El Alamein – 'Bob was in the trenches and a plane came over and sprayed them with bullets. His eyes were full of sand and he thought he was blinded.'

On demobilisation, Paisley finally got his Liverpool career moving and played 33 times as Liverpool won that 1946/47 League championship. Peculiarly this is less celebrated than Paisley's subsequent omission from the 1950 FA Cup final team.

Stubbins saluted Paisley's contribution as a player: 'Bob Paisley offered so much energy in the course of a game that I often thought he would be stretchered off when the final whistle sounded.'

The omission from the 1950 Cup final team, two days before Wembley, was a heartache that would never go – 'I felt sick, really sick,' Paisley said, while his wife Jessie said that when the news reached Co. Durham: 'He had the whole of Hetton up in arms. Dear me, there was nearly a riot. They were very loyal.'

But it taught Paisley a lesson about selection and non-selection, about ruthlessness. It was a concept to which the avuncular Paisley would return with incisive success, a knife inside a cardigan.

Lawrie McMenemy once said of Paisley: 'Canniness in Yorkshire is carefulness, canniness in the north-east is niceness. A canny lad is a nice lad and that's what he is'; whereas Brian Clough said of Paisley: 'Sometimes his smile is genuine. Sometimes it hides his true nature. He's as hard as nails, and crafty.'

Kenny Dalglish once recalled Paisley saying: 'I'm only a modest Geordie, but back me into a corner and I'm a vicious bastard.'

And Paisley himself understood: 'Where I come from in the north-east, we were all brought up with the need to better yourself. That, and the belief in football as a religion, produces a certain kind of driving force for this job. It gives you that little spark of ruthlessness, that need to win.'

Paisley had left Hetton in 1939 and stayed in Liverpool for the rest of his life, but son Graham says: 'He never lost the accent. The north-east was very much a part of who he was. Even though he left when he finished playing for Bishop Auckland, those were his roots. He came from a coalmining community. He lived the major part of his life in Liverpool but the north-east was still very much home to him.'

✦

IF THE WORLD OF FOOTBALL thought David Moyes had a difficult job succeeding Alex Ferguson in the summer of 2013, imagine how it reacted in 1974 when Bill Shankly stunned Liverpool with his impromptu retirement on the day he signed Ray Kennedy from Arsenal.

Few considered Bob Paisley to be the man to follow a legend. Shankly was a giant of the game, a national figure, a messianic character. Paisley was a former Liverpool player, a physio, a coach, a quiet assistant. He was not the man to front a football club. So it was thought.

Paisley changed that notion. But it was not straightforward. He does not receive much credit for use of language but Paisley's words convey the difficulties of succession when the predecessor is not just legendary and omnipotent, but still around.

'I never applied for the job, I wouldn't have applied for the job,' Paisley said. 'It came at us overnight. Bill decided to retire and I thought if I don't take it, I'd worked with backroom staff, if someone new came in… I thought I've got to make a go of it to keep this. There's such a family spirit at Liverpool. I thought I'd give it a go. It was for the staff.

'There's no doubt about it, Bill was a great manager an' that, so well liked, everybody held him in such high esteem. Everywhere you went [he was there]. Bill wasn't unique for nothing. I don't use that term loosely when I say that Bill was unique as a manager. I mean, his very presence, all the rooms seem to be filled, you opened a drawer and you felt Bill was there an' that. Aw, it was a tremendous sort of pressure and something I'd not given a thought.

'There's no way anyone imitating can be great. You've got to be yourself. If that's not good enough, you've just got to accept that. I couldn't go on and say things like Bill did. But I could do them – in a more cunning sort of way.'

In his first season as manager of Liverpool, Bob Paisley won nothing. Liverpool were out of Europe before Christmas, they lost to Middlesbrough in the League Cup and to Ipswich in the FA Cup. They had been the holders.

Liverpool finished second to Derby County in the league. Never again, in Paisley's time, would a season go by without silverware.

There was no revolution, Paisley changed odd positions, such as bringing in Phil Neal from Northampton Town at right-back. In Paisley's second season Liverpool won the league title and the Uefa Cup, a two-legged final against Bruges.

Paisley was on his way, he was on his way to three European Cups, six league titles, three League Cups and one Uefa Cup – 13 trophies collected between May 1976 and May 1983. Paisley's understated intuition, his cool, ruthless decision-making – his 'cunning' – saw him inherit a fine team and make it better.

As Hugh McIlvanney put it in 1982 after a visit to Paisley's office: 'His authority on the game has grown like a tree during more than 40 years at Anfield and if the acquired wisdom is passed on too obliquely for some tastes, often through muttered, unfinished asides in the idiom and accent of the coalfields of North-Eastern England, its substance is unmistakable to anyone who listens carefully enough.'

It is probably over-simplification to say that Paisley's genius was simplicity but it was the idea he preached. 'We don't want purists or theorists at Liverpool,' he said, 'football is a simple game but one of the hardest things in soccer is doing the simple things regularly.

'Take concentration. That's too easy to bother most so-called deep thinkers, but is it? Geoff Boycott stayed at the very top so long because of it. They decry him and say he's too professional but if Geoff Boycott were a footballer, he'd be welcome here.'

Although there was no revolution in playing staff when Paisley took over, he gradually changed players and earned a reputation for it. Status, and certainly not age, did not protect a player from Paisley's continual assessment.

'A birth certificate doesn't tell me a players' age,' he said, 'the training ground and matchday does that. That's how I knew when to unload. A player isn't necessarily finished when he leaves us, he's just finished here.'

Even after a haul of trophies, Paisley told McIlvanney: 'I'm not as soft a touch as people think. I never was on the pitch but some seem to think I am here.' To which McIlvanney added: 'Paisley never allows the word transitional to be applied to his teams – he sees it as the kind of word people hide behind and he hates hiding in football.'

Of the team that won the FA Cup in 1974, only Ray Clemence, Phil Thompson and Emlyn Hughes started the European Cup final of 1978. Phil Neal, Alan

Hansen, Jimmy Case, Graeme Souness, Terry McDermott, David Fairclough and Kenny Dalglish were all added by Paisley.

By the 1983 League Cup final, only Neal, Hansen, Souness and Dalglish started. Bruce Grobbelaar, Alan Kennedy, Mark Lawrenson, Sammy Lee, Ronnie Whelan, Craig Johnston and Ian Rush had been brought in.

'It's always fascinated me how Liverpool have let players leave the club without causing even a little ripple,' said Brian Clough. 'A star drops out but the team keeps on winning.'

Clough sang loudly of Paisley's achievements, but while Paisley was voted Manager of the Year five times by his peers, and received and rejected a job offer from Real Madrid, there was a broader sense that he was under-valued. Every season the bible of the game, *Rothmans Football Yearbook*, nominated six people or clubs for awards. In his nine years at Anfield, Paisley was not nominated once individually. When knighthoods began to roll into football, Paisley was again overlooked. There was a failed, posthumous petition about it on Merseyside.

But Brian Clough knew. 'There is no magic formula, there is no mystery about Anfield, it's just down to pure talent,' Clough said as Paisley approached retirement in 1983. 'Bob Paisley epitomises that and I am amazed that people in football, who ought to know better, do not just accept the fact.

'He is on the same level as Sinatra in his field and nobody should question his talent. It's not the fact that he's got a bigger band or sings on bigger stages, it's just down to ability. The man oozes talent and he talks more common sense than ten of us other managers put together. He probably works harder than the ten of us put together as well.'

Clough was particularly smitten by one unforeseen Paisley decision: his conversion of Ray Kennedy from striker into left-sided midfielder: 'An absolute masterstroke.'

Even the unassuming Paisley was prepared to say: 'Ray Kennedy was one of the best moves I ever made.'

Ray Kennedy was a graceful tank of a player. He had balance and power. Kennedy had won the double with Arsenal in 1971, when he was 19, and in 1974 had become Shankly's last signing at Anfield. He arrived on 12 July, the day that Shankly left, but Shankly was unworried what his sudden departure would do to the player. Kennedy, Shankly said, 'reminds me of Rocky Marciano'.

Paisley inherited Kennedy who was bought to play up front. When Paisley eventually got round to his autobiography after leaving Liverpool in 1983, he wrote: 'Apart from all the other problems I had to contend with so soon after succeeding

Bill Shankly as manager, I was left with the legacy of harnessing Ray Kennedy's talents to Liverpool's pattern of play.'

Kennedy was supposed to rival John Toshack as Keegan's partner but Paisley quickly discovered 'Ray had really lost his appetite for playing up front.'

Kennedy came from Seaton Delaval, north of Whitley Bay. His father Martin, a miner, worked at the local pit then at Longhirst Drift pit near Morpeth. Paisley reached back into north-east past to speak to a schoolteacher of Kennedy's and 'learned that he had played midfield as a schoolboy'. Paisley added that Kennedy 'was surprised I had found that out'.

Kennedy was impressed, too. He was not an easy man at times according to others at Anfield, who christened Kennedy 'Albert Tatlock', after the grumpy Coronation Street character. But Kennedy didn't half play well for Bob Paisley. Converted to left midfield, Kennedy missed five league games in five seasons and won five league titles, those three European Cups, the Uefa Cup, League Cup and 17 caps for England.

'In my view he was one of Liverpool's greatest players and probably the most under-rated,' wrote Paisley. 'At England level he was totally mis-used.'

This is scorching criticism from someone like Paisley.

'At Liverpool things were built around him [Kennedy], and we played according to his abilities which were recognised throughout Europe – except in England. He never received the acclaim he deserved in this country and at international level England wrongly asked him to "pick people up."'

Not receiving due acclaim may have felt familiar to Paisley.

'I had a lot of time and respect for Ray,' he wrote. 'With both of us being from the north-east we could talk to each other and we had a good rapport – something that is not too common between a manager and a player.'

Paisley's affection for Kennedy flows off the page. But when Kennedy's form began to dip, the rapport did not prevent Kennedy being moved on to Swansea City. No one knew then that Kennedy was suffering from the onset of Parkinson's disease.

Kennedy joined Toshack at Swansea, then returned to the north-east, this beautiful trophy-laden force moving to Hartlepool United in 1983. Kennedy made his Hartlepool debut in a 5-1 defeat at Reading. Kennedy scored Hartlepool's goal.

The club was on the brink. Finishing second-bottom meant another bout of seeking re-election. Kennedy travelled to London to help make Hartlepool's case. They won and the club's official history records: 'He [Kennedy] played just over 20 games for Pools, but his respect and standing in the game probably kept the club in business during the re-election vote.'

Kennedy had been told of his Parkinson's by then. He took over a pub in his native Seaton Delaval and remains in the area.

Kennedy's 1982 exit from Anfield meant that he missed Paisley's final season at Liverpool, 1982/83. Liverpool won the league by 11 points and the League Cup at Wembley against Manchester United. Ray's namesake, Alan, scored Liverpool's opener that day.

At its end, the Liverpool players, knowing it was Paisley's last Wembley appearance, broke with tradition and pushed him up the 39 steps to receive the trophy ahead of captain Souness. It was Souness's idea.

Paisley looked flattered and embarrassed, but he took off his cap and skipped up those steps to collect the trophy and shake hands with the occupants of the Royal Box.

'The honour was theirs,' observed Dalglish.

THE MAN WHO SCORED the only goal of the 1981 European Cup final came from Sunderland.

Alan Kennedy was born and raised in Shiney Row, on the city's southern outskirts. Kennedy was playing for Liverpool, managed by a man from nearby Hetton-le-Hole, and to score his historic goal, Alan Kennedy received a throw-in from a lad from Seaton Delaval, Ray Kennedy.

Given what Bob Paisley said to Alan about his erratic Liverpool debut in 1978 – 'They shot the wrong Kennedy' – he might have called this goal a north-east conspiracy.

It was the 83rd minute in the Parc des Princes, Paris, 27 May 1981; Real Madrid were the opponents. As Real defender Vicente Del Bosque looked on, Alan Kennedy did what came naturally. Until his late teens when he was converted to a left-back, Kennedy had been a left-winger. Now he raced into the Madrid area and scored from a tight angle to give Liverpool, and Paisley, their third European Cup. It was three in five seasons.

Three years on, back in Rome where Liverpool had won their first European Cup in 1977, Liverpool and AS Roma drew 1-1. The 1984 European Cup final went to penalties.

Liverpool led 3-2 and needed one more successful kick to reclaim the trophy. Joe Fagan was now Liverpool manager but he had the left-back signed by Paisley. Alan Kennedy stepped forward and scored. Once again he had produced the decisive strike in a European Cup final.

No relation to Ray, Alan Kennedy came to mean a lot to Liverpool and Bob Paisley. There had long been one-way appreciation and it began before Alan Kennedy was born. Conforming to a Paisley pattern, it started in Hetton-le-Hole.

That is where Alan Kennedy's mother and her six sisters grew up. In an upstairs restaurant at Anfield called the Boot Room, Kennedy recalls his north-east childhood and says: 'My mother knew Bob Paisley back in the 1940s – I was aware of him probably from the early stages of my life. He lived in the same village as my mother and her sisters and many a time I'd hear my mother say: "Oh, I remember Bob Paisley".'

Sarah-Anne Donnelly, later Kennedy, worked in Worlock's fish-and-chip shop in Hetton and would see the aspiring player that was Bob Paisley on a Friday. It is uncanny – or canny – that decades later Paisley would sign her son for Liverpool.

'There wasn't much to Hetton,' says Alan Kennedy. 'My uncle used to go into the local bar and have a couple, and inevitably the talk would be about football, and about Bob. 'Oh, Bob did this, Bob did that, Bob made good.'

'They were very proud of him and what he did at Liverpool – though they would have loved it to have been done at Sunderland or Newcastle.

'My grandmother used to talk about him playing for Bishop Auckland. But Bob decided that his future was away. It was tough back then to get a job. So they understood.

'In the area – Easington, Hetton-le-Hole, Houghton-le-Spring – they were proud of him. These were all mining people, my uncle was a miner. They were hard, rugged people but good, honest and homely. That was epitomised in that village.

'Around the time I got into the youth team at Newcastle, I used to go back to Hetton to see my grandmother. She still lived there and two of her daughters still lived there. By then everything was about Bob Paisley, what he was doing, and I felt pride about him coming from Hetton-le-Hole, very much.'

Kennedy had still not met the man he heard so much about, and would not until, remarkably, they shook hands at Wembley Stadium.

The 1974 FA Cup final which ended Liverpool 3 Newcastle United 0 provokes many and varied memories: Kevin Keegan's two strikes against the club he would later save, David Coleman's 'goals pay the rent' commentary, the fact it turned out to be Bill Shankly's last match in charge of Liverpool.

Alan Kennedy, as with all Newcastle's players, had reason to rue the team performance. He had reason, too, to rue the purple tracksuits and the pre-game photo-op of him dressed as a zebra in a Durham wildlife park. But it was also the day he met Bob Paisley. Kennedy was 19.

'Of all things, I get to meet Bob Paisley and Bill Shankly at Wembley in 1974,' Kennedy says, impressed still.

'It was amazing to me that this man from Hetton, who my mother had talked about, who'd played football and gone on to do well at Liverpool, that I'd be meeting him at an FA Cup final. We didn't realise then that he was going to be the Liverpool manager.'

Neither Paisley nor Kennedy knew in 1974 that one would be signing the other. But in August 1978 a north-east journalist, Bob Cass, turned up at Kennedy's parents' council house. Kennedy still lived at home and for 18 months Terry McDermott lived there with them.

Kennedy, by then an established Newcastle United player, had his TR7 parked outside. 'It was white with a go-faster stripe. I bought it in Newcastle. Cars were very important in those days.'

Yet while Alan Kennedy had a TR7 and his older brother Keith had also made it as a professional at Newcastle, then Bury, the Kennedy home did not have a telephone. Kennedy had the number at Anfield of chief executive Peter Robinson but no phone.

'Some people probably had phones in their house then, but I didn't know anybody who had,' Kennedy says. 'We're talking 1978. We were in a council house. It was a case of finding the nearest telephone box, which was at Barnwell shops, and going down there and phoning up Anfield. I was shaking like a leaf, I really was, like.

'I remember the number, it was 051 then, not 0151. I remember dialling slowly and thinking: "Who's going to be on the line, like?" The secretary came on and I asked: "Can I speak to Mr. Peter Robinson, please?"

'Peter then said the deal was more-or-less done but that I would go into training with Newcastle the next morning as normal. Then I would go down to Liverpool. It was amazing how it happened. Bob Cass knew Liverpool were interested in me. I thought I was going to Leeds United, they were number one to sign me – or so I thought. It wasn't like that. Liverpool came along, offered the money.

'The Barnwell shops at Penshaw: my mother worked in the fish-and-chip shop there. Before that she'd worked in the fish-and-chip shop in Hetton.

'I walked down to the phone box, 60 or 70 yards – this is a true story. There were three or four people in front of me using the phone. I was standing there, like, telling people Liverpool want to sign me. They're going, "Huh?" I was trying to get them to hurry up, but their telephone calls were important too. I must have waited an hour. It must have been an hour.

'If you remember, at six o'clock it used to get cheaper, didn't it? Half-price, something like that. You'd be there with your 2ps.

'That was about your background and Liverpool knew that. We couldn't afford very much, we lived in a three-bed council house. We had a washer, an old-fashioned one, then you'd use your mangle. We'd a coal fire. We lived basic.

'But it was great. And everything was about football. We were on the River Wear, it was close, near Penshaw Monument. Plenty of hills. We actually played football on a hill, it sloped away to the river. I'd go on cross-country runs, miles.

'The shipyards were too far away to see, it was more rural. I felt more of a country lad than anything else. Yet everywhere around us was work, work, work. There was an ironworks near us, a factory that made iron. I could see it from my bedroom window. It glowed at night, every night, until they closed it down. We'd get wood from the local joinery about half a mile away. I'd push my barrow down, get the cut-offs, wheel it back up. The things you did – but it was physical, all physical.

'In Co. Durham there were lots of little villages, all linked by one road. There was Shiney Row, Philadelphia, Newbottle, Houghton, Hetton, Easington and on. I've run that road. It'd cost tuppence on a bus, and you didn't have tuppence.'

The £330,000 transfer was concluded within 24 hours of his 2p phone call. Kennedy was thrilled to be joining Liverpool, the European champions, and also to be leaving Newcastle United.

'The players at Newcastle felt the problem at the club was the directors interfered too much. They appointed Gordon Lee as manager, who came with Richard Dinnis. He wasn't up to it and we knew that. We lost 10 of our first 11 games. The club was going nowhere. After Dinnis, they said they'd get a trouble-breaker in – Bill McGarry. I was off. I didn't like McGarry. He didn't like me. The club wanted a lot of money for me.'

Newcastle's demand caused a delay in Kennedy's sale. Increasingly frustrated, he chose to express himself in an unusual fashion. There was no knock on the manager's door, or the chairman's. Alan Kennedy describes what he did next:

'I grew a beard.

'Look at me! I'm a rebel, I'm tough. I've got a beard on. When I came to Liverpool I'd a beard. I looked 36, I was 23.'

Some 30 years later a beard of greater notoriety would resurface in the north-east, on the face of Sunderland manager Roy Keane.

Kennedy's facial hair did not put off Bob Paisley. He collected his new signing from a Liverpool hotel the next morning and drove him to training.

'We didn't talk about the north-east, he talked to me about getting into the team. I remember Bob saying: "I can't promise you anything. Work hard. I've got Joey Jones and Emlyn Hughes still here. But I've brought you here to make that position your own. If you can't do it, we've got two others. Although we won the European Cup three months ago, no-one here is guaranteed their place. I've changed it around before and I'm looking at better players all the time."

'You were immediately under pressure, that first day. That was in the car from the hotel in town where he picked me up. That's pressure. Straightaway. I'd not had that at Newcastle. There, I knew I'd be playing.

'I'd had a bad injury in 1977 and Liverpool were a bit sceptical as to whether they should take me. But the knee was fine. I didn't know then, but it was the best day of my life.'

Kennedy would go on to play for England, but what he and Paisley had in common – knowledge of Hetton-le-Hole and Kennedy's mother – did not translate into favouritism.

Kennedy says Paisley had 'a soft centre' but he saw other characteristics.

'When I first arrived at the club in '78 he wanted to look after me. I looked at him, cardigan, tie, jacket, hair brushed back – he was like a fatherly figure, a grand-fatherly figure. I was 23. He was nearly 60. But he didn't care how he dressed and he didn't say much until you talked about football, then you'd see his eyes light up.

'When he first talked about Liverpool to me, it was like he was telling a story about his family. It was about the love of Liverpool Football Club. It was his, though he had so many good lieutenants around him, it was family-run. Bob was the reluctant leader thrust into the limelight. He wouldn't like it today.

'He was an intelligent man but he didn't like speaking too much. He didn't want to speak to the media. He always said the players did the talking. He would speak to fans one-to-one but in front of people he looked uncomfortable.'

At other times Kennedy experienced Paisley's toughness, that cunning: 'Bob wasn't sentimental.'

That was a reference to the day in 1982 when Sunderland needed to win at Anfield to stay up and did so, Stan Cummins scoring the only goal. Paisley's support for Sunderland was quiet but there was champagne in the away dressing room and the rumour was it had been sent in by the home manager.

Kennedy was there, he says it wasn't like that because: 'Bob Paisley wasn't sentimental when it came to things like that.

'Listen, Bob loved the north-east, he loved the people, but when it came to "business", he would want to win the game. He'd always pick his strongest team. He picked a strong team that day.'

Kennedy already had direct experience of Paisley's hardness. It came three months after scoring that winning goal against Real Madrid. That was the last game of season 1980/81. For the first game of season 1981/82, Kennedy was dropped.

'I'd scored that goal in Paris and I was in every newspaper in the north-west, pictures of me with champagne, whatever. We'd won the European Cup but when we got back to training we'd a practice match at Anfield. It was the younger players versus the older and established players. I was in the young team, so was Ronnie Whelan, Ian Rush. Others. We beat the first team 6-1.

'As far as I know, the manager summoned the coaches and said: "That wasn't good enough. We're going to get rid of him and him and him." Gradually they all went.

'I was left out for a while. Mark Lawrenson came in. Mark was a great player. He could play anywhere. When I came back into the team he was at left midfield in front of me. Then Bob decided to play him at centre-back. I knew then that if I missed a game I'd never get back in the team. I didn't miss a game for four years – 205 games.'

Alan Kennedy stayed seven years at Anfield. He won five league titles, four League Cups and two European Cups.

After Paris in 1981 he took his medal back to Sunderland. 'I was very proud. I was in the Penshaw, the local CIU working-men's club – I was a member. I showed the medal off and the look on the faces: 'God, is that all it is?' They went back to talking about greyhounds.'

After Liverpool Kennedy joined the doomed Lawrie McMenemy experiment at Roker Park which ended with Sunderland in the Third Division. Kennedy had returned to the north-east, as he had done 'most weekends' while at Liverpool. Though he briefly later played for Hartlepool, Kennedy would re-settle in the north-west.

He recalls one north-east to north-west journey after a victorious Liverpool trip to St James' Park.

'Bob was very proud. He told the driver to go by Penshaw Monument. We didn't go into it but Bob was pointing at it saying: "That's where I used to roll me eggs down." He'd also organised [scout] Alex Smailes to sort out sandwiches. Ham and pease pudding. The lads were looking at them thinking: "What's this?"

'I was loving it. We're driving by Penshaw Monument eating ham and pease pudding.

'Bob said: "This is it."

Don and Brian on Wearside: Revie prepares to join Sunderland in 1956; Sunderland's Clough consults Sinatra in 1964. (Mirrorpix)

CHAPTER FIVE

BEFORE (I): DON & BRIAN

THERE IS A CONVINCING STATUE IN ALBERT PARK, Middlesbrough, of a man on his way to work. The statue is on ground slightly raised and the figure is leaning forward as if in motion, his work boots slung over his left shoulder, a look of relaxed purpose on his face. His direction is Ayresome Park. The statue is of Brian Clough.

Brian Clough was born and raised at No. 11 Valley Road about 300 yards away from where his statue rises in Albert Park. A man who would play for England, become a national personality in Britain and an international football figure across Europe, spent the first 26 years of his life in Middlesbrough.

Clough was far from unhappy about that. He said some might think of his end-of-terrace home on Valley Road as 'just another council house, but to me it was heaven'.

Albert Park was one of the venues of his life. Some of the earliest association football in Middlesbrough was played there, years before Ayresome Park was constructed. Ten years old in 1945, Clough said: 'I learned how to play by covering every single blade of grass in Middlesbrough. I learned my skills on Clairville Common, in Albert Park, and on a cinder pitch just down the road. Often we played in the road itself.' The motor car had not yet changed street-life forever.

Today there is a green plaque on the house on Valley Road informing passers-by of the boy who grew up here with his seven siblings, father Joseph, a sugar boiler at Garnett's sweet factory, and mother Sarah whom Brian worshipped.

Clough's statue is walking away from Valley Road bound for Albert Park's iron gates, then Ayresome Street and the ground where Clough would make his name as a prolific natural goalscorer good enough to play for his country. Clough scored 204 goals in 222 games for his hometown club. They were Second Division goals but that did not deter England.

On the way to the ground was Rea's café, where Clough met his wife

Barbara, who worked at ICI. And it was where he and his other love, Peter Taylor, a goalkeeper from Nottingham, would talk football. Clough and 'streetwise Pete' would go on from Rea's to win the European Cup. There's an estate agents and a pawnbroker there now.

Ayresome Park staged three games at the 1966 World Cup, one of which was North Korea's defeat of Italy. It was Middlesbrough's home for 92 years but it is no more, pulled down after 1995 when the Riverside became Middlesbrough's new stadium. There are some cobbles left on Warwick Street hinting at a different time.

A housing estate was built where Boro once played. One of the streets is called Clough Close. He might have preferred Clough's Way but he could not complain: in a ten-minute stretch of Middlesbrough, there is a plaque, a statue and a street named after Brian Clough. The town has not forgotten one of its own.

Another of the streets on the Ayresome site is Camsell Court. It is named after George Camsell, from Durham, who joined Middlesbrough in 1925 and over the next 14 years scored even more goals for the Boro than Clough did. In doing so Camsell became a hero to many, including a young lad who lived about 200 yards away down the other end of Ayresome Street from Clough and Albert Park. His name was Don Revie.

'Being born on Teesside, my boyhood idol was George Camsell,' Revie said. 'As a youngster I stood outside Ayresome Park for many an hour to get his autograph. I was then only about seven but I could sense the magic which surrounds a goalscorer.'

That Don Revie and Brian Clough should have Middlesbrough, Ayresome Park and George Camsell as their mutual starting point is a knot of a detail given the unravelling thereafter. The two men went their separate ways from this spot only to meet again decades later in the opposite corners of a boxing match at the heart of English football. That was a fight about Leeds United, about style, about England. The shared Middlesbrough past mattered not.

Eight years older than Clough, Don Revie came from Bell Street, a five-minute stroll from Ayresome Park. He was the youngest of three children. His father Donald was a joiner who knew unemployment in a town that had lost some of its Herculean purpose after the Wall Street crash; his mother Margaret took in washing.

Much has been made of Revie's poor childhood. He referred to it in a thin autobiography from 1955: 'There was no television in the north. Even radios were a luxury in many homes on Teesside.'

Given his dour image, that Revie called this book *Soccer's Happy Wanderer* will delight many.

But when he stood at the Holgate End waiting for Camsell, Revie and other children would have known of the workhouse next door. Physically it was closer to the Revies, yet the Cloughs had eight children to feed and clothe.

If proximity to poverty helped mould Revie, so did the death of his mother when he was 12. 'Only a boy who has lost his mother knows what heartache it means,' he wrote.

Two years later Revie started a bricklaying apprenticeship and playing for Middlesbrough Swifts, a local youth team. Leicester City saw him there and a month after his 17th birthday Revie was signed at Filbert Street. He would return to the north-east as a Sunderland player in 1956 but he would never play for Middlesbrough or manage them.

On Teesside there is a feeling that Revie never looked back – he had the chance to join Middlesbrough in 1958 and did not take it. But he knew his Boro history and 40 years after the event was still talking about how unlucky George Camsell was to have scored a record 59 goals in 1927 – 'The year I was born' – only for Dixie Dean to score 60 the next season.

In 1955, the year Clough made his Middlesbrough debut, Revie was named Footballer of the Year. He is the only Middlesbrough man ever to win that award, but Revie was a Manchester City player by then. Later, of course, he was the force behind Leeds United's surge from Division Two to greatness, and after that Revie was manager of England, but despite it all, he still had the capacity to leave his home-town cold.

That explains why for all Revie's success there is no plaque outside No. 20 Bell Street, no statue on the way to old Ayresome Park and no street named in his honour. Revie's place is elsewhere. Leeds.

Middlesbrough's reaction to Clough and Revie is as different as the men themselves were supposed to be. It was future MP Austin Mitchell who compared Clough to John F. Kennedy and Revie to Richard Nixon.

Yet Revie and Clough shared much: that background, England caps, managerial innovation, and Leeds United; but whereas Clough became popular nationally as a loud iconoclast, Revie became known for the whiff of quiet subterfuge, 'dirty Leeds'. Clough is celebrated for John Robertson, yet Revie had Eddie Gray.

Something the men also shared was time in the Roker Park dressing room and, much later, allegations of financial shadiness. Those two things could be connected: Revie would be lambasted for his alleged greed when leaving the England job for Saudi Arabia – 'Don Readies'. And Clough would be tainted by Terry Venables' reference in a court case to 'Cloughie liking a bung'.

Accounts from players at Sunderland in the 1950s shine with anger, personal and collective, over money. Len Shackleton, one of the most gifted English players of all time, was so good the young Bobby Charlton tried to be him. Shackleton was aware of his own ability, the tens of thousands who paid to see it and the little he received at the end of the week. Revie played with Shackleton at Sunderland, while it was 'Shack' who set up the meeting with Derby County that saw Clough and Taylor leave Hartlepool, where they had started management together.

These were days of enormous attendances and enormous gate receipts, not just at Roker, but it was Sunderland who were labelled the Bank of England club. In 1957 Sunderland were fined the then enormous sum of £5,000 for illegal payments, a record. Directors were suspended.

Shackleton was furious daily and became increasingly militant. Trevor Ford, signed by Sunderland in October 1950 for £30,000 – 'the world's costliest player' – was fined £100 by the FA for asking for more than the nominal £10 signing-on fee.

When his book 'I Lead The Attack' was published in 1957, among Ford's chapter titles were 'Under the Counter', 'Drugs and Drink', 'The Transfer Racket – and the Cost'.

Ford wrote: 'Footballers, the last bonded men in Great Britain, are tragically underpaid.'

Even someone as mild as Stan Anderson says: 'Bank of England? That was gate money, not directors' money. They were getting absolute fortunes. It's a bygone time but it still rankles with me. Shack said it was a bloody joke. There was a goalkeeper playing for Bishop Auckland then. Middlesbrough tried to sign him and the going rate was £15 per week. The keeper laughed, he was getting £20 from Bishop Auckland, an amateur team.'

Shackleton and Ford were two stars in one team and the tension showed, Anderson says. 'Shack hated Fordy because he was being paid more – or because Fordy's backhander was bigger.'

The north-east's dressing room culture was such that even Jackie Milburn, not remembered as Shackleton is, had a chapter in his book titled: 'Are Directors really necessary?' and eventually this would see George Eastham take Newcastle United to court over 'the retention and transfer of players of professional football'.

In July 1963 Eastham won on the basis of restraint of trade. Immediately some players' salaries improved, though not all. Even those with increased pay were still entitled to feel they had been ripped off before.

Revie and Clough both missed out, just, on the personal salary consequences of Eastham's victory, but they had absorbed this sense of injustice inside Roker Park.

They could scarcely have avoided it – Anderson and Revie roomed together.

'We were like-minded,' Anderson says. 'We were similar players at Sunderland – don't give the ball away. To be fair to Don, he was a super player, a possession player, a ball-playing inside forward.

'He'd probably been better at Man City, and he was nearly 30 when he came to Sunderland, but he was such a delicate player, never put his foot in to anyone. So when people started talking about Leeds, I thought: "It can't be, it can't be Don." At no time could I ever see him kicking somebody or punching somebody. He just moved into space.'

Anderson's portrait brings another player to mind: Nigel Clough.

Anderson would later see and experience a different kind of Revie, and the golf partners fell out after Revie rang Anderson the night before a match against Leeds when Anderson was at Newcastle.

'I told Joe Harvey straightway,' Anderson says. 'I thought, I'm not having this on my conscience. Joe just started laughing.

'I've no idea why a bloke should change that much. Leeds just kicked lumps out of everybody. Without kicking people they were a good side. For some reason he brought that bit into them – Billy Bremner, Norman Hunter.'

One of the reasons why Anderson was perplexed by Revie, the manager, was a memory of Revie, the player, at night in their hotel room. Asked about the theory that Revie was motivated by a win-at-all-costs desire to escape the poverty of his Middlesbrough childhood, Anderson replies: 'Don never gave the impression of being from a poor background.

'He spoke eloquently. I roomed with him and he said his prayers at night. He wasn't embarrassed about it. I thought it was a bit strange – he used to get down on his knees and say his prayers before he got into bed. I don't know, do you do that coming from a very poor background? He never gave me that impression.'

Revie's son Duncan has spoken of his father's regular church-going, though it was Revie's superstitions that were known – he sent a car to Blackpool in 1967 to collect 'Gypsy Laura Lee' to come and lift 'a curse' on Elland Road.

Bob Paisley had a typically pithy understanding of the change Anderson witnessed: 'Like so many managers I felt Don looked for something in his own teams that he did not have as a player.'

It was a comment that could apply to Clough. As a manager, Clough had his teams organised and focused on work. As a player, Anderson says: 'Cloughie was intuitive, everything he did was instinctive.

'He understood the game but it couldn't have been anything else but instinct.

He wasn't a particularly good header of the ball but some of the goals he scored with his head, well…

'If you looked at him technically, you'd say: "No. No." But if you said: "What about positional play and the knack of scoring?" Absolutely top of the class. I played behind him umpteen times and I was so surprised how many goals he scored from so many positions. I remember George Mulhall saying: "That lucky bastard." And I said: "Well, yeah, but how is it always luck?"'

Given his career was ended at 27 through injury, Clough's luck was hard at times. Even the man who was to become his enemy acknowledged that.

Clough placed a value on hard-won praise – in Rea's café on Linthorpe Road, Taylor had been the first to offer it – and before the acid, before the venom infected their relationship, when thinking again of Ayresome Park, Revie said: 'Over the years since Camsell, my hometown club has built up a tradition of finding youngsters with the flair for scoring, Mick Fenton, Brian Clough and Alan Peacock.

'And if it had not been for a serious knee injury, Clough, now a successful manager with Derby County, might have gone on to emulate Camsell's feats.'

Once upon a time, Brian Clough could have been Don Revie's new goalscoring Middlesbrough hero.

World Cup-winning brothers: Jack and Bobby back in Ashington, 1966. Mother Cissie, in hat, and father Bob, await their sons. (Mirrorpix)

CHAPTER SIX

BEFORE (II): JACK & BOBBY

'WE COLLECT GENUINE "GEORDIE" WORDS,' Bobby said.

'Jackie will come over to Manchester and say: "I have come across a couple of new ones – 'snags' and 'baiggies' – do you know what they are? The first is a turnip and the second is a turnip too – but a different kind!"'

Back when things were different, back when the World Cup of 1962 was in the future, never mind 1966, back when the coal-dust of Ashington was still part of them and their lives, Bobby Charlton and his brother Jack were pals, or 'pels' in their Ashington dialect.

Jack would head across the Pennines from Leeds to Manchester to see his younger brother, and vice versa. Jack was a centre-half at pre-Revie Leeds United and Bobby was Bobby Charlton. As Bobby shows, they both still had Ashington on their minds.

This was 1960. Bobby was 22 going on 23. He was already England's Bobby Charlton, had been to the 1958 World Cup, won the League with Manchester United and survived the Munich air crash. He was still coming to terms with the loss of his friends and his old world, and the shock of his new world, his fame – 'Why, nearly every month one young lady sends me a box of kippers.'

The stories come from *Bobby Charlton's Book of Soccer*, published as the 1960s dawned. Bobby wasn't swinging.

The opening six words were: 'There is nothing special about me.' Granted, the next word was 'except', but all that Charlton went on to say was that he came from a line of footballers and was pretty useful, as opposed to arguably the greatest Englishman ever to kick a ball.

Charlton shared his uncle Jackie Milburn's gifts, for the game and modesty – though Bobby notes the honour in being named 'favourite sportsman of the readers of the *Eagle*' two years in succession. Apart from that, and playing football, Bobby's 'greatest joy is to escape to my Ashington home'.

There were four Charlton boys but Jack and Bobby were closest in age and the two spent much of their days together, though the elder by two years, Jack, would complain to their mother: 'I'm not tekkin' wor kid, he's ower soft.' But they went as one.

'Jackie and I used to enjoy scouring the beaches for coal washed up by the sea,' Bobby said. 'At places like Seahouses, the beaches are black with sea coal.'

He recalled fishing at Craster and his father Bob having a horse. Bob Charlton, who had a son called Robert, called his horse Bobby.

According to Robert: 'Dad is a typical pitman, suffering from pneumoconiosis like most of his mates, but not letting it bother him.'

Yet Bobby left that home for Manchester United aged 15. It says here for reasons such as 'those gruelling inquests after every game. In Ashington, nobody talks about anything else except last Saturday's game. Manchester has its football fans too – plenty of them – but at least they have some other distractions.'

Lest that sound the whole reason, Charlton adds that Duncan Edwards left the Midlands for Old Trafford despite having Wolves next door. Matt Busby was clearly an attraction in himself but this was an era when professional football operated a dual economy – one legal, one illegal – and Bobby was the most sought-after boy in England. The Charlton door was knocked constantly. It was 1952 and one club offered £800 for a 15-year-old's signature.

'You needed to be fairly nifty to avoid the traffic of football scouts back at number 114 Beatrice Street,' said Jack.

Manchester United may well have dug deepest. What is curious is that Bobby, and Jack, supported Newcastle United and their uncle Jackie Milburn was the star player. But Jack said that his mother, Cissie, the key football influence in the Charlton household, had an 'aversion to Newcastle United'.

Jack is unspecific – 'I think it may have had something to do with the club's reputation for not looking after kids properly' – but he later said that it was Milburn who advised Cissie not to let Bobby go to St James' because of that reputation. And this was when Newcastle were good.

Jack followed his father down the mine, having declined an invitation to go to Leeds United for a trial. What he saw there made him grateful when Leeds returned with a second invite and he left immediately. The sheer scale of the underground world amazed then and now. Jack was once taken to see his father at work at Linton, five miles from Ashington. That five-mile journey was underground.

Coal, and its dust, shaped their lives. The house on Beatrice Street belonged to the colliery and when Bobby settled in at Old Trafford, he fell in with David

Pegg, who came from a mining family near Doncaster. 'David was my particular pal – pitman's folk, like me,' Bobby said.

'Just before the accident he got a new car, and we used to go out in it together – to the pictures, dancing or to his home in Doncaster. We had a great time and to make it still better our parents chummed up as well, and they still exchange visits.

'Then came Munich, and the great emptiness.'

Munich was 'the accident'. The vast sadness of 1958 was expressed on Bobby Charlton's young face. David Pegg had died and Bobby had lived. But he was changed forever. In the words of Newcastle-born writer Gordon Burn, Bobby's face thereafter contained 'the under-colour of worry'.

It was the colour of Jackie's face, too, when he heard the news from Munich. He was getting changed after a Leeds training session and followed his instinct. He caught a train to Newcastle, a taxi to the Haymarket and the bus to Ashington. It would have been easier to phone home but the Charltons did not have a phone. Jack had not bought a newspaper for fear of bad news but at Haymarket, he saw one and read the Stop Press: 'Bobby Charlton among survivors.'

When Bobby was released from hospital in Germany, it was Jack who collected him from London. He drove him back to Ashington, not Manchester. It was in the backstreet at home that the photograph was taken of the recuperating Bobby playing football with some youngsters.

After that, Bobby's returns were less frequent, although he and Jack rode around the town after the World Cup had been won in 1966. Jack bought his parents a new house, which they called Jules Rimet. Brothers winning the World Cup: it had been done once before, Fritz and Ottmar Walter with West Germany in 1954, but not since.

Golden years: in 1966 Bobby was voted Footballer of the Year. In 1967, Jack was voted Footballer of the Year. 'I felt a bit guilty about that,' Jack said, 'because the one thing I couldn't do was play.'

Brother Bobby had already sprung to Jack's defence. Seven years earlier he had said: 'Although our kid is as brash as I am retiring by nature, he never had any opinion of his own ability. He is wrong, though. Jackie is a good player, and will show it if he ever has the luck to figure in a really good side.'

Don Revie's arrival at Elland Road ensured Jack Charlton featured in a very good side. In all he played 773 games for Leeds United over 20 years and was never substituted. Bobby played 758 times for Manchester United over the same period, 1953 to 1973.

But along the way from playing together for Ashington's YMCA team to

England's World Cup team, cracks had begun to appear. Bobby mentioned the differences between the brothers in the 'brash' and 'retiring' contrast and gradually those differences created a separation.

In Ashington it was felt that Bobby forgot, forgot where he came from and forgot what he came from. The town was pole-axed by Margaret Thatcher's pit closures; Bobby said she deserved a minute's silence from football fans on her death.

Jack could not have agreed. He became a close friend of Arthur Scargill when he was manager of Sheffield Wednesday and loaned his car to striking miners. Its registration was traced. When manager of Newcastle United in 1984 he would hand out tickets to striking miners' families. He still lives in Northumberland but he and Bobby are far from close. The Charlton brothers don't collect Geordie words together any more.

Taking on football: Newcastle United break the world transfer record in August 1996 by spending £15m to sign Alan Shearer, who grew up on their doorstep. (Mirrorpix)

CHAPTER SEVEN

SHEARER: RETURN OF THE NATIVE

BOBBY AND JACK LEFT. They followed Stan and Harry, Bob and Don. Jimmy went too, and Howard, then Colin, and Norman, and Bryan. Ray left. Later Peter, Paul and Chris would go in a rush, the family silver. There was always a lot of leaving. Alan was another.

But Alan came back. And one of the reasons Alan Shearer stands out from the others who departed the north-east was not just that he was one of English football's greatest strikers, but that he came back when his best days were not gone. Others came back too but Shearer returned just before he turned 26 and just after being top scorer at Euro 96. He came back at his peak.

Shearer came back despite being wanted by Manchester United. He could have gone to Old Trafford first, won his medals, then had a last hurrah at his hometown club. It is possible to conceive Manchester United wining the European Cup before 1999 with Shearer at the club.

But he didn't do that. The reality of professional football is money, and Newcastle United had to smash the world-record transfer fee to get Shearer from Blackburn Rovers, who did not want him to go to Manchester. But there was also symbolism that August day in 1996 when Shearer was unveiled in front of 15,000 outside St James' Park and spread his arms wide in his new black-and-white kit, 18 months before the Angel of the North was installed.

If it was the day he gave his country and western line about being 'only a sheet metalworker's son from Newcastle', it was a true, meaningful homecoming.

That was because of something else Shearer said that day: 'Everyone knows I've always wanted to play for the club, but if I'd gone elsewhere I would have had the best years of my career behind me, now at Newcastle I have got the best years in front of me.'

That is why Alan Shearer was and is exceptional in Newcastle United history and north-east football. It is about geography.

'The whole city's waiting for him,' said Albert Stubbins, once rapid bearer of the No. 9 shirt, then aged 77, and back in town.

'When you buy someone like Shearer, you begin to realise what you've missed,' says Stan Anderson. 'Look at the strength of the man. Have you seen the goals he scored? Just incredible.'

That talent was another factor of course. When Luis Suárez scored his 30th Premier League goal in 2014 there was praise and wonder at his achievement. Shearer scored 30 Premier League goals in three consecutive seasons at Blackburn. He was fast, brave and certain, the personification of attacking aggression. His innate vigour drove Rovers to the Premier League title in 1995. In 1994, aged 23, Shearer was already Footballer of the Year.

And then he joined Newcastle. For £15m – with Blackburn charging £600,000 on top of that in interest payments.

It was a fee that made even football swoon. It almost doubled the British record, set when Stan Collymore joined Liverpool. By £2m it beat the fee AC Milan paid Torino for Gianluigi Lentini four years earlier. Shearer was joining Alf Common on the list of world-record transfers.

But it was not all coming 'hyem' folksiness. Shearer had needed persuading. Just as Common left Wearside, Shearer had left Tyneside.

He was a teenager then and the mythology was that he had a trial at Newcastle and was put in goal. That happened, but it was not the full story, in fact two clubs pursued him: Newcastle and Southampton. Both made apprenticeship offers; Newcastle United were not quite the incompetents they were made out to be.

'I chose Southampton,' Shearer said of his stark geographic choice. 'I loved the people there and thought the coaching was superb. As well as that, I felt I owed something to Jack Hixon.'

Hixon was the scout who had taken all those players to Burnley. Now he was working for Southampton and Shearer trusted him. Shearer got on the 'Clipper' – or 'Clipp-ah' – the non-stop bus service from Newcastle to London Victoria that still has a special ring to Shearer's generation.

At Southampton Shearer scored a hat-trick on his debut, aged 17, and got married. It was in the city's St James' church. When he joined Blackburn in the summer of 1992 it was for a British record £3.6m so when the £15m came along, Shearer already understood the pressure of expectation.

Keegan, a former Southampton player, was just a few months into his job as Newcastle manager when Shearer was leaving The Dell. He made a phone call. He would have to wait.

And Keegan would be made to wait, and sweat, four years later. Not only was Alex Ferguson involved, there was interest from Arsenal, Everton, Inter Milan, Juventus and Barcelona. Then there was Jack Walker at Blackburn. The self-made multi-millionaire industrialist had two portraits on his office wall: one of Winston Churchill, one of Alan Shearer.

At 25, Shearer was offered the player-manager's job at Blackburn by Walker. It was unheard of and the pressure of Jack Walker's personality temporarily swayed Shearer. He was staying.

Then Keegan called again. By his own admission, Shearer was 'Keegan daft', as were most in Newcastle in the early 80s. Shearer had queued to see Keegan's first game in Magpie black and white and he was a ballboy in Keegan's last. And now Keegan was on the phone. Shearer, having wavered and having heard of Liverpool's late interest, said yes. When Newcastle announced the deal BBC Radio FiveLive changed its programming.

'He is the outstanding English player of his era by a mile,' Keegan said.

But either intentionally or not, Shearer had gradually created a public image for himself by then as straight, tough, dull. His teammate Tim Flowers called him Nigel Mansell. He was as wary of the media as his manager at Blackburn, Kenny Dalglish, who was as wary as his manager at Liverpool, Bob Paisley.

Shearer had constructed a shield that made him appear terse, hard. Even he called it 'Shearer-speak'. It all amounted to a picture of Shearer as single-minded, narrow, selfish. It was a contrast with the soft-perm affability of Keegan – or Waddle, Beardsley, Gascoigne.

That trio of names mattered as much as any on Tyneside in the late 1980s. Beardsleywaddlegascoigne became one word. It was the word for loss.

Waddle left first, when he was 24, Beardsley when he was 26 and Gascoigne when he was 21. Had Keegan been the manager, they would not have left. If they had not left, would Shearer have gone to Southampton? They left because the club was adrift and they had a hard, professional choice and made it.

The reverse of that is what Keegan, the John Hall regime and Shearer achieved in 1996. But Shearer's choice also entailed an unforeseen element in this hard-boiled hero – sentimental attachment to home, to Keegan, to the Gallowgate – and five years later Shearer sat in the St James' Park press room and reviewed himself and his decision.

'If I was this hard, single-minded individual then I would have chosen to go to Man U,' he said, 'because they were the ones winning everything at the time. So you can look at it and say there is a bit of sentiment in me.

'And there was – there was the pull of Kevin, there was the pull of Newcastle, the whole thing: the No.9 shirt, St James' Park, the Gallowgate, Newcastle United has always been the dream. That was always the ultimate ambition.

'Also, there was the pull of going on to win things. Newcastle had blown the title the season before and I was well aware they could kick on and be a major force. I'd say that the only thing that is missing, and it's a big "only thing", is the silverware. That's the disappointment, but I wouldn't change anything. If someone had said to me then: "There's your situation, would you do it again?" I most definitely would.'

Shearer was content then, relatively content. He was entitled to be otherwise, as within seven months of joining Newcastle the brochure had not brought what it said it would. Keegan went. Within 12 months Shearer snagged his studs in the turf at Goodison Park and sustained a grim knee injury.

Dalglish came and went as Keegan's successor and Ruud Gullit dropped Shearer. Shearer could have used that to crowbar his way out of the club, and there was always speculation about Barcelona. When Bobby Robson came there was speculation about Liverpool – and Robson seemed keen to sell.

But Shearer stayed. Over ten years he played 395 times and scored 206 goals. He broke Jackie Milburn's record, came second in the Premier League and played in two lost FA Cup finals. Shearer's last game, aged 35, was a 4-1 win at Sunderland. He scored.

Shearer moved into television when he retired and as each week went by his rampaging past was a week older. It goes. In 2016 it will be the 20th anniversary of the day Alan Shearer and Newcastle United tried to alter geography.

PART THREE

THE CLUBS

Dockers and players: from a 1951 Picture Post essay – 'The Team is the Town's Concern' – Middlesbrough footballers meet workers on Teesside docks. (Getty Images)

CHAPTER EIGHT
MIDDLESBROUGH

30 AUGUST 1997: Midnight in Madrid. In a small, suffocating hotel room off the city's main drag, Gran Via, the window is open. The day has been hot, the night is still hot, the hotel is hot. Everyone is desperate to cool down. Beneath the window a river of traffic roars along the famous street. There will not be much sleep.

Madrid had Saturday night fever. The old Spanish computer that delivered La Liga's 1997/98 fixture list had produced a Madrid derby for the opening day: Real versus Atlético, the reigning La Liga champions against their eager neighbours, and long before kick-off the atmosphere inside the Santiago Bernabeu Stadium was smoking. A fire started among Real's Ultras caused a delay.

Real Madrid had a new manager, Jupp Heynckes, who had made signings – Christian Karembeu, Fernando Morientes – and, it turned out, a significant other.

Atlético Madrid manager Raddy Antic had new players as well, such as Christian Vieri, bought from Juventus for £12m. The night held new beginnings, for Spain and La Liga, but it had meaning elsewhere, including a thousand miles away on Teesside. That was because of Antic's other £12m signing: Juninho.

Osvaldo Giroldo Junior – Juninho Paulista – or simply Juninho, was a fair-haired boy from Brazil who in October 1995 made the then unprecedented, astonishing move from Sao Paulo FC to Middlesbrough FC. To call this a step-change signing for the Teesside club, and the three-year-old Premier League it had just rejoined, understates the moment. This was not even an engine change. This was a new model altogether.

Not long before, Middlesbrough's record signings had been men like Hull's Andy Payton. Juninho was Brazil's No. 10.

He had made his Brazil debut in February 1995, on his 22nd birthday, alongside Bebeto, Dunga and Cafu. It was the day after Middlesbrough had won 2-0 at Wolves in England's second division, Steve Vickers and Uwe Fuchs scoring.

Four months later Juninho was part of the Brazil squad that came to England for the Umbro Trophy, a preparation tournament for Euro 96. Brazil had won the 1994 World Cup and Mario Zagallo was in the process of changing an ageing squad. Juninho was part of that change.

At Wembley Brazil won 3-1 and Juninho scored Brazil's first, a free kick of swaying beauty. He was playing up front with Ronaldo. On England's bench, sitting beside Terry Venables, was Middlesbrough manager Bryan Robson.

Boro had just won promotion to the Premier League and played their last-ever game at Ayresome Park, a 2-1 victory over Luton Town. The club had a young, driven local chairman called Steve Gibson, and fresh belief.

It was not even a decade since liquidators had padlocked the gates at Ayresome. Debts of £2.1m forced the team to start 1986/87 playing a 'home' game at Hartlepool United's Victoria Park – in the old Third Division. Refused access to Ayresome Park, Middlesbrough had to wait for Hartlepool to play their game against Cardiff, before 3,456 watched Boro's 6.30 kick-off against Port Vale. The score was 2-2. Archie Stephens got both Boro goals.

From that turmoil Middlesbrough Association Football Club, formed 1875, became MFC (1986), which is how it remains.

Gibson, who was only 28 then, once sat down with a group of north-east reporters and recalled that period. It was with a mixture of cheer and loathing.

'If we hadn't gone ahead with the game, we were out,' he said. 'Hartlepool played first and we were having all kinds of problems with the Football League, they were useless. We'd applied to the Gola League. We were going to rebuild it that way.

'It was an early-evening kick-off and about 100,000 people now tell me they were there.

'It was a strange period for me. I was quite young and was asked to get involved. Then I was up to my neck in it. It was so intense, you never knew how bad the situation was. Every time you picked up a stone, something crawled out. It was horrendous. I thought originally that the debt – and this was a long time ago – was £1.3m. To put it into context, the turnover of the club was about £200,000. Then the £1.3m became £1.5m and then £1.7m, £1.8m, £2m and then £2.1m.

'And then the old directors said that the club owes them "this amount". The biggest amount of money that went out was to the old directors. You couldn't lose sight of the fact that your role was to save the club, because in any other walk of life you would have picked up an axe and chopped people's heads off. You were saving the club to give all this money to these individuals who had already killed the club. I'm quite open about it, I'll give you names, it's whether you'll print them.'

Gibson, Middlesbrough-born and Middlesbrough-bred, has a cherubic face and is usually mild and charming, but he also possesses a ferocity that would have shocked people he dismissed as 'third-generation shareholders... talking about what they were having for lunch.'

Gibson's energy has seen him be saviour, strategist, benefactor and chairman and a decade on from Victoria Park, Hartlepool, his ambition meant that MFC (1986) had a new 31,000-capacity stadium, the Riverside, and a queue to fill it. They also had, as Juninho later explained, Bryan Robson. Gibson was responsible for that too.

Bryan Robson was born and raised in Chester-le-Street, between Durham and Newcastle, and became the heroic captain of Manchester United and England. Despite his outstanding talent and geography he was not signed by Newcastle United, Sunderland or Middlesbrough as a boy. He joined West Bromwich Albion.

Robson was revered in England but what Juninho stressed was that Robson was revered across the globe. So when Bryan Robson arrived in Sao Paulo a few weeks after Brazil's match at Wembley, Juninho was impressed. Everybody was impressed.

It turned out that Juninho's contract had just ended and he was in negotiations with Sao Paulo about a new one. Middlesbrough sensed an opportunity. When, some 15 years later, Philip Tallentire of Middlesbrough's *Evening Gazette* travelled to Brazil to retrace the transfer, Juninho said to him: 'That was the unique thing Middlesbrough had at that time, the name of Bryan Robson.'

It did not happen straightaway, and Juninho was not on Teesside when the Riverside staged its opening game – Middlesbrough's 2-0 Premier League victory over Chelsea. Craig Hignett scored the first goal in the new stadium.

Eventually, after agreeing a £4.75m deal with Sao Paulo, Juninho arrived in October to be met by thousands at the stadium, including a samba band and an atmosphere combining euphoria and disbelief. It was a taste of the affection to come.

'Mardi Gras with fried onions,' wrote Harry Pearson.

'Today it would be like Middlesbrough signing Neymar,' says Tallentire.

Juninho made his Boro debut in a 1-1 home draw against Leeds United. He supplied the pass from which Jan Age Fjortoft gave Middlesbrough the lead.

Boro would rise to fourth after Juninho's first goal, against Manchester City in December, but he would score only one more goal that first season as Boro slumped. They won two in 19, though during that run a second Brazilian international was signed – Branco, who had played in the 1994 World Cup final. Middlesbrough had Juninho, Branco and Jamie Pollock.

The season had fizzled out but Boro had stayed up and Gibson was not stopping. As Euro 96 progressed, the club stunned football again by signing Fabrizio Ravanelli from Juventus. Having scored in that year's Champions League final, Ravanelli moved to Teesside for £7m. This was almost as exotic and unexpected a signing as Juninho's.

Boro had already signed a third Brazilian. For £4m, a robust midfielder left Bobby Robson's Porto team. He was Player of the Year in Portugal but in England not much was known about Emerson Moisés Costa. That would change.

'We had a good team in the first year but not good enough to climb the table,' Juninho said. 'Bryan and the chairman saw that. We had to buy those players.'

Ravanelli's impact on the pitch was instant. In front of over 30,000 at the Riverside, Middlesbrough began season 1996/97 with a Ravanelli hat-trick in a 3-3 draw against Liverpool. But that was not the Italian's only impact.

'Ravanelli wanted things to be done his way,' Juninho said. 'If it happened differently from that, he would shout and think players were jealous of him. We had trouble after the Liverpool game, he spoke to Bryan Robson and thought that I was jealous of him because he came and scored a hat-trick. I explained that I had no problem with him.'

Teesside, which had never been the home of silverware or glamour, was being talked about. On 22 September 1996 Arsene Wenger was introduced at Highbury as Arsenal's new manager and said of his own origins: 'Everything is internationalised today. Could you imagine four years ago that Ravanelli and Juninho would play in Middlesbrough?'

After six games, Boro were sixth in the Premier League. Juninho and Ravanelli clicked in a 4-0 defeat of Coventry, each scoring twice. Nick Barmby had been another major investment and the attacking trio were supplemented by the piledriving force from midfield that was Emerson. Ravanelli scored four in the second round of the League Cup against Hereford United, the beginning of a journey that would lead to Wembley. It was the season that Middlesbrough would also reach the final of the FA Cup at Wembley.

But it was a season memorable for other reasons. Branco scored against Hereford, too, but it was one of his last acts before Boro instructed him to leave the premises. This affected Emerson, whose wife from Rio was said to be struggling in north-east England.

Rumours began to grow of turbulence within the club and they exploded when Emerson flew to Brazil just after Robson had named him in the squad for a match against Leicester City. Emerson had flown once already and the *Sun* had published a detailed interview with him in which he demanded to be released from his recently signed four-year contract, estimated at £16,000 per week.

'The bottom line is that my wife Andrea has found it impossible to settle in England,' Emerson told the *Sun*. 'We both knew this within three weeks of her arriving.'

Emerson then denied speaking to the *Sun*.

This came a few weeks after Barmby decided to leave for Everton. It was even said Juninho was starting to harbour regret. Having been sixth after six games, Boro won none of the next 12. They were collecting injuries and suspensions. Things would get worse.

At the end of November, with Middlesbrough now 15th, I sat in Juninho's front room in the red-brick Stockton suburb of Ingleby Barwick with Brazilian reporter Leonardo Roca and listened to Emerson and Juninho pledge their allegiance to the club.

Juninho's parents and sister had moved to Teesside with him; Emerson was in a house across the road. The setting felt incongruous but there were smiles as Juninho's mother poured Brazilian coffee. Her son nibbled a Bourbon biscuit and said: 'This idea that we have a miserable life in awful Middlesbrough, it's just not true.'

But there was a get-out: 'As long as the club keep to their assurances and are ambitious, we will stay.'

Emerson nodded at it all. He offered a picture of coiffeured personal contentment. That very night he flew away again. Truculent, gifted, difficult, Brazilian – Emerson sparked a furore on Teesside and no little consternation within the club. Robbie Mustoe didn't behave this way. It was all new to Boro, and alarming.

Except it wasn't that new. In a different corner of Stockton, Willie Maddren must have laughed to himself.

Maddren, from Billingham, had been a definitive Middlesbrough player on the pitch and in 1984 had succeeded Malcolm Allison as manager at Ayresome Park. Tragically, in 1995, Maddren, known for his physicality, was diagnosed with motor neurone disease. He died in 2000 aged 49, having written an autobiography called *Extra Time*.

Maddren was around to witness Emerson's antics and it took him back – more than it took him aback.

Maddren thought of Middlesbrough's end-of-season tour to the Far East and Australia in 1977. Maddren roomed with Boro's star player of that time, Graeme Souness, and recalled that after bumping into a dancer in the hotel bar in Hong Kong, Souness felt her company would be preferable to MFC's. Souness missed the flight to Australia.

'A single guy, good-looking and immaculately dressed, Graeme didn't always think with his head so I wasn't surprised that he had got himself fixed up,' Maddren said. 'What did amaze me was his audacity to simply walk out on the team. I guess Graeme was the Emerson of his time.'

Souness turned up three days later and was accepted back. It took Emerson a fortnight but strident midfielders are always valued and he was quickly in the team. It was for a 5-1 defeat at Anfield that left Middlesbrough 16th, two points off relegation. The next match was Blackburn Rovers away, on 21 December. It was a non-event, a momentous non-event.

With Boro saying that they had an injury epidemic on top of suspensions leaving them with 23 players unavailable, 24 hours before the game, Middlesbrough declared they could not fulfil the fixture. There was uproar. The Blackburn-Boro match was cancelled. Rovers were furious, the Premier League was unimpressed, fans and observers were bewildered. Middlesbrough said they had sought Premier League advice.

By the time of the next game, Boxing Day, Boro were able to field a team that beat Everton 4-2. Juninho scored twice, and the arguments raged.

Juninho had not suffered the sickness bug that had afflicted the squad and part of the reason for his popularity on Teesside is that resilience. In this season he played more league games than any other Boro player. He was a jockey-sized talent with conspicuous commitment. He had been signed as 'the boy from Brazil'; he had become 'the boy from Ingleby Barwick', 'the Little Fella'.

Twenty-five days after failing to turn up at Ewood Park, Middlesbrough felt the full force of official disapproval and were docked three points by an FA Premier League commission. Having been advised they would be fined rather than receive any other punishment, Boro were outraged. Gibson employed the most expensive lawyer in Britain, George Carman, to fight their case. Carman said he would have won in a court of law. This was a Premier League commission. Boro lost three points. The repercussions would be long-lasting.

Boro were bottom of the table but they had reached the League Cup final against Leicester City and had started to win in the FA Cup. Ten years earlier Middlesbrough could not have afforded a horse, now they were trying to ride three.

This was Middlesbrough's first major Wembley final. Their previous visit had been seven years earlier in the Zenith Data Systems Cup final against Chelsea. Chelsea won 1-0.

Seven years on, Middlesbrough were a club unrecognisable and all the season's stress would be worth it with victory at Wembley. After a goalless 90 minutes, there was extra-time and when Ravanelli scored, it seemed Boro were about to collect the first piece of major silverware since joining the Football League 98 years before.

Then Emile Heskey equalised. That meant a replay at Hillsborough. Leicester won 1-0.

It was 16 April 1997. Middlesbrough were despondent; they were weary. Three days earlier Boro had taken part in an epic FA Cup semi-final against Chesterfield. Reduced to ten men in the first half, Boro went 2-0 down when future Burnley manager Sean Dyche scored a penalty, and it could have been worse, Jon Howard having earlier had a legitimate goal for the underdogs ruled out. But strikes from Ravanelli and Hignett brought extra-time, more extra-time, and Gianluca Festa made it 3-2. Then Chesterfield equalised to force a replay, another replay. Middlesbrough won it, setting up an FA Cup final with Chelsea.

The season had become an endurance spectacular and just 48 hours later, Boro had to play a league game at White Hart Lane and lost. They were 19th, five points off safety, but had two games in hand. One of them was at Ewood Park, scene of December's cancellation. It finished 0-0. There was still some hope.

In the last league game of the season Middlesbrough could stay up if they won and Sunderland lost. Sunderland did lose, and were relegated. But that was because Coventry won, not Middlesbrough. Boro were at Elland Road and though Juninho equalised, the score was 1-1. Middlesbrough were relegated.

A defining image was of Juninho in tears on the pitch. 'I was very emotional after the game because of how I felt about the club,' he said. 'I learned to love Middlesbrough. I learned to love all the people around the club and I saw all the commitment of the directors, of Steve Gibson, so it was very sad.'

There was still an FA Cup final to come. Middlesbrough lost it, too.

On the day there were tales that Neil Cox had thumped Ravanelli at the team hotel, of which Juninho said: 'I remember that, though it wasn't on the day of the final.'

In the space of 31 days, Middlesbrough played nine games, lost two Cup finals and were relegated from the Premier League. Had they not been deducted three points over the Blackburn non-game, they would have finished 14th. Had they not been relegated Juninho would not have been in Madrid on a hot night four months later.

'I think I would have stayed,' he said. 'But I wanted to play in the 1998 World Cup. I thought it would be difficult if I was in the English second division.'

✦

AUGUST 1997: Middlesbrough's first game of the next season was at home to Charlton Athletic.

Juninho was gone, worried about that World Cup place. No one expected Ravanelli or Emerson to be around either, but they both were. Ravanelli scored in front of 29,000. He played in the next game, too, but then departed for Marseille. 'Want-away' Emerson stayed longest, until January, when he joined Tenerife.

Of the £12m Middlesbrough received for Juninho, £5m was immediately re-invested in Paul Merson, who left Wenger's new Arsenal for life in the north-east and life in the second division. Merson started 45 of Boro's 46 league games, which ended with promotion. Merson was at Tranmere Rovers the day Juninho was making his debut for Atlético Madrid.

Juninho looked at home in the Bernabeu. It was some game and he crowned it with a goal. He played as he had on Teesside, pulling wide on tip-toes to take possession before making zig-zag thrusts at Real's defence. He was dancing his way back into Zagallo's squad for France 98.

Downstairs afterwards, he smiled and said: 'I see they won 2-0.' Middlesbrough had beaten Tranmere.

On my return to the hot hotel room on Gran Via, the television was not showing replays of a ferocious match, it was carrying footage from Paris of a car crash involving Princess Diana.

There were 80,000 in Madrid, there were 12,000 in Birkenhead. Juninho looked exhausted by the scale of the occasion and said he tired in the second half, and the pace of the game is what a significant other debutant from that night recalls.

'I remember it was very high tempo,' says Aitor Karanka.

'It was a Saturday night. It was like a daydream for me to be playing for Real Madrid, at the Bernabeu, against Atlético Madrid. Amazing. We drew 1-1. Seedorf scored an amazing goal. What a goal.'

Clarence Seedorf was one of Karanka's new teammates at Real Madrid. Karanka had been signed from Athletic Bilbao, where Real's new manager Heynckes had been previously.

'Jupp knew me,' Karanka says. 'I played for him in Bilbao when I was 19, 20. He brought me to Madrid and five years later he brought me back to Bilbao. Obviously I have a very good relationship with him.

'I knew a lot about Juninho because he had a very good relationship with Roberto Carlos. They lived together, not in the same house, but in the same complex. I was a good friend of Roberto. I was with them a few times, not a lot, but a few times, and when Juninho was injured he was treated at the Atlético physiotherapist's practice, which was in front of my house in Las Rozas. So I went to see Juninho a few times when he was getting treatment. He got a bad tackle, Michel Salgado against Celta.'

Salgado, who later joined Blackburn Rovers, broke Juninho's ankle and damaged surrounding ligaments. The injury was so severe Juninho didn't make the World Cup in France. He then struggled for form, Atlético changed managers three times and in September 1999 he returned to Middlesbrough on loan.

'I have not seen him since he left Madrid,' Karanka says. 'He was unlucky when he was injured, he was an amazing player and if he'd not had the injury he would have been even better. He was young, his career was going up.

'He still played at a high level. The people here still love him. He wasn't a typical player for Middlesbrough, the Premier League. He wasn't big, he came from Brazil, in the beginning that must have been curious. I've heard a lot about him since I've been here, everybody talks about Juninho.'

When Karanka says 'here' he is referring to Middlesbrough's training ground. On 13 November 2013, Aitor Karanka was named as Middlesbrough's new 'head coach', the first foreign manager in the club's history.

IN FOOTBALL these things tend to be franked 'Second Coming' and Juninho's lasted the bulk of season 1999/2000. After their re-promotion, Middlesbrough had come ninth in the Premier League, Juninho then helped them to 12th. It wasn't miraculous; it was pleasantly steady.

However, midway through 2000/01 Boro were in the bottom three of the Premier League again and Bryan Robson was under sustained pressure. There was paper talk that the man who sat beside him at Wembley back in 1995 – Terry Venables – would be brought in to 'help' Robson. This was denied right up until it happened. Robson stayed as manager but Venables was 'head coach'.

Middlesbrough were second-bottom when Venables came in. In his first game, Boro lost 1-0 at Sunderland and dropped a place. But in the next game, at home to Chelsea, a goal from Dean Gordon gave Boro a 1-0 win and gradually the table was climbed. It wasn't glorious, apart from a 3-0 win at Highbury, but Boro finished 14th.

Steve Gibson knew that Robson would be made uncomfortable by the Venables option, but Gibson also knew that he had to act. The decision was justified.

On the last day of the season there were over 33,000 at the Riverside to see Middlesbrough beat West Ham. Joseph-Desire Job scored. 'One Job on Teesside' became the chant in his honour.

After seven years as a player and manager at Middlesbrough, during which time he helped re-invent the club, Robson left by 'mutual consent'. It was a fading away that none had wanted but it felt inevitable once Venables had been asked to come in. There is a lot of sentimental behaviour in football; there is a lot of ruthlessness too.

Gibson paid tribute at a press conference: 'Bryan brought his own style and charisma to the club. We had never gone beyond the sixth round of the FA Cup or the semi-finals of the League Cup and we were regarded very much as a yo-yo club. Bryan took us beyond the sixth round to the final of the FA Cup and then beyond the semi-finals of the League Cup and into the final twice. We had five years as a Premiership club and two seasons outside, during which we won the First Division championship and won automatic promotion. The average crowds were 10,000 prior to Bryan's arrival and they are now 35,000. Bryan's legacy will live long at the club.'

Terry Venables left, too; he had a contract with ITV. Boro were searching for their first manager since Robson replaced Lennie Lawrence and in June 2001, one month after his 40th birthday, Steve McClaren was named as Robson's permanent successor.

While Robson's status as the club's hero player-manager, then manager, had been whittled at, McClaren's had been growing in his role by Alex Ferguson's side at Manchester United, and as an assistant to England manager Sven-Goran Eriksson.

Much was expected of McClaren. He was viewed as part of England's future, the coming coach, and to get him Middlesbrough had to fight off interest from West Ham and Southampton. In McClaren's first game, Middlesbrough lost 4-0 at home to Arsenal.

Sport is supposed to be about joy, excitement and, if possible, glory. But just as Gibson will never forget, or forgive, Middlesbrough's three-point loss at Blackburn in December 1997, McClaren will never forget August 2001. Sport is also about agony.

The 4-0 defeat by Arsenal was followed by a loss at Bolton, then by another at Everton. In his fourth game in charge, at home to Newcastle, 'Steve McClaren's Middlesbrough' lost 4-1.

'Pointless and clueless,' concluded the *News of the World*. Middlesbrough were 20th of 20, again.

McClaren had his managerial character shaped, perhaps warped, in those opening four defeats. They are not too far away from him, even now. It is he who mentiones 'Pointless and Clueless'.

McClaren had signed a five-year contract and, unlikely as it seemed then and at several moments later, he stayed five years. Along the way Middlesbrough won the first major trophy in their history, the 2004 League Cup. Boro then had two seasons in Europe – for the first time.

'We're just a small town in Europe,' crowed the fans.

In the second of these Middlesbrough reached the Uefa Cup final against Seville in Eindhoven. As in McClaren's first game, this also finished in a 4-0 defeat.

McClaren then became manager of England. He had not won over most of Teesside for most of the time, but he was Middlesbrough manager when they won their one and only trophy. In that respect he fulfilled the brief set by Gibson in 2001.

In his office at Derby County's training ground in April 2014, McClaren gave his account of that League Cup run, the 2003/04 season, and the seasons around it. He gave it two days before Derby went to Middlesbrough in a Championship match. It was the first time McClaren had been back to the Riverside since his departure in 2006. The score was Middlesbrough 1 Derby County 0. McClaren got a good reception. He had been unsure about that.

ON THE OPENING DAY OF 2003/04 Middlesbrough travelled to Fulham in the Premier League and lost 3-2. Malcolm Christie had a penalty saved by Edwin van der Sar but the game was not as tight as the scoreline suggests, or as McClaren remembers. 'We were hopeless at Fulham,' he says.

'Carlos Marinelli played, and scored. But we lost and I remember saying: "He'll not play again."'

Middlesbrough had signed Carlos Marinelli when he was 17 from Boca Juniors. He was called, as many promising Argentinian teenagers are, 'the next Maradona'. Marinelli starred at youth team level, but it turned out he was not the next Maradona, or the one after that. He scored four goals over three years, and as McClaren says, the one at Fulham would be his last. It was. Marinelli never played again for Middlesbrough. He left for Torino.

Szilárd Németh was Christie's next partner but it got no better. In front of 30,000 at the Riverside Arsenal were 3-0 up in 22 minutes and won 4-0. To McClaren it was all too like his first game. But this was his third season.

Two days later at Leicester City there was some sanctuary in a 0-0 draw and a debut for Gaizka Mendieta.

Mendieta was part of Middlesbrough's improbable exotic pattern. Two years earlier he had left Valencia for Lazio in a €48 million deal, then the sixth most expensive player of all time. But it had not worked out in Italy and after one season Mendieta returned to Spain. He joined Barcelona on loan and played regularly for Louis van Gaal. Now, still a Lazio player, he was joining Middlesbrough on loan. Valencia-Lazio-Barcelona-Middlesbrough. It cannot have been his planned career trajectory.

Four days after Leicester, Mendieta made his home debut. Boro lost 3-2 to Leeds and Middlesbrough had one point from a possible 12. In their next game, at Bolton, Boro lost 2-0. Five games into the season, Boro were second-bottom with one point.

In Derby McLaren reviews the sequence of results, thinks of the amount of time he had been given and says: 'My God, how did I survive?'

The answer lies in the office of chairman Gibson. In McClaren's first two seasons Middlesbrough had finished12th and 11th and averaged just over a goal a game. Scintillating, it was not. But Gibson stuck with it. There were often audible tensions at the highest level of the club but Gibson has the knack of patience. He is a rare football man.

'I remember Terry Venables had come in and he got 1-0 wins to stay up,' McClaren says of the squad he greeted in 2001. 'We inherited that. We established ourselves in the first season but it was tough. We struggled really to find a way to play. We didn't have a lot of goalscorers. We would win 1-0 or draw. It was about survival, that first season.

'In the second season Steve Gibson put some investment in and we got George Boateng, Geremi. Juninho came back and I started to build a core of players. Boateng was a big part of that, we already had [Gareth] Southgate. But we weren't playing the kind of football I wanted to play, we weren't exciting people. The games were dour. I said to Steve we needed to brighten things up, get a few characters in. Bringing Juninho back was a statement. We wanted to excite the crowd.'

Juninho's third era on Teesside had false-started a year earlier after the 2002 World Cup, where he was a late substitute for Ronaldinho in the final. Juninho had started the first four Brazil games but when Brazil met England in Shizuoka in the quarter-final, he was on the bench. Steve McClaren was on the one opposite. He approached Juninho afterwards.

The Little Fella had re-established his reputation on loan in Brazil and Atlético cashed in. Juninho returned to Boro for £6m.

He was immediately injured, seriously, in a pre-season friendly and was out for eight months. So it was not until February 2003 that Juninho was seen again in red. It was in a reserve game against Bradford City. The Riverside attendance was 19,450. 'Unbelievable,' he said.

He was part of the optimism about 2003/04. One point from those first five games sucked at it and Juninho started all of them. So he was dropped. Teesside gulped. But Middlesbrough beat Everton 1-0 and McClaren signed Danny Mills from Leeds and Boudewijn Zenden from Chelsea.

It was two days later that Middlesbrough's historic League Cup campaign began. Boro hosted third division Brighton in the second round. There were 10,400 there. The score was 0-0. Four minutes into extra-time, Christie scored the only goal and Middlesbrough were through.

'The first game is always the hardest,' McClaren says. 'The previous season we went out to Ipswich and Steve Gibson said to me after that how important the cups were to Middlesbrough. He stressed that. He told me: "We can't play weakened teams", which I think I did at Ipswich. So we became a cup team.

'One of the things he said when I came [in 2001] was that he wanted to win a trophy. We did actually start to build a cup team – inconsistent in the league, capable of winning in the cups. We went from being dour to wanting to be more open. But I remember Brighton, thinking "extra-time". We'd put a big emphasis on it and we scraped through. I've said to teams since about that first step being the hardest. We scraped through. We hadn't livened the place up.'

Ten games into the Premier League season, Middlesbrough were one place above relegation. In the League Cup third round they drew Wigan Athletic away. Boro won 2-1.

'Wigan were top of the Championship then, that was tough,' McClaren says. 'We put out a good team. Compared to the first two seasons, that was a decent team. I remember it because Mendieta scored a great goal. We hadn't started to look ahead. We got Everton in the next round and I thought: "Oh, my word".'

At least the fourth round was at the Riverside. Wayne Rooney was in the Everton team. It was another 0-0, even after extra-time. That meant penalties; Boro scored all theirs and won 5-4. Mark Schwarzer saved Leon Osman's.

'Everton were similar to us,' McClaren says. 'But we'd got it together then, we'd gone on a run in the league, won at Man City.

'We scraped through this one too – on penalties. It can't have been a classic, can it, 0-0?

'Mendieta had settled and become a big player for us, scored at Wigan. There was a part of me thinking: 'What's he doing at Middlesbrough?'

'It was a major signing for us. It showed intent. We were trying to excite the supporters. I was aware of Steve Gibson's view that the club was for the community, that its traditional role was to bring some excitement into the town. Middlesbrough's focal point was the football club. He'd had that with Bryan Robson, and with Juninho the first time round, and Ravanelli. I had to buy into that. It wasn't easy. I agree that it was flat and dour in the beginning.

'I'd come from Manchester United, so it was a shock to me. But I just had to survive that first season, that was my first and only objective. After that, buy a bit of time to build a team. I was very fortunate that Steve gave me that. Look at the start of this season we're talking about, it wasn't the best, but I knew we'd brought in some characters. You must have a pretty decent team to go to Manchester United and win 3-2, which we did in that February.

'It just shows that it was in the third season that we started. In modern football, how many coaches are given the first two seasons? You know what I mean? It shows how long it can take to build something.'

McClaren puts down his glasses and says: 'I was given time. I was given time.'

By mid-December, Boro were 11th in the league and into the fifth round of the League Cup. They were drawn away to Tottenham, who were 1-0 up in the second minute. Four minutes from the end, Michael Ricketts equalised. That brought more extra-time and when it finished, more penalties. Once again Middlesbrough won 5-4. This time Mendieta missed but Gus Poyet and Mauricio Taricco missed for Spurs.

'Tottenham had a good team out, [Freddie] Kanoute and [Robbie] Keane up front,' McClaren says. 'I picked [Massimo] Maccarone!

'Michael Ricketts scored. He was a certain type of player; he never fitted in. He'd had a good spell at Bolton but it was a bad signing by myself because he didn't fit into how we wanted to play. He wanted to run onto the ball, not into feet. That was my mistake.

'I was attracted by his goals. It didn't work out, but he delivered in that game. [Franck] Queudrue scored the winning penalty. Two penalty shoot-outs, three extra-times, we were hanging on in there. We were going for it, and then we'd a semi-final.'

Middlesbrough drew Arsenal; Bolton and Aston Villa were in the other semi. The first leg was at Highbury on 20 January 2004. On 10 January Middlesbrough lost 4-1 at Arsenal in the Premier League; on 24 January Middlesbrough lost 4-1 at Arsenal in the FA Cup. But in the game in between, Middlesbrough won 1-0. Juninho scored.

'We played them ten days earlier and lost at Highbury,' McClaren says. 'That was in the league, they'd beaten us 4-0 at home too. Then we got them in the FA Cup, at Highbury, lost 4-1. I hated going there because we never won – we were once 3-1 up there with 20 minutes to go and lost 5-3. I was glad it [Highbury] went.

'But when we saw their team that night, we thought we'd have a chance. He [Wenger] didn't play [Ashley] Cole, [Patrick] Vieira. That was Juninho's game, that's when he really came back to life. When he first came back, he'd struggled, in the second half of the season he was tremendous. And that was his game, I call it The Juninho Game. He played ever so well and got the goal.'

Middlesbrough were now 90 minutes from the Millennium Stadium, Cardiff, but in the return leg, Arsene Wenger had Cole and Vieira back. His new £17m signing, Jose Antonio Reyes, was given a full debut. Unfortunately for Wenger, Martin Keown was sent off on 44 minutes and unfortunately for 20-year-old Reyes, after Edu had equalised Zenden's opener, Reyes scored an own goal. Middlesbrough had won 3-1 on aggregate. They had the chance to make history.

McClaren felt some excitement had at last been delivered: 'That was the first time I really felt the Riverside was rocking. That was the night. The crowd were with us. That was a breakthrough.'

The final was three weeks away and in that period Middlesbrough went to Old Trafford and won 3-2, a result about which McClaren says: 'That was pivotal. That was the game when we felt we had a team. We went there and beat a Man United team with Giggs, Van Nistelrooy and Scholes in it, Cristiano Ronaldo on as sub. Juninho got two, Joseph Job got the winner. That day made us believe we could win big games. It was two-and-a-half weeks before the final. We knew we could handle Cardiff after that.'

Middlesbrough had the opportunity to win the first trophy in a history dating back to 1875. But they had had that opportunity in the League Cup finals of 1997 and 1998 and in the 1997 FA Cup final. All three had been lost and for McClaren this became the agenda.

'It's strange,' he says, 'because most people would be happy that we'd got to a final, but instead they were thinking: "Well, we've been here before and lost." It wasn't euphoria. It was: "Now you're here, you've got to win this".

'So, while it was great, there was also a lot of 'Oh, no'. There was a lot of pressure, I felt, and maybe that was to our advantage. Maybe Bolton felt it was great just to be there. Our fans didn't think it was great just to be there. It was: "We've got an opportunity to put the other three to bed."

'I call the final, The Staff's Final. We prepared meticulously. I over-prepare. We'd been beaten at Newcastle the Saturday before. The first thing the staff said before it was: "If we lose at Newcastle, don't let it affect the final".

'We met on the Sunday morning – me, Bill Beswick, Steve Round, Steve Harrison and Paul Barron. We planned the week. I put my plan up, all sorts on it.

'I said: "What do you think?"

'They said: "We can't do that! It's too much. It's over-preparing, over-coaching. Why don't we try easy?"

'That became our motto for the week: "Try easy". We got the press out of the way on the Monday; tickets, transport, all sorted on the Monday. Tuesday, I'd a day with the team. Wednesday, we had a tennis tournament. Thursday, we had off. Friday was a bit more of a ball session. Saturday was travel and a fun session. We didn't train at the stadium, we trained at Ninian Park. That was all to do with the staff. They took away the pressure.

'On the Sunday, kick-off was 2.30 and it was all about being ready for 2.30, not 2.50, not 3 o'clock.

'At 2.32 we were 1-0 ahead.'

In an extraordinary opening, Teesside's one Job gave Middlesbrough a second-minute lead. Just five minutes later, Zenden added a penalty, while slipping. Kevin Davies scored for Bolton but it was McClaren, not Sam Allardyce, who was the first English manager to win a domestic trophy since Brian Little led Villa to the same Cup eight years earlier.

McClaren missed Job's opener. 'I wasn't ready but that's typical, I was over-preparing. I was changing from suit to tracksuit. I sat down, then it was 2-0. I thought: "Well, if there was pressure before, it's just doubled."

'No, it wasn't enjoyment. We had to win now; at 2-0 we could only lose it. That was my first thought.

'I didn't change anything. When Bolton scored, it took some tension away, it made it more of just a game. We knew it could go either way. Mark Schwarzer made a mistake for the goal but he was instrumental in winning after that. We'd built a strong defence: Schwarzer, Mills, Southgate, [Ugo] Ehiogu, Queudrue, with Boateng and Doriva in front. Bolton were direct but we were big and tough enough.

'It was the culmination of two, three seasons. It was just relief. So tense. It was for Steve Gibson, we forced him into the celebrations. It was great for him, and it was great for the fans. I saw old men crying, people were emotional.'

Middlesbrough had their breakthrough. There were tears because of all that had gone on in the decade leading to Cardiff; and Juninho was there, he played, and when Juninho looked back, he said: 'The preparation was much different from 1997, the club learned, the club knew how to prepare for the final.

'The Cup run was very difficult, we played Arsenal, who were a great team and Bolton at that time were a good team, [Jay-jay] Okocha was doing well, they were a strong team. But we were solid, we had players with experience, it didn't matter if we had to play Arsenal away. It was a team that was properly prepared to win the Cup. Cardiff was great.'

It had been far from smooth but now there was tangible progress and in the following season Middlesbrough faced Sporting Lisbon in the fourth round of the Uefa Cup, they reached the FA Cup semi-final – lost to West Ham – and came seventh in the Premier League. That placing brought another season of European football and it was momentous, good momentous. Middlesbrough reached the Uefa Cup final.

Ten years on from Cardiff, McClaren is in Derby talking about appreciation, about winning the League Cup.

'I don't think it was appreciated,' he says, 'not fully. We were always battling the excitement of the Ravanelli-Juninho era. We were always up against that.'

There is no anger in McClaren's tone, but there is disappointment. There is also some acknowledgement that his tactical and personal caution was part of the reason for the distance between himself and Middlesbrough fans. There were times when Boro felt like a club divided between boardroom, dressing-room, dugout and fanbase.

Does he accept that he was too cautious, particularly in the beginning?

'Absolutely. I was pragmatic, that's how I'd describe it. I'd come from Manchester United wanting to play a particular brand of football but after my first four games – 'Pointless and Clueless' – I had to be pragmatic, I had to be. My first game, we lost 4-0 at home to Arsenal, second home game we lose 4-1 to Newcastle. I had to re-think.

'I wouldn't have got through without the staff. It was us five, we were rock solid. We had to get through it pragmatically. I say to everyone my first season at Middlesbrough was two banks of four: "Don't move". It was awful. I remember thinking: "I don't want another season like that."

'Gradually we built. Steve Gibson was great, he had opportunities to sack me. He gave me time. Many would not survive. He's the one who deserves all the credit. At the end of the first season I said to him that he needed to spend some money. And he did. We had lots of fights about players. "Ridiculous money," he'd say. In the end he always went and got the player, always. Southgate, he went and got, Boateng, Juninho. Mendieta! Then I said "I want rid of Juninho, I want Hasselbaink and Viduka and Yakubu." And he went and got them. It goes on and on. They got us to Eindhoven.'

✦

EINDHOVEN AIRPORT, THURSDAY 11 MAY 2006. Middlesbrough's beaten squad and management were standing waiting for their flight home to Teesside. There was a loud silence. The 4-0 scoreline from the night before had done them no favours. Mark Viduka had missed a great chance to equalise at 1-0.

The air was one of weariness. There had been 15 matches in the Uefa Cup alone, it had turned into a 64-game season. Steve McClaren was leaving for England and for the World Cup in Germany. Everyone just wanted to get home.

Then, suddenly, noise. As Middlesbrough's players contemplated their feet a gang of jubilant Seville fans entered the hall. Their raucous joy clashed with Boro's dejection. Southgate and Viduka just stared at the Spaniards. It was all they could do. They didn't need this.

What noone knew in that Eindhoven departure lounge in 2006 was that Middlesbrough would bustle their way to 12th and 13th in the next two seasons before dropping from the top-flight in 2009 and staying there. Eindhoven's departure lounge was the scene of the end of Middlesbrough's golden period.

Chairman Gibson was there. 'It has been two great years in Europe and we wouldn't have swapped them for the world,' he said, 'but we're probably looking forward to not playing so many games next season, and it gives us a chance to regroup.'

Perhaps because he did not wish to sound like a tired chairman, Gibson added: 'In the context of our history it would have been a pipe dream to get to the Uefa Cup final not so many years ago.'

He was the man who would know. Gibson knew that while in May 2006 Middlesbrough were in a European final, and in May 1996 had just completed a first Premier League season at the Riverside, in May 1986 Middlesbrough had lost the last game of the season at Shrewsbury Town and were relegated to the old Third Division.

He had witnessed it all, from bottom to top. Now he had a shortlist for the future. There were three names on it: Martin O'Neill, Alan Curbishley and, once again, Terry Venables. Three-and-a-half weeks later, Middlesbrough announced Southgate would be their new manager.

Southgate was Middlesbrough captain, it was he who had lifted that League Cup in Cardiff. He was an England international and had been at the club for five years. He had been McClaren's first, signature purchase. Southgate was respected as a thoughtful footballer. As the years went by, like many insiders, he was prone to say that he no longer liked the game he loved.

This was new, though; his playing career ceased immediately. Southgate was 35, had no coaching or management experience and, crucially to critics, such as Alex Ferguson and the League Managers' Association, Southgate had no qualifications. Middlesbrough had to argue for months with the Premier League to get Southgate's appointment ratified.

While that went on in the background, Southgate got on with the job. It started brilliantly. On the opening day of season 2006/07, Middlesbrough travelled to Reading and were 2-0 up in 21 minutes – Stewart Downing and Yakubu scoring.

Then Reading scored three. Boro did win their next game, at home to Chelsea, but they took two points from the next 15 and by New Year's Day were fourth-bottom. After that came some form and Southgate's first season ended with a twelfth-place finish. Attendances, 28,500 the previous season, dropped 2.5 per cent.

Season 2007/08 brought 13th place. During the course of it Yakubu was sold to Everton for £11.5m, Mido was bought from Tottenham for £6.5m and there were ten consecutive games without a win lasting from September to December. In January Middlesbrough broke the transfer record set by the £8.5m McClaren advised be paid for Maccarone.

Boro paid £12m – for another Brazilian. This one came from Heerenveen in the Netherlands, Afonso Alves, and he looked a good player the day he scored twice against Manchester United. Alves rounded off the season with a hat-trick against Manchester City in a remarkable 8-1 final game. 'Embarrassing,' said City manager Sven-Göran Eriksson.

Attendances at the Riverside had fallen a further 3.5 per cent and it had gained an unwanted reputation as a venue with empty red seats. Yet there were 32,600 there on the opening day of the next season, an indication of local appetite and hope. Mido scored the winner against his former club, Spurs, and by early November Boro were eighth, four points off a Champions League place. Then, collapse. Middlesbrough won none of the next 14 games and scored just five goals.

They were second-bottom in February and in April were still there. Then came a relegation six-pointer against Hull City. Redcar-born David Wheater, who had been an extra in *Atonement*, filmed on Redcar beach, helped sell a match marketed with two tickets for £20 as 'One Hull of a Deal'. More than 32,000 saw

Middlesbrough win and score three goals for the one and only time that season.

But Boro did not get six points. They got three. And on the season's last afternoon, at Upton Park, Middlesbrough lost again. They had been in the Premier League since 1998. It was over. Attendances had gone up 6 per cent.

Southgate stayed on. The club received £6m for Alves, who moved to Qatar. He had scored ten league goals in 42 games. He had eight Brazil caps, which caused wonder on Teesside. Mido had already left for Wigan.

The ambition of bouncing back, as Boro had under Robson, began well. They were second in the Championship after seven games, but then lost 5-0 at home to leaders West Brom and lost the next two home games, so even after beating Derby on 21 October 2009, leaving Boro a point off top, Southgate was sacked.

Gibson described it as 'the hardest thing I've had to do in football' and said of Southgate: 'Gareth has given Middlesbrough Football Club magnificent service as a skipper and, in very difficult circumstances, as manager. I appointed Gareth in a situation that was greatly unfavourable to him.'

There were 17,500 present for the Derby game. Relegation had cost Middlesbrough 30 per cent of their matchday support. Southgate was sacked because of results other than Derby and because Gordon Strachan had agreed to take over. One week later he did so, his opening day marred by a photograph of a list of players he wanted on loan such as Arsenal's Jack Wilshere.

Strachan had been having time off since leaving Celtic but he returned to Scotland for players, bringing a rash across the border including Barry Robson, Scott McDonald and Kris Boyd. It was something of a referendum on the quality of Scottish football and it was lost. 'I really should have used the players that were there and used a system for them,' Strachan would say of Middlesbrough once he left.

Having been one point off top when Southgate left, Boro finished the season 29 points off promotion. Gibson gave Strachan more money but the first game of 2010/11 was lost 3-1 at home to Ipswich and by the time of the next home game there were 14,500 in the Riverside.

When, in October 2010, Middlesbrough lost to Leeds at home, Strachan and Gibson held a farewell meeting. He had lasted less than a year and offered his resignation. To the admiration of Gibson, Strachan 'tore up his contract – he sought no compensation and walked away from the club with empty hands. It's a measure of the man.'

It is tempting to write that Middlesbrough were at a crossroads, but actually the were on a back road, 20th in the Championship. They were parallel with the main road and desperate to get across. They decided to turn back. The past would be the future, they brought in Tony Mowbray.

Mowbray, from Saltburn, is core Teesside. Appointing himwas akin to Newcastle United appointing Alan Shearer or Sunderland Niall Quinn.

Mowbray meant – and means – more to the Teesside public than simply appearances on the pitch. Mowbray was there in Hartlepool in 1986, at 22 he was club captain. He became 'Mogga', the man of whom Bruce Rioch said he'd want beside him on a flight into space. That became the title of the club fanzine 'Fly Me To The Moon'. Mowbray is heart-and-soul Middlesbrough and when he was appointed the club chief executive Keith Lamb, not known for romantic declaration, said: 'The reason we appointed Tony is because he cares.'

Lamb added that 'Tony has been manager of the year in England and Scotland', and experience gained at Celtic, Hibernian and West Brom helped the feel of this appointment as the perfect fit. Mowbray had joined Celtic as a player and it was he who initiated the first 'Huddle' on a pre-season game in Germany.

For his first Riverside game, Mowbray's presence put 5,000 on the average gate, but it was lost to Bristol City. It was October 2010 and Middlesbrough were 23rd in the Championship.

By season's end they were twelfth and having won their last four games, there was renewed belief that 2011/12 would see Middlesbrough challenge for promotion. On New Year's Day 2011 Middlesbrough were second in the Championship behind Southampton. But those clubs went in different directions and unfortunately for Mowbray, Middlesbrough went down to seventh, outside the play-offs, while Southampton rose to the Premier League.

That led to a fourth season in the second tier. It began with a defeat at Barnsley. Eindhoven felt decades ago.

But in November 2011 Middlesbrough went top with victory over Sheffield Wednesday in front of 28,000 at the Riverside. It seemed as if Gibson's patience would again find a reward, and as 2013 dawned Boro were third.

Then collapse. Again.

Of the next 21 matches Middlesbrough won three. They finished 16th. The average attendance was 16,800, which is a triumph of perseverance and in some way a tribute to Mowbray's standing.

When 2013/14 started with another home defeat, to Leicester, background doubts about Mowbray's ability to steer Middlesbrough upwards stepped forward. After 12 games Boro had won two and were 17 points adrift of leaders Burnley.

Mowbray's last game was back at Barnsley. Middlesbrough took 2,200 fans to Oakwell and saw their team 3-0 down at half-time. Two days later the club issued a statement thanking Mowbray for his 'dedication and integrity'. The hometown dream was over. The feeling on Teesside was one of sadness, and a sense that Mowbray, without millions in the transfer market, had paid for some of the signings under Strachan.

Jonathan Woodgate, club captain and local lad, offered a programme apology to Mowbray: 'If it wasn't for him and the chairman back in 1986, we may not be sitting here talking about this. As players I feel we have let the club and him down.'

AITOR KARANKA LANDED ON TEESSIDE three weeks after Mowbray departed. Although the previous 20 years had seen Middlesbrough sign players from all around the world, Karanka, 40, was the first foreign manager in the club's history. Nine of the club's last ten managers had been English.

Karanka came with that playing pedigree from Real Madrid, with whom he won the Champions League, and that connection to Juninho. Karanka also had three years' experience working alongside José Mourinho as a Real coach and he had other knowledge of Middlesbrough.

'I knew something about the club because in 2005 I'd an offer to come here,' he explains in his office at the training ground.

'At that time Geremi was here and we had been together at Real Madrid. I called him, he told me, and it's everything I'm tasting now. The atmosphere is perfect, the training ground, the chairman. I'm very happy. And I spoke to Gaizka Mendieta to ask about Middlesbrough.'

Karanka is relaxed as he walks through the corridors past his new staff: 'I'm very proud to be here. I tell people in Spain I couldn't choose a better place to start my career.

'Middlesbrough has a similar feel to Bilbao. The people are the same, the weather is similar, sometimes. The economics are the same in Spain, everywhere is suffering. The club is good for the supporters, gives them some good news. It's the same with Bilbao, if you're living in a bad moment, your team can make it better.'

It was two days before the last game of the season, at Yeovil. Middlesbrough would win it 4-1 to come 12th once again. He had started planning for the next season but the six months in post had shown him enough ups and downs to re-evaluate early thoughts.

For Karanka's first home game there were 23,600 at the Riverside to see a 1-0 win over Bolton. For his second home game there were 13,600 to see a 1-0 defeat against Brighton.

In between there had been two away games: Derby had beaten Middlesbrough 2-1 with a 90th-minute winner and Birmingham City made it 2-2 with a 90th-minute equaliser.

When Brighton scored their winner in the 86th minute, Karanka said: 'Of course I'm angry.'

Six months on, Karanka reveals that he was worried as well as angry. Middlesbrough were 19th after the defeat, three points above relegation. The mood inside the stadium was miserable. 'Merry Christmas from all at MFC' said a Tannoy voice as people drooped off into the mid-winter darkness.

In the small press room, once buzzing with reporters, a couple filed short reports for national newspapers now accustomed to looking the other way when Middlesbrough becomes the subject. It doesn't even matter that a Mourinho right-hand man is manager. The Riverside was built on an isolated slice of the town and it felt like it that night.

'The day against Brighton was my worst here,' Karanka says. 'I was here for one month, five games, and we lost three in the last minute. For this, I was doubting why I was here but I learned a lot and then we started to win. I don't have a good memory of Brighton but it is a strong memory. After that game, I knew we had to change.'

Change came: Middlesbrough won their next three games without conceding a goal. Some attributed this to a pet hamster called Holly acquired by the players. But any uplift sagged in January when the team embarked on a seven-game run without scoring.

Karanka's first visit to north-east England had been as a 21-year-old Athletic Bilbao player in October 1994. Bilbao drew Newcastle in the Uefa Cup. Karanka took home a bottle of Newcastle Brown Ale as a souvenir. 'I still have it,' he says.

The game gave him an impression of English football but six months in the Championship gave him experience. Craig Hignett returned to the club as Karanka's number two.

'I have learned we need to improve our mentality,' Karanka says. 'When we got near to the play-off positions, I don't know if we were afraid, but we need to improve. I know the league much better now.'

It has made him re-consider bringing players over from Spain. 'In the beginning I thought maybe that was a good option but now, six months here, I need to be sure. Bringing young Spanish players here, I need to be very sure.'

One teenager is expected on Teesside in the summer of 2014, though, Diego

Ghidoni, son of Doriva. Doriva is manager of the Sao Paulo club Ituano owned by Juninho. Boro's Brazil connection continues.

Karanka is a suitable judge. Vicente Del Bosque brought Karanka into the Spanish Federation's system to coach Spain's Under-15s, U-16s and U-17s.

'I'm impressed with the Academy here,' Karanka says. 'I like to work with young players, that's what I was doing with the Spanish national team. I've used some players from the Academy – Williams, Reach, Morris, Gibson. I want to play with young players.'

But as he surveys the future, Karanka does not look to Del Bosque or his Galactico past for inspiration, nor to Mourinho, though they speak weekly; he instead looks south-west to Lancashire. After six months in England Aitor Karanka knows what he wants Middlesbrough to be if they are to win promotion back to the Premier League and fill the Riverside once more.

'Burnley is the example for us next season. They're a very good team with a very good mentality. When I look in the mirror, I want to see Burnley.'

The man who changed the direction of traffic: Kevin Keegan tries to get to his car outside St. James' Park. (Mirrorpix)

CHAPTER NINE

NEWCASTLE UNITED

9 MAY 2014 Thirty-one years, eight months and nine days after the man who would be King first pulled on the black and white stripes at St James' Park, he is back. And it's like he never left, at least at first it is.

Downstream from St James' on the other side of the Big River in Dunston, there are around 60 tables with ten on each. The light nights are here and a summery breeze of anticipation is billowing through the velvet drapes and around the room. Tickets cost £45 and up but no-one is questioning value as the first sups of Friday night drinks are taken. This is the old Federation Brewery's Lancastrian Suite, a giant working-men's club on Gateshead's industrial fringe with stock beer, stock food and a Scouse compere-comedian doing a convincing impression of Roy Hodgson morphing into Frank Spencer.

Then the act cuts off. The hubbub descends to murmur, silence. There is a flurry at the double doors at the back. Suddenly music booms into the huge space filling it with the sounds of 'Right Here, Right Now' as two giant screens illuminate one word: 'King'.

Everyone is instantly on their feet, there is a scrum to one side. Here are bouncers shielding the star from the human press. It is the entrance of a gladiator, a boxer, a revivalist preacher. There is a swell of emotion within the roaring crowd. Grown men, and the audience is mainly grown men, can be seen gulping air. It's Kevin Keegan.

This is what football can do in a place obsessed with it. You go back to Arthur Hopcraft's phrase: 'Football can make a man more ridiculous than even drink can.'

If sometimes it seems in Britain, and in places like north-east England in particular, football carries a disproportionate daily importance, then this was one of those scenes that confirm its absurd power.

This was no confection, this was sincere. This was everything Bill Shankly told Keegan it could be. Keegan makes his way to the stage, the noise reaches a crescendo, then falls amid smiles and shuffling seats. It's time for the first course: vegetable soup with dumplings.

✦

19 AUGUST 1982: the Gosforth Park hotel on the northern fringe of Newcastle, a city where professional football has stagnated.

Newcastle United had finished the 1981/82 season ninth in the Second Division, where they had been since relegation in 1978.

Despondency could be measured in the last two home attendances of the season – 9,419 against Wrexham – and not many more against QPR three days before that. QPR had to borrow Newcastle's away kit, then thumped them 4-0.

Arthur Cox was Newcastle's manager. Cox had been Bob Stokoe's assistant at Sunderland when they won the FA Cup in 1973 and so knew the north-east. He did not express that knowledge or feeling charismatically, but Cox did something behind the scenes more eloquent than anything done by a Newcastle United employee for a decade and more. In the summer of 1981 Cox had a meal with Kevin Keegan's agent Harry Swales and at its end Cox spelled out a vision he had: 'I want a player to do for us what Dave Mackay did for Derby County. I want Kevin Keegan to come to Newcastle.'

Keegan was at Southampton at the time, having joined them from Hamburg, where he not only won the Bundesliga and reached the 1980 European Cup final, he was named European Footballer of the Year in 1978 and 1979. He was as famous a footballer as there was on the planet, first made captain of England in 1976.

And in the summer of 1982, Keegan was captain of England at the World Cup in Spain having scored 26 goals for Southampton to make him the league's top scorer. Cox could well have seemed delusional to Swales.

But when the first stories emerged that Keegan could be leaving Southampton for Manchester United, Cox got back in touch and set up a meeting with Keegan, Swales, the Newcastle board and Alistair Wilson from Newcastle Breweries.

Keegan was intrigued by the idea of Newcastle United but he was also a sporting celebrity who knew his economic value. Informed by Newcastle chairman Stan Seymour junior that attendances would double at St James', Keegan replied: 'If you think that is going to happen, Mr Chairman, would you be interested in giving me 15% of the increase in your crowd? If there is no increase then it won't cost the club a penny.'

Newcastle agreed. The deal was mutually beneficial and Keegan sensed that it would work as he prepared for his unveiling that early evening in Gosforth.

He wrote in his autobiography: 'Word had spread like a bushfire throughout the city and hundreds of fans turned up. They were all over the place and I could hear them saying: "He's in there, he's in there." The response surprised me at the time, but the strength of feeling of both the fans and the press was to become familiar to me over the years as both a player and a manager. Eventually I taught myself to anticipate it by imagining the most extreme reaction in any given set of circumstances – and that was what always occurred.'

In the penultimate game of season 1981/82 there were 10,700 to watch QPR win at St James'; on the opening day of season 1982/83, when QPR were again the visitors, there were 35,700.

The 35p match programme carried the headline: 'We've Got Kevin!' and reflected on a summer when the Rolling Stones had played at St James', and now this: 'Even a man of Kevin Keegan's enormous experience could never really imagine what lies in store for him,' it said.

North-east football's great chronicler Arthur Appleton wrote a column in the Newcastle programme in those days and thought back over the decades, concluding: 'For shock impact, for instant explosive excitement, the signing of Kevin Keegan is greater than the two comparable signings, those of Hughie Gallacher and Malcolm Macdonald.

'We've all known that the area was a tinder box for the game, in spite of the recession . . . And now we're alight again.'

Newcastle beat QPR 1-0 that day, it barely needs stating who scored. Fans queued outside for hours, among them a boy called Shearer. Keegan was overwhelmed: by the adoration, by the noise, and by the money charging into his bank account.

England's new manager, Bobby Robson, was also there to witness Keegan's debut. A month later Robson named his first England squad and Keegan was not in it.

Keegan's England career was over. On his next visit to St James', Robson was spat at by Newcastle supporters and nearly 15 years later, when Sid Waddell interviewed Keegan for *Loaded* magazine, Keegan had not forgotten: 'Robson never had the guts or whatever to ring me up.'

The north-eastern response was so strong in 1982, and later, because Keegan had done something few major players had done since the 1950s or before, including Robson: he changed the direction of travel.

The north-east had grown accustomed to wearily waving goodbye to either unseen indigenous talent or under-appreciated indigenous talent and here was Kevin Keegan reversing that trail of departure. The captain of England was stepping into the Second Division and with a club that appeared to be dying from self-induced indifference. This, above all else, is why over 30 years later grown men are on their feet.

For Newcastle United August 1982 should have been the equivalent of Shankly arriving at Anfield, of Ferguson finding his feet at Old Trafford. Of course, it wasn't.

Keegan's effect upon the club was immediate but the team took longer to adjust. He signed for one season and at its end Newcastle had finished fifth. He said he would stay for another but that the club needed to buy. They brought Peter Beardsley back home from Vancouver Whitecaps and allowed Chris Waddle to develop further.

Season 1983/84 climaxed with Newcastle United's promotion. There was delirium on the last day at home to Brighton because it was Keegan's last match, but Newcastle had not stormed the division, they had come third behind Chelsea and Sheffield Wednesday. So Keegan took to the Tannoy at St James' after the 3-1 victory (scorers: Keegan, Waddle, Beardsley) and urged the board to back Cox: 'Now is the time to go into debt,' Keegan said.

The directors may have been shaken by this idea, and the bluntness, but the following week Keegan gave them some ammunition. His farewell match, against Liverpool, saw 36,000 rocking the ground again and Keegan leaving from the middle of the pitch on a helicopter, dropping his No.7 shirt as he took off. It was theatre, yes, but it was real too.

Mark Lawrenson was there, in Liverpool red. He had unknowingly signalled the end of Keegan's playing career by taking the ball off him with rather too much ease in a 4-0 FA Cup defeatat Anfield earlier in the season. Many years later Lawrenson told me comparisons with Shankly 'are valid – because Kevin gave people pride, he gave the region a smile. I played in the helicopter game with the likes of Dalglish, Souness. It was like a bloody cup tie.'

Keegan was 33. His playing career began as a 17-year-old for Scunthorpe United in 1968. This was his last match, though he said: 'This wasn't my night. This was for Newcastle United, to celebrate their promotion and raise the money they needed to buy new players. I did a brochure for them called *Auf Wiedersehen Kev* and all the profits from everything went to the club.'

John Gibson of the *Evening Chronicle,* who even then had seen a lot of Newcastle United, wrote: 'Bringing Keegan to Tyneside was like opening your own bank.'

Keegan wanted the money re-invested in the squad to support Cox. Cox also required a new contract. The club blinked. Unused to the sort of ambition – sporting and financial – personified by Keegan, they peeved Cox with a new offer to the extent that he left the club within a fortnight.

Cox later gave his reasoning in the book *Newcastle United, Fifty Years Of Hurt*: 'I didn't feel the directors respected what we'd achieved. They had asked me what the plans were, so I said I wanted the following three players: Steve Bruce, Kevin Sheedy and Mark Hateley. They were all gettable.'

Given the obstacle the under-rated Bruce would become to Newcastle in the red of Manchester United, Cox's frustration was justified for years.

Post-Keegan, but promoted, Newcastle now had to find a new manager. He was on the doorstep but Jack Charlton was reluctant. He was persuaded to take the job on a year-long basis by Jackie Milburn. Milburn, who had advised Bobby Charlton to avoid Newcastle's youth system, now coaxed his brother Jack into taking it on.

Unknown to most outside Tyneside was that in it was a gem that Newcastle had not overlooked: Paul Gascoigne. Charlton gave the teenager from Dunston a debut.

At the end of the season Newcastle sold Waddle to Tottenham for £590,000. Instead of going into debt to build a team, Newcastle's board balanced the books. They had come 14th and for some at the top that seemed enough.

Not for others, in the dressing room and on the terraces. In a pre-season game at St James', Charlton was barracked by some fans and simply walked away.

In came Iam McFaul, Newcastle's goalkeeper the last time they won an important trophy, the 1969 Uefa Fairs Cup. McFaul made 18-year-old Gascoigne central to his team and Newcastle finished 11th in 1985/86. They then dropped to 17th but remarkably, in 1987/88, even though Newcastle had sold Beardsley to Liverpool for a British record £1.9m, they finished eighth in the First Division. Newcastle had made an international splash by signing Mirandinha for £575,000, the first Brazilian to play in English football, It was their first top-flight top-ten finish since 1977.

Gascoigne was 21 in May 1988. Two months later he joined Waddle at Tottenham for £2.3m. He had played 99 times for Newcastle. Despite becoming a global Geordie at Italia '90, Gascoigne would never wear the black and white stripes again.

Cox, Keegan, Waddle, Beardsley, Gascoigne – in the space of four years all left St James' Park. The consequence was predictable. In May 1989 Newcastle were relegated back to the Second Division. They finished bottom, winning seven games all season. Middlesbrough went with them; they joined Sunderland there.

During the course of that season, Jackie Milburn died and so did Joe Harvey, Newcastle's last trophy-winning manager. They got around to putting up a plaque for Harvey in 2014.

Also during that season came a new anthem: "Sack The Board." And from the old, disappearing collieries of Northumberland, another figure, John Hall.

THE STORY IS NOW PART OF FOLKLORE. When the telephone rang at Kevin Keegan's Hampshire home, the voice on the other end was Sir John Hall. 'The only two people who can save Newcastle United are speaking on the phone to each other,' Hall told Keegan.

It was March 1992 and Keegan had returned to Hampshire after just 40 days as manager of Newcastle United. 'The more I thought about it the more incredible it was,' he would recall.

Keegan had flown off in his helicopter in 1984, not just from Tyneside, but from football. He had gone to live in Spain and had been happy to stay away from the game.

He had said over the St James' Tannoy that the club needed to invest and instead they sold their best players and still fell into debt. There was an acrimonious battle for boardroom power between Hall's Magpie Group and the existing board, who had been rebuffed by Howard Kendall, appointed and dismissed Jim Smith and who now had Ossie Ardiles and a very young team struggling at the wrong end of the Second Division.

The club was a mess again and a decade after Keegan had come as saviour-player, he was coaxed back as saviour-coach. He had never been in management.

Keegan's first act was to fumigate the training ground at Benwell and re-paint it. It was not just symbolism. Adding a second magpie to the one in a cabinet at St James' was.

But after seven games – four wins, a draw and two defeats – Keegan and his 'buffer' Terry McDermott thought Hall was 'playing political games' with the other directors over money promised for players. They walked away.

This was another moment when Kevin Keegan knew his value, this time politically. He challenged Hall from a position of popular strength.

Hall relented, Keegan returned and Newcastle stayed up, just ahead of Plymouth.

Hall still did not have full control in the boardroom and Keegan was only contracted to the end of the season. There was another hiccup, another contract rejection from Keegan before Hall seized control and his new chief executive Freddie Fletcher began to shape Newcastle's future.

Having just avoided relegation to the Third Division, Keegan re-ordered priorities and aimed for promotion. Newcastle United won the first 11 league games of season 1992/93 and the club took off. Keegan was building more than a team, he was firing a city whose football imagination had been under curfew. Whenever critics discuss what Keegan got wrong, they forget from where he started.

From losing 5-2 at Oxford United in Ardiles' last match in charge, Newcastle won promotion by eight points and the energy now coursing through the club, from dugout to boardroom, from dressing room to stands, lifted Newcastle to third in the Premier League in their first season back. When 8,000 fans were locked out of a home game against Grimsby, police warned that it was getting dangerous. Future home games had to be all-ticket.

Keegan and Hall were doing one of the hardest things in football: they were challenging geography and perception. In 1992 Keegan had signed Brian Kilcline from Oldham Athletic; three years later he signed David Ginola from Paris St-Germain. It was the difference between bricklaying and architecture.

Even Ginola couldn't believe it, he thought he was joining Barcelona. The Tyneside club were competing in the Catalans' market-place.

Third in the Premier League in 1994, Newcastle slipped slightly, to sixth, in 1994/95 – but then they had been playing in Europe. The rise had not been without turbulence, but the club was an unrecognisable force and one benefit of coming sixth in 1995 was no European football the next season.

On promotion in 1993, Keegan had the ambition and belief to say to Manchester United: 'Watch out, Alex, we will be after your title.'

Now Newcastle United would make their greatest effort to deliver on that promise.

✦

ON THE AUGUST DAY IN 1992 when the Premier League was born, Newcastle United were not at the birth. They were facing Southend United in something called 'Division 1', even though it was England's second division.

Robert Lee was playing in that same division for Charlton Athletic, alongside Alan Pardew. Seven games into the season, with Newcastle top of 'Division 1' and Charlton second, Newcastle bought Lee for £700,000.

Charlton came 12th; Newcastle finished first.

This was Keegan's first full season in charge at St James'. The club had bottomed out and were on the up. When, in their first season in the Premier League, Newcastle came third, they scored 82 goals, more than champions Manchester United. Keegan's Newcastle were dubbed 'The Entertainers'.

In their second season the goal-count dropped but at the end of it Keegan signed Les Ferdinand, Ginola, Warren Barton and Shaka Hislop. On 19 August 1995, three years after facing Southend, Newcastle United defeated Coventry City 3-0 in the opening game of the fourth season of the Premier League.

Newcastle won nine of their opening ten league games and scored 26 goals. A club that had not been champions of England since 1927 began to dream. Rob Lee scored the opening goal of that season against Coventry. By then he was club captain. This is his account of Newcastle United season 1995/96.

'I REMEMBER THAT COVENTRY GAME,' Lee says in a Newcastle hotel. 'I scored the first – Keith Gillespie cross. Header.

'But the goal I remember most was Les Ferdinand's at the end because we were desperate to get him off and running. We'd brilliant team spirit and the atmosphere was great that night. We knew we were better than the season before.

'Kevin had signed Les, David Ginola, Shaka Hislop and Warren Barton and the transfers were done early. Bang. I didn't feel we had a good team, I knew we had a good team. On the opening day of that season, I looked around and I saw presence. Les was big, Ginola was big. We had pace. We had goalscorers. We annihilated Coventry.'

Les Ferdinand had cost £6m when he was bought from QPR. Three years earlier Newcastle's record transfer fee was still the £850,000 paid to Wimbledon for Dave Beasant. Newcastle United were breaking records and changing perspectives. Lee was part of that change.

Keegan had wooed Lee to Tyneside by telling him that Newcastle was closer to London than Middlesbrough, who also wanted to sign him. Then Keegan drove Lee around house-hunting, while eating midget gems in Keegan's car. Lee could not quite believe that 'Kevin Keegan' was making this effort for him.

'If I'm honest, the north-east all blurred into one,' Lee says. 'I always played well up here for Charlton.

'I don't think you realise the magnitude of the club and the intensity of the people until you get here. Kevin Keegan sold me Newcastle. I wouldn't have joined if he hadn't been in charge. Les Ferdinand wouldn't have either, no way. I think this club needs a charismatic manager because of its situation, where it is, it's miles from anywhere.

'After promotion, we finished third in our first season in the Premier League. I don't see that happening now. We got into Europe, an amazing achievement really.

'In our second season we again started really well, but we sold Andy Cole during it. Wimbledon away in November, I think it was – Coley had a bit of an argument with Keegan, challenged him. He was sold not too long after that. Huge decision. There was something going on behind the scenes.

'I challenged Kevin once myself. That didn't go well. He left me out once after I'd passed a fitness test. He asked me to go on the bench. In my stupidity I said "absolutely not". I refused to be sub. It's never got out. The next day I went and apologised. It was forgotten after that, but he didn't let many get away with it.

'With Andy Cole, I always believed Kevin had something up his sleeve and I knew how much he liked Les Ferdinand. I was always tapping him up when I was away with England. Not under orders, just by myself.'

Ferdinand scored in the Coventry game, as Lee says. Ferdinand then scored two at Bolton in the next game. By game ten of the season, Ferdinand had scored in eight of them – 13 goals.

Tyneside was beginning to bounce, as Lee says: 'The atmosphere around the place was great. We trained at Durham University's facilities. It meant we'd be changing with students. I remember one day a big fat lad came and changed between me and Ginola. Ginola said: 'Is that a new signing? He's a bit out of shape.'

'We had thousands at training, ice cream vans, burger vans. We had nothing to hide. We played eight-a-side. Very rarely would we work on tactics. But it was always high tempo. We got a lot of injuries in training. I got injured on a Friday once. I was out for four weeks. You noticed that some couldn't cope with the intensity of the training. Within two months Kevin could see if they could cope with us.'

More often than not, Premier League opponents were struggling to cope with Newcastle. There was a defeat at Southampton, 1-0, the only dropped points in the first ten games. Manchester City and Chelsea were both beaten at St James' after Southampton, then Newcastle made the 350-mile round trip across the Pennines to Everton.

'I remember Everton away vividly,' Lee says, 'because Ginola played up front with Les. Kevin liked to tinker now and again. Everton had their "Dogs of War" and it's never easy, Goodison Park. We battered them. We knew we'd said something that day.

'"The Entertainers" tag had come the previous season, we just carried it on. Team-talks were very short. Kevin would go down the opposition and say: "He wouldn't get in my team, he wouldn't get in my team", and on and on.'

It was something Keegan must have witnessed in his playing days at Liverpool under Bill Shankly. Bob Paisley recalled dressing room speeches when, according to Shankly: 'Cruyff, Best, Charlton, Law – they couldn't play. I've seen Bill take the magnetised figures representing these players off the board and put them in his tracksuit pocket during a team-talk.'

Keegan's Shankly-esque motivational powers extended to the fans. 'At home games Kevin would say we had this crowd, "Go and entertain them – attack", Lee says. 'We used to fly at teams in the first 15 minutes. It's easy to say the crowd make a difference but here it does. It was huge. I'd come from Charlton. Keegan told me the numbers through the turnstiles here had exceeded their budget and that it was the crowd who bought me. He knew the importance of the crowd. I believed him.'

After game ten of the season, there was a pause, a 1-1 draw at Tottenham. Liverpool and Blackburn were then beaten at St James' and by the end of November, when Leeds United lost 2-1 on Tyneside, Newcastle United had a five-point lead over Manchester United and a ten-point lead over Arsenal in third.

Lee has a particular memory of that Leeds game, in which he and Beardsley scored.

'We had a thing going on that if you said the wrong thing, or made a mistake, you had to do three press-ups. Scott Sellars kicked a corner flag in a game, got down and did three press-ups.

'When we played Leeds at home this season, we were winning 2-1 and the game was into the last few seconds. The ball went out for a throw-in. Keegan thought it was the final whistle, he jumped up. Warren got the ball and said: "Gaffer, it's a throw-in. Give us three." And he did, Kevin got down and started doing press-ups on the side of the pitch. We were on the pitch looking at each other laughing our heads off.' Given what was to happen at Leeds the following April, when Keegan produced his 'I'd love it' rant on TV, this was a contrast.

By the time Newcastle travelled to Old Trafford two days after Christmas, they had won 14, drawn three and lost two of 19 games. At the season's halfway stage they had a 10-point lead over Manchester United and there were Christmas cards for sale on Tyneside showing Keegan holding the Premier League trophy. They were not produced by the club, and after a 2-0 defeat at Old Trafford, the lead was seven points.

Andy Cole scored Manchester United's first. Newcastle had played as normal and attacked; there was no sense that they would protect their lead in the table by frustrating Ferguson's team.

'Man U away was a must-win game for them,' Lee says. 'We didn't play well and Coley scored for them.

'Could we have played differently there? With the personnel we had, I don't think so. We played 4-4-2 but Peter [Beardsley] went everywhere. Our collective defence wasn't strong enough. We attacked at Man United when others wouldn't. I liked that.

'We tried to change it once,. play three centre-halves. That was Wimbledon away, we were two down in a matter of minutes, hadn't a clue.

'After Man U, we knew we didn't play well. They were better. But we still looked around the coach on the way home and thought we had good players. We did, we beat Arsenal 2-0 in our next game. After Man U we won five in a row. I genuinely thought we could and would win the league then. It wasn't cockiness, we just had a good team. We could win different ways. That run took in Middlesbrough away when Asprilla made his debut.'

The £6.7m signing of the brilliant, eccentric Colombian striker Faustino Asprilla from Parma has long been regarded as a turning-point moment in Newcastle's title pursuit.

Asprilla arrived on Tyneside on a snowy February day in a fur coat. Where would he fit in? Did Newcastle need him? These were the questions being asked. Then, on his debut at Middlesbrough, Asprilla sauntered from the bench with 23 minutes remaining and used his elastic talent to turn a 1-0 deficit into a 2-1 victory.

Asprilla had not expected to be even on the bench and was still digesting his sale from Parma, as well as his lunchtime glass of wine.

'My exit from Parma was controversial,' Asprilla said when we met in a Jesmond café over 15 years on. 'The only reason I left was because Fabio Capello was going to be their new manager and he said he didn't want me.

'Newcastle is very different from Parma. I was very close to joining Leeds United, very close. I chose Newcastle because of Kevin Keegan. The love and desire he had for the club, the love he had for me to come and play, that convinced me. I had been voted one of the top three players in the world at the time but Keegan talked to me with such passion, the love he had for the club and the city was amazing. He was transferring that love into me. I knew I'd be loved. Keegan was right, I was.'

Rob Lee shares that view. Some have blamed Asprilla as a disruptive influence on Newcastle United, but Lee has never agreed with that.

'I think in a way Tino was bought for the bench initially, to make an impact, but he played so well, Kevin wanted to find room for him in the team. Maybe that altered how we played, a little bit.

'We had a hard-working team. We could cope when Ginola didn't play well. On his day Ginola was brilliant; when not, we could cope. Everybody else worked their socks off.

'When Tino came into the team, we had two players like that. But I don't blame Tino and I never have. We had balance and a settled team but Kevin wanted Tino in. Sometimes he left Keith Gillespie out, put Peter wide. That meant Peter was out of position. He was trying to find the chemistry. I think Tino should have been a direct replacement for Peter, but if you do that you lose Peter's work-rate. He was getting older but he was still Peter Beardsley. With hindsight you would maybe have started with Peter, then brought Tino on for him.

'But honestly, Tino was brilliant, fitted in straightaway. He never learned English but he loved it here. Players look at Newcastle as a stepping stone now; he didn't, and he was one of the best players in the world.'

During the five-game winning run that followed the loss at Old Trafford, Newcastle defeated Bolton at home 2-1. It was 20 January, 23 Premier League games had been played and the table showed Newcastle had a 12-point advantage over Liverpool and Manchester United. Twelve points – it would become stat of the season.

After Asprilla's debut at Middlesbrough, Newcastle lost at West Ham and drew 3-3 at Manchester City, the only two games Lee missed.

In that period Manchester United played an extra game, and won, so that by the time Ferguson and his squad arrived at St James' on 4 March, those 12 points had been sliced to four, though Newcastle had a game in hand.

Around the time of Asprilla, Keegan made another purchase, spending £3.75m to bring David Batty from Blackburn Rovers. Keegan described Batty as the 'final piece in the jigsaw'.

Lee was pleased. 'Kevin was always one for asking players about other players. I remember him asking me about who I would want to play alongside. I said either David Batty or Paul Ince, I was playing with both for England. Kevin listened. Managers should. I knew who I found tough and Batty was one of them – tough, kept the ball. He was good. And I got on great with him. He came in for that game, David Batty made his debut against Man U.

'I'd missed two games injured, then came back in. We battered them. David Batty played as well as anyone that day. But Peter Schmeichel was unbelievable, some of the saves he made . . . They had one shot – [Eric] Cantona, goal.

'We heard that a lot: "How did Man United get on?" – "1-0, Cantona; Schmeichel was brilliant."

'Look at their record: Newcastle away – 1-0, Cantona. QPR away – 1-1, Cantona. Arsenal home – 1-0, Cantona. Tottenham home – 1-0, Cantona. Coventry home – 1-0, Cantona. In five of six games, that's how it was. None of his goals were in the first half. Check back, I bet the reports all say how brilliant Schmeichel was.

'I'm not blaming anyone, but, if we'd had Schmeichel, we'd have won the league. I've never seen anyone like him. People forget how good he was.'

Gary Neville's recollection also included Schmeichel's reflexes at St James', and Steve Bruce's resilience. Neville has said that at half-time, with Newcastle utterly dominant but not in front, Ferguson lambasted him:

'Asprilla is beating you on the ground, he's beating you in the air. What's going on? Play like that in the second half and you've cost us the title. Out we came for the second half, and this time we had the slope. It's a big old slope at Newcastle, the biggest in the league. In the first half it felt like we were stuck at the bottom of a hill being pounded, but now we were up at the top and, while it might sound odd, I felt taller.'

In the second half, Cantona had one chance and took it. Newcastle's lead was now one point and Neville said: 'We weren't playing well but we seized the moment and the whole world knew then that Newcastle were never going to win the league.'

Lee did not think that way. At that moment he still believed Newcastle could and would win the title. In the next game West Ham were beaten 3-0 at St James', which left Newcastle three points clear and still with a game in hand.

But then Newcastle went to Highbury and lost 2-0 and then went to Anfield for arguably the most celebrated match of the past 30 years and lost 4-3.

By then Manchester United had caught up, but Newcastle United had two games in hand. The way the sequence was going, Newcastle were always playing second. The Liverpool game was on a Wednesday night, live on TV.

'Everyone wanted to watch us. We played a lot of games on Sundays and Mondays. TV wanted every game we played. It can be off-putting because you're playing catch-up.

'We lost at Highbury, we were poor. Liverpool? What can I say? We'd lost to Arsenal but nothing had changed. At Anfield we went 1-0 down then 2-1 up, 2-2, then 3-2 up, 3-3, then [Stan] Collymore's goal. At the near post.

'We've probably played in the best game the Premier League's ever seen – because we attacked. They attacked, we attacked. And we got nothing out of it.

'Man U would not have played the way we did. They got their results differently. Kevin Keegan's philosophy was to entertain and, genuinely, I wouldn't change anything. I loved those five years of Keegan, loved training, loved playing. I hated missing games, I played with injuries I didn't admit to because I wanted to be part of it so much. I'm a great believer in players being happy. It was such a great place to be.

'Kevin was devastated at Anfield. In the dressing room he was devastated, we all were. We should have got at least a point.'

After that, Newcastle were second three points behind, but with a game in hand. They beat QPR three days later and, two days on, faced Blackburn at Ewood Park. Rovers had Shearer up front but it was to be another Geordie striker, Graham Fenton, who made headlines. Fenton was 21 and came from Whitley Bay.

Twenty minutes from time, with the score 0-0, Fenton replaced Mike Newell. Five minutes later Batty scored against his former club and Newcastle were looking at a precious away win. Then, with four minutes left, Fenton equalised. That was bad, but worse, in the 89th minute Fenton scored the winner. Newcastle had again been flattened at the last. They had taken 6,000 fans to Blackburn. A potential three-point deficit, with a game in hand, became six points.

Although Newcastle immediately won their next three matches, beating Villa, Southampton and Leeds, Manchester had a decisive advantage.

'We still believed, even after the Blackburn game, when Graham Fenton scored those two goals,' Lee says. 'We were 1-0 up. I still believed Man United would trip up. But the Forest game – Ian Woan scores a wonder goal. I believed until then.'

Manchester United had tripped, losing 3-1 at Southampton to reduce the gap to three points, and Newcastle still with a game in hand. Goal difference was now against Keegan's team and after a 1-0 win at Elland Road, Keegan raged at Ferguson's alleged mind games – 'I'd love it, love it, if we beat them.'

Lee says the televised post-match outburst was nothing new to Newcastle's players: 'Kevin used to rant and rave all the time. When he used the word "pal", you knew there was trouble – "I'll tell you, pal." He could rip people apart with words. He ripped Warren Barton apart after the 2-0 at Arsenal. Five of us were going off with England. He battered every one of us: "And you five can fuck off to England." I always remember that.

'He slaughtered me a few times. But his man-management was brilliant.

'I once got new boots, Diadora, yellow stripe on them. I wore them against QPR, never got a kick against Ray Wilkins, who was about 48. Keegan slaughtered me at half-time: "Get those fuckin' boots off."

'I changed them. About ten minutes into the second half I was taken off. I said: "Why? I've changed the boots."

'He said: "Yeah, but you're still shit."'

After the victory at Leeds, Newcastle were still three points adrift, but they had that game in hand, the penultimate game of the season at Nottingham Forest. Beardsley gave Newcastle a 1-0 lead but 15 minutes from time Ian Woan equalised.

From joining Manchester United level on points, albeit with a worse goal difference of five, Newcastle were two points behind with one game to play. Even Lee knew it was all over. Newcastle had a home game, against Tottenham, while Manchester United were at Middlesbrough, or as Lee puts it: "Bryan Robson's Middlesbrough".

'That's what we were thinking. I'm sure it's not, but Middlesbrough weren't going to win that game.'

Middlesbrough lost 3-0. The title was won in the north-east, but not by a north-east club.

'We knew it was over by Tottenham. I don't remember the lap of honour. That was how it felt. Depressing.

'But look again at Man U – they lost one of their last 15 matches. Drew one. That's a better record than our start. Compare our results to Man U's results after they beat us. People say we lost the title; they won it.

'The only thing I regret is that if we'd won, it would have changed coaching. People said: "You can't play the way Keegan plays and win." Teams are a lot more defensive now, they pack midfields. It's all about results. We were cavalier, great entertainment. Would a manager survive today playing the way Kevin did?'

Lee has no over-riding criticism. He thinks, maybe, that a central defender should have been signed to assist Darren Peacock, and Des Walker, back from Sampdoria at Sheffield Wednesday, has since told Lee he would have 'walked across the sea' to play for Newcastle, but then that might have altered the team's impulse.

And Lee noticed the geographic factor sometimes.

'What I did find was that the travelling back after games was tough. We didn't have planes, we were always on the coach. We'd be getting back from Anfield, after that game, at 3am. After England games we'd not get back til' 4am – the London players were home in half an hour.'

After an hour of memories Lee slumps in his chair. He knows this is just the beginning.

It was February 2014. Lee was back in Newcastle as he was speaking at a fans' forum that Wednesday night. There was another on Thursday and another on Friday. Eighteen years on, Tyneside talks and talks about 1995/96.

✦

NEWCASTLE UNITED'S REACTION TO THE DISAPPOINTMENT was to break the world transfer record to sign Shearer from Blackburn. Yet Keegan and Shearer were together for only five months before Keegan resigned, saying he was disenchanted with the board's decision to turn the club into a plc.

'I still don't understand why he left,' Lee says. 'I know he wanted to run the club like Alex Ferguson. I understand that, he has principles. I know the plc thing was around, but I don't really understand that.

'What I know is that Newcastle United had to keep Kevin Keegan, no matter what a plc meant. Sometimes people don't want to hear things and they needed to be told Kevin Keegan had to stay. But there are egos. I look back to when I left and I wish I hadn't, but Bobby [Robson] messed about with my contract.'

The author Jonathan Tulloch met Keegan near the end of this period. Tulloch's novel *The Season Ticket*, about two boys obsessed with St James' Park, became the film *Purely Belter*.

'We approached Kevin about making a charity record and he was brilliant,' Tulloch said. 'He was referring to the directors as "them up there" and said quite a few things about them. I think he was upset that Newcastle United were being turned into a trade name. Freddie Fletcher came in and was spitting feathers. You could see the friction.

'Keegan was on the people's side in the way the directors weren't. He means a lot to the area because he understood that for them football was about self-esteem. Basically one of the oldest parts of the industrial world was in decline and football represented the last flower of that old sense of co-operation and community. Keegan might not have articulated it that way but he certainly understood it. That's why the name Keegan represents something.'

Freddie Fletcher was the chief executive. One of his most-used business words was 'maximise'. He saw what the Premier League was becoming materially and wanted Newcastle United to exploit its merchandising potential. Keegan understood this – his personal economic calculations were undisguised – but he could feel a loss of control as the club expanded.

He hoped that he could resign privately and remain in post until the end of the season. The club accepted his resignation and suddenly it was in the *Sunday Mirror*. Within 48 hours Keegan was gone and Newcastle United had planned a trip to Sitges near Barcelona, where Bobby Robson lived.

Robson had left the England manager's job in 1990 and joined PSV Eindhoven. From there he went to Sporting Lisbon and Porto before landing the Barcelona job in July 1996. Robson would say he 'bleeds black and white' but he had been at the Nou Camp only six months when Keegan left Newcastle.

Sir John Hall found a corner of Wynyard Hall and looked back.

'We went to Bobby,' Hall says. 'He was the right choice and we'd heard he wanted to come back, that Elsie [Robson's wife] wanted to come back. They'd been everywhere.

'Joe Melling, a journalist, set up a meeting for us in Barcelona. Freddie and Douglas flew out and I flew up from Marbella and met surreptitiously at Bobby's house in Sitges and sat in the garden. Bobby said: "Yes, I want to come back." And we did a deal with him. He was coming. Absolutely great.

'We flew back, but I thought that evening I'd just talk to him about coming and on the telephone I knew straightaway he had changed his mind. Various reasons, said he wanted to stay loyal to Barcelona.'

In the background was informed speculation that Barcelona would be moving Robson aside for Louis van Gaal at the end of that season and Hall says: 'We told him about Louis van Gaal but Bobby could not believe this would happen to him at Barcelona.

'Maybe he thought he could use this [approach] as a way to negotiate a deal with Barcelona. Van Gaal came in, Bobby went upstairs.

'Two years later, after we'd tried Kenny Dalglish and [Ruud] Gullit, [we got Robson]. But if we had got Bobby at the time . . .'

Dalglish required no introduction. In the history of English football he was one of only four managers to win the title with two different clubs – Tom Watson, Herbert Chapman and Brian Clough the others. Dalglish had followed Keegan as a player at Anfield and was now doing so as a manager at St James'. He had signed Shearer for Blackburn, where he had won the title as manager to add to the three he won as manager of Liverpool.

Newcastle finished second again as Dalglish picked up from Keegan. But on the weekend in late July 1997 when Newcastle agreed to sell Ferdinand to Tottenham, Shearer damaged ankle ligaments in a pre-season tournament at Goodison Park. Dalglish had already sold Ginola to Spurs.

It meant that on the opening day of the 1997/98 season Newcastle had Asprilla and new signing Jon Dahl Tomasson up front. They won, Asprilla scored two. Then he scored three the night Newcastle beat Barcelona 3-2 in the Champions League. The vibrant quality embodied by Asprilla, Gillespie and Lee stunned the new Barca manager Van Gaal, who, as predicted, had replaced Robson.

The defeat of Barcelona was a euphoric landmark for the club: in September 1992 Newcastle won 2-1 at Bristol Rovers in the second division; in September 1997 Newcastle beat Barcelona in the Champions League.

But by Christmas the Champions League was over and Newcastle were 20 points behind Manchester United in the league. There was progress in the FA Cup, though the draw with Stevenage saw Dalglish embroiled in a row about safety that reached *Newsnight* and Jeremy Paxman, no football man, asking Dalglish: 'Are you a big girl's blouse?'

Not long after, Freddy Shepherd and Douglas Hall were exposed in the *News of the World* sneering at the club's fans. The two directors were forced to resign but made their way back.

Dalglish's team reached the FA Cup final, a chance to end a domestic trophy drought then 43 years old, but Arsenal won 2-0. Two games into the next season, Newcastle's lamentable planning saw Dalglish replaced by Gullit.

The calibre of name matched the expanding stadium, soon to rise to 52,000-capacity. Only Old Trafford held more. Gullit watched his first game from the stands as Liverpool won 4-1 at St James', Michael Owen scoring a first-half hat-trick. Stephane Guivarc'h, a £3.5m signing by Dalglish, scored his one and only Newcastle goal that day.

Under Gullit, Newcastle again reached the FA Cup final but again lost 2-0, this time to Manchester United. Five games into the next season, in another display of zero forward planning, Gullit walked before he was pushed.

Newcastle were looking for a fourth manager in under three years and Robson was asked again. This time he came and Newcastle won their first match at St James' under him 8-0. Shearer scored five. Welcome home, Bobby.

Robson's Durham roots, his miner father, meant that he grasped the Geordie Nation talk of Hall. Robson had been in professional football since 1950 and had survived in management for over three decades. He inherited excellence in Shay Given, Gary Speed, Nolberto Solano, Lee and Shearer but Robson knew success was underpinned by investment. He bought pace in the shape of Craig Bellamy and defensive assurance in Jonathan Woodgate.

Gradually Newcastle gelled as a team and began to flow again. There was a night in late 2000 when Newcastle won 3-1 at Highbury to go top of the Premier League and Robson told an irritated Arsenal camp that 'some people around here need to learn how to lose'.

Robson had gravitas and personality and Tyneside was growing fond of a man who contrasted with much that had gone on recently at the club. He had his 70th-birthday in 2003 but he was a regenerative force.

IN SHAY GIVEN AND GARY SPEED, ROBSON HAD TWO OF HIS "blue-chip" players. Given joined Newcastle in August 1997, Speed five months later. Given played 463 times for the club, making him third in its all-time appearance list. Speed played 285 games in black and white. They were vital players as Newcastle rose again under Robson and they became close friends and room-mates. After both departed St. James', their friendship endured.

On November 27th 2011 Speed was found dead aged 42. One month later I spoke to Given. He was still in shock and searching for the vocabulary to express a desperate situation.

"The last thing I want to do is cause upset," he began. "I want to say something and I've been asked a lot about it. I want to remember Gary, speak of him as a friend. I don't want to repeat the other great tributes that people have paid. But they're true. Gary was a natural. I am proud to call him a friend. I'll do it this once. I won't go on."

Given, then with Aston Villa, had heard the news from Alan Shearer and Craig Bellamy as he prepared for a match at Swansea.

As Speed was manager of Wales, it was expected the game would be called off. But it went ahead and Given was in tears on the pitch.

"I was trying to get my head around it," Given said, "and I was all right in the warm-up. But then there was the minute's silence, or the applause it turned in to, and the man on the microphone started speaking about Gary.

"Dunney [Richard Dunne] and James Collins had their arms around me just keeping me up. I was just trying . . . But you can't help how you're feeling . . . Just devastating . . . It sunk in then.

"But then we had a game to play. I had to try to keep my eyes clear. Maybe I'd have been better heaving in my hotel room. It's tough. It's shock. The tears just come. You can't keep it in.

"When Alan had called and spoken, he was kind of shaken as he spoke. I was shaking as I heard. It's disbelief. Are you sure this is true? But Gary's best friend John [Ratcliffe] had called and it was true. This was about 20 minutes before the team meeting. I had to tell the gaffer [Alex McLeish] and he was shaken once he heard. I don't know what he said at the meeting, I was in a daze."

Given spent the following days trying to be of comfort to Speed's wife Louise and their sons Eddie, then 14, and Tommy, 13. He told the boys about the death of his own mother, Agnes, when Given was just five.

"It's tough, it's hard for the boys, so hard," Given said. "I'll miss Gary but you can't put into words how much they'll miss him, how they're going to cope. I don't know what to say.

"You can say 'everything's going to be all right', but they are going to have bad days. There's no magic wand. Everything's changed.

"I've told the boys about my mother. I lost her when I was five. I know how much it hurts. It's hard even getting the words out. There are going to be tough months and years ahead but they need to know there's support from relatives and friends. You just try to help because you never get over things like this; you've got to learn to live with it. You never get over losing your mum at five years of age. It's something my brothers, sisters and myself have had to live with.

"We have had to get on with our lives as best we can. Obviously we'd love our mum to be here. It's not going to change. We'd love Gary to be here, to pick up the phone to him now. It's not going to be. We'll always miss him. But you've got to learn, you've got to keep living."

Given subsequently picked up the first hamstring injury of his long career, he thought due to stress and fatigue.

"Hindsight says I shouldn't have played but I know Speedo would have played. You think all those kinds of things as well. I could hardly walk after and it meant I thought I couldn't carry the coffin."

Given did not wish to discuss the funeral. He wanted to focus on Gary Speed, the man and the player: "Even people who never met Gary were impressed by him."

ON THE PITCH NEWCASTLE WERE RECOVERING THEIR strength and mounted real challenges in 2002 and 2003. They finished fourth then third and qualified again for the Champions League. Robson was in charge on unforgettable occasions for Newcastle fans – Feyenoord in 2002 and Inter Milan in 2003.

Robson's image was of the wise old owl, sometimes forgetful, and people loved the purity of his enthusiasm. That image developed once Robson left St James' and his funeral in 2009 in Durham Cathedral, featuring a passionate eulogy from Alex Ferguson, was a state occasion for English football. The feeling was sincere.

But that image must be set against the reality of Robson's last 18 months at Newcastle, when he was ready to sell Shearer to Liverpool so he could buy Emile Mpenza, and the cost of poor signings mounted up. Robson spent £11m on Hugo Viana when he was not needed; there was £5m on Titus Bramble and previously £7m on Carl Cort, among others.

While beyond the fanbase and the club attention was on Robson the man, on the terraces and in the boardroom the weekly focus was on performance. This uncomfortable fact of life revealed itself to Robson on 9 May 2004.

It was the last home game of the season and Newcastle needed to win it. They were chasing fourth place in a race with Liverpool. Wolves, bound for relegation, were the opponents. The score was 1-1.

As the players emerged for the end-of-season lap of honour they found a ground three-quarters empty. The game had ended amid boos. Robson gave an angry critique of Newcastle's fans after a television interview, when his microphone was still on. It was broadcast through the stadium.

This was three days after Newcastle had lost the second leg of the Uefa Cup semi-final in Marseille to two goals from Didier Drogba. At Marseille Airport, Hall raged audibly, and Robson was his target.

'Where you there?' Hall says, startled, when reminded of this. 'I was very, very annoyed that night.'

Ultimately another season had ended silverless. Newcastle went to Anfield on the last day of the season knowing fourth place had gone. Liverpool took it but the manager who got them there, Gérard Houllier, was immediately replaced by Rafael Benitez. Newcastle had the appetite to do the same with Robson but stuck with him. Newcastle's support noted the difference.

Four games into the next season – in another example of non-planning – the board changed their mind. Having not chosen to sign Patrick Kluivert, Robson accepted him reluctantly and picked him in place of Shearer at Villa Park. Kluivert scored but Newcastle lost 4-2. Newcastle were 16th. It was over.

Tellingly, there were no protests. Those fans who chant Robson's name now weren't chanting it then. Maybe they were simply weary.

The club was unhappy. The Robson era had also included numerous stories about player behaviour, dressing room unrest, and there was a risible attempt to sign Wayne Rooney. People were fed up.

'He did very well for us, a very nice fella,' Hall says of Robson. 'But we got a lot of players in who weren't very nice. He bought some younger players and there was a caucus in the dressing room of younger players he'd lost control of. It was not a nice place to be. There was a divide.

'We wanted Bobby to go upstairs but he wouldn't do that. Freddy had to make a decision, he was the chairman. There was a way to do it, but it was four games into the season. It wasn't a happy time, but we'd to make a decision.'

Newcastle wanted Martin O'Neill; they appointed Graeme Souness. There was instant conflict with Bellamy – then an on-pitch scrap between Kieron Dyer and Lee Bowyer – but Newcastle reached another semi-final, in the FA Cup and the quarter-final of the Uefa Cup. The second leg of that game at Sporting Lisbon came three days before the Manchester United semi in Cardiff. Newcastle lost both, 4-1, 4-1. The joke was it was their new formation.

Souness spent around £50m on players such as Jean-Alain Boumsong and Scott Parker, although the Scot may not have been the driving force behind the £16m vanity purchase of Michael Owen in 2005. Owen's face as he walked in the entrance at St James' was that of a man keen to locate the exit.

It had become predictable that Souness would not last and he was sacked, mid-season, in February 2006. Glenn Roeder, once Keegan's teammate, stepped in and the ship steadied. Roeder lasted 15 months, his departure, apparently, a resignation.

It was 6 May 2007. On 15 May Newcastle appointed Sam Allardyce. No-one knew then that 48 hours later Hall would receive a call from an Icelandic bank on behalf of someone called Mike Ashley.

3 MAY 2014. Some 90 minutes after the final whistle had blown on the final home game of the season, St James' Park was all but empty. The groundsmen tended the pitch, cleaners shuffled along the rows upon rows of grey seats that had been filled with particular noise, and the last few players made their way out. It was calm.

But it was an illusion. Even though Newcastle had just beaten Cardiff City 3-0 to confirm their place in the Premier League's top ten, and relegate Cardiff, there was nothing calm about this day.

Newcastle's manager, Alan Pardew, was one of the last to leave. Newcastle's home season had finished with a win but it was an afternoon when Pardew lost.

He had been losing for some weeks, ever since Newcastle travelled to Hull at the start of March and won 4-1 only to have the result obliterated by Pardew's touchline spat with Hull player David Meyler. Some said it was a head-butt; it seemed a bit less than that. Pardew was fortunate that Meyler chose not to make more of it, then or afterwards.

All knew this was not frivolous; Pardew had crossed a line and Newcastle United fined him £100,000 that night. They could have sacked him.

The television loop ensured Pardew's head-jolt was on constant replay and the authorities acted: he was banned for seven games, the first three of which were from the stadium in which Newcastle were playing. In terms of punishment this broke new ground in the Premier League.

For the other four games Pardew was not allowed in the Newcastle United dugout, but he was able to attend the games and be with his players in the dressing room.

It was inevitable a soft-focus image of Robson would be brought up after the incident at Hull, which rather ignored Robson's fist-fight with two of his own players while manager at Ipswich.

'Punches were thrown,' Robson had remembered. 'It is not an incident I recall with any pride.'

Robson was hard when required to be; he was also gracious.

Hull had come six weeks after Pardew had verbally abused the Manchester City manager Manuel Pellegrini. Pardew had been fortunate then, too. This verbal attack was in some ways more unpleasant than the Meyler confrontation. It was gross conduct and Pardew apologised.

Two weeks after that Newcastle sold their best player, Yohan Cabaye, to Paris Saint-Germain, and chose not to replace him. A week after that, Joe Kinnear departed St James', his seven-month role as director of football having apparently changed little at the club. It had bemused a few inside and attracted ever more supporter criticism from outside.

Not for the first time, Newcastle United felt like a splintered club. Kinnear's exit came three days after Newcastle had lost 3-0 at home to Sunderland. The next game was a 3-0 defeat as well, at Chelsea, then came a 4-0 defeat at home to Tottenham.

Yet Newcastle were ninth in the richest league in the world. A superficial reading of the club's situation would show mid-table stability under a manager given a rare amount of time in a sacking culture. The club was operating an annual profit and had sold Cabaye for around £14m more than they had paid for him two-and-a-half years earlier. Under the ownership of Mike Ashley the club had moved to – some might say stumbled upon – an economic model.

But when, after this last home game of the season, a banner was held up at the Leazes End proclaiming 'Newcastle United: Balance Sheet Champions', it was not congratulatory. The club's model yielded profit but it pushed some fans away and others into mockery.

The banner was on view as Newcastle's players walked around the pitch after victory over Cardiff, a farewell to the season rather than a lap of honour. It is a custom but a difference at Newcastle was that the manager felt sufficiently uncomfortable to not join his players and coaching staff on that walk.

Pardew had been baited all afternoon. Two minutes into the game the chant of 'Get out of our club' came forth from the Gallowgate End. It has been aired at Ashley for several years, the B-side of an earlier Tyneside favourite, 'Sack The Board'.

The mood inside the ground, almost full again, was such that when Pardew made motions to leave his seat to speak to his players on the pitch, he was howled down. This was Pardew's first match at St James' since his seven-game ban but it turned out his movement was no less restricted.

In the 59th minute, with Newcastle 1-0 in front, a banner appeared with three pictures on it, one of Ashley, one of Kinnear and one of Pardew. 'Liar, Liar, Liar' it read. Then, ten minutes later, a walk-out, though not a mass walk-out.

In the days leading to the game Newcastle's support had been in debate as to whether they would stage an organised protest and, if so, what form this would take. Newcastle's fanbase, like most, is fractured. There are degrees of militancy and for all that it is portrayed as demanding, many, perhaps a majority, could be described as passive.

Part of the reason the three local newspapers, the *Chronicle*, *Journal* and *Sunday Sun,* had been banned by the club from the press box at St James' seven months earlier was that the club felt those papers' reporting of a protest march through Newcastle city centre before the Liverpool match had been 'disproportionate' given, they said, around only 300 people participated.

There may have been 500, even so, the club's stance was that hundreds do not represent 52,000. But, having walked alongside it, the march made an impact as it headed up Barrack Road in silence, white hankies waved, because it was representative of a broader attitude. At the bandstand in Leazes Park, an organiser made a measured speech about 'regaining self-respect' and asking those gathered to 'think about where you spend your money'. The spending and not spending of money had become a theme.

Minute 69 had been chosen to remind people that 1969 was the last year Newcastle United won a trophy, the Fairs Cup. As the clock ticked over, around 2,000 fans got to their feet and did the hardest thing of all, they left.

The club were entitled to again say that this was unrepresentative. And again, they could have a point, because the fanbase is changing. At the previous home game, against Swansea, I'd walked up an hour before kick-off to the ticket office and bought one for £21. It was for the Level 7 section high in the Leazes End near the away fans.

While queuing, I noticed the ticket price was £20. £1 had been added as a 'booking fee' despite there having been no booking. In this way football clubs, not just Newcastle United, skim money from fans.

Up on Level 7 the atmosphere was like a playground. There was a stag party, a hen party, a group of Dutch lads, a group of Scottish lads and a lot of children with parents. There was lots of eating. There were not lots of traditional football supporters and when Swansea won via a last-minute goal, there was no outcry. People had come for an afternoon out, had something to eat, and left.

Crucially for the club and Premier League, seats were filled. Television does not like empty seats. It could suggest the Premier League is not all it's cracked up to be.

Against Cardiff, in the 69th minute, those who left knew what they were doing. Pardew, meanwhile, was unable to move.

The chorus of 'Alan Pardew, it's never your fault' had rung around, a reflection of a feeling locally that Pardew has blamed circumstance more than his own failings when things have gone wrong.

A neutral might claim, for example, that Pardew did not sign Cabaye, nor did he sell him, both decisions were taken above Pardew's head. A Newcastle fan would reply that part of Pardew's job is to win arguments against those above.

Part of the reason Pardew may not is because his position within the hierarchy is not as strong as it might be. The eight-year contract he signed at the club in September 2012 apparently does not alter that reality. In the eyes of Newcastle's fanbase Pardew's position was weakened by events such as Hull and Pellegrini, and an appearance on Sky TV's *Goals on Sunday* programme earlier in the season.

Then Pardew said of Ashley: 'Mike is a strong character who has been a success in his whole business life and is a genius in that world – but football isn't his world and when you come to football the logic doesn't quite fit. He loves football but he sometimes can't understand how it works and it confuses and upsets him, and when he is upset he does things that aren't brilliant for the football club.'

Ashley's private response to seeing one of his business managers on TV saying he makes decisions that 'aren't brilliant' and calling him confused is unlikely to have been mild.

Three weeks later, when Newcastle beat Chelsea, Pardew said: 'This win is for

Mike Ashley and all of our fans – trust me, he is a fan.'

The victory over Chelsea in November came three days after Newcastle had gone out of the League Cup at home to Manchester City. Newcastle have never won the League Cup and supporters are understandably vexed. If 2013's version of Newcastle United cannot win the Premier League or reach the Champions League, then the domestic cups are the only opportunities for seasonal glory.

So there was a degree of anticipation when Newcastle were drawn at home to Cardiff in the third round of the FA Cup in January. But Tim Krul, Cabaye and Loic Remy, Newcastle's key striker, were absent from the starting XI, Cardiff won 2-1 and Newcastle's club policy had been unveiled on their pitch.

It would later receive official confirmation at a fans' forum nine days after the season. With prize-money and television payments soaring, Newcastle stated: 'The club's priority is the Premier League.'

When asked about a cup run, the club's reply was that they had 'research' and look what happened to Wigan Athletic and Birmingham City – they won cups and were relegated the same season.

They accepted that Swansea City's 2013 League Cup win ran against that, though there was no mention of Tottenham's win in 2008 or Middlesbrough's in 2004. The response also failed to take into account the excitement generated, for instance, at Sunderland that season by winning League Cup ties against Chelsea and Manchester United.

The statement was a joyless end to a soured season. The club also confirmed at that meeting that Pardew, despite being unable to walk around his own pitch, would remain as manager.

After Hull City, Newcastle had ten games left. They lost eight of them.

Sixth on Boxing Day, three points off a Champions League place, Newcastle's season had a further 21 games: they lost 15 of them.

MIKE ASHLEY HAD MADE A PUBLIC SHOW of turning up to games while Pardew was banned. But in general Ashley was attending fewer games and was nowhere to be seen at the Cardiff match. One of his contacts was around however. Keith Bishop is a London-based PR man who represents Newcastle United, Glasgow Rangers and showbiz others.

Bishop walked down from the directors' box with what looked like a mother, father and two late-thirties sons of apparently Asian origin. There had been takeover talk in the corporate section at the game but then there is always takeover talk at St James' Park. Wishful thinking is one of north-east football's afflictions.

Why would Mike Ashley sell? TV income is booming, Premier League profile is booming. Season 2013/14 ended with Newcastle tenth and with TV and prize money of £77.4m, a rise of £32m from the previous season. The new television agreements make owning a mid-table Premier League club so lucrative that trying to win the League Cup, for example, is secondary.

And Ashley's Newcastle have proved that you can be part of this club without spending vast amounts. Newcastle's last permanent first-team transfer had been Moussa Sissoko's £2m move from Toulouse 16 months before.

Two transfer windows had come and gone since then without Newcastle buying a player. Yet Newcastle finished in the top ten. They had done the work of two transfer windows in January 2013, when Sissoko was joined by Mapou Yanga-Mbiwa, Yoan Gouffran and Massadio Haidara, and they had coped. This was surely good management at two levels, Pardew's and Ashley's.

Besides, just look around: Mike Ashley was everywhere. The emptied stadium revealed just how full it was of Ashley's Sports Direct publicity. Some continue to ask what it is that Ashley gets from owning Newcastle United – it was possible to count 137 Sports Direct signs and logos from one side of the pitch.

That included the 18 logos on the top of the home dugout seats and the 13 in the away dugout. Across the top of each is another series of logos. During games, cameras always focus on the dugouts.

There were advertising hoardings, smaller boards all around the ground and the two giant red signs either side of the black 'Newcastle United' sign on the East Stand. The 137 did not include the logos on the walls on the inside of the tunnel or the one on the sign that greets the players as they line up to leave it.

Where Liverpool have the 'This Is Anfield' sign, Newcastle have 'Howay The Lads'. Newcastle's has a Sports Direct logo underneath it.

A first-time visitor could well think that this stadium was called the Sports Direct Arena. Buy something from the club shop and the till receipt will inform that it is registered in Nottinghamshire, where Sports Direct has its HQ.

In 2007 Sports Direct had the profile of one of its rivals, JD Sports; now it's got a High Street profile akin to the major chains around its new shop on Newcastle's main drag, Northumberland Street. In that time Sports Direct's share price has more than quadrupled.

Maybe this was the plan all along. Sir John Hall says so. But still it is asked: Why? Why did Mike Ashley buy Newcastle United?

In 2014, Hall recalled the unexpected days of May 2007. The man who built the Metro Centre was then encountering the man who was the rising name in British retail. They had some common background.

'In the way we started, yes,' Hall says. 'The similarity between ourselves is that we both started, in a sense, from the front room of our mothers' houses. There's that similarity, though he took his business way beyond me. He would probably take more of a gamble than I would. But he's built up this business, which is tremendous.'

Hall had arranged to go to London to see potential buyers of his 41 per cent share in the club who came from Malaysia.

'To go back,' he says, 'we were in control of the club, we became a plc to bring more money into the club. But when [Roman] Abramovich came into football – to me, as the strategist for the family business – I could not compete with a billionaire.

'Why did Abramovich come into football? By doing that and pouring wealth into Chelsea, he made it impossible for most of the local millionaires in football – Bill Kenwright, myself, people like that – to compete with a billionaire. I would not risk the family's wealth. It was a lose situation, so I said: "It's time to get out."

'I had a lot of hassle from Freddy [Shepherd] and Douglas [Hall's son] but I made my mind up that I was going to sell the shares. It took me two years travelling round Europe and it ended up, one day I got a call.

'I was negotiating with some Malaysians, who wanted to buy Newcastle United, and who were coming over for the Cup final [2007, Chelsea v Manchester United]. I said I'd go to London to meet them.

'On the Monday of that week, I arranged to meet them at a London hotel to do a deal to sell Newcastle United. On the [previous] Thursday I got a call from an agent on behalf of an Icelandic bank. He said: "We have someone interested and we'll give you your pound per share. Can we meet?"

'I said: "Well, I'm meeting these Malaysian businessmen at 11."

'He said: "Don't go. Come and see us."

'I said: "I'm honour-bound to go and see them."

'I was met off the train at 10 and I was taken around to see Ashley's people and lawyers – I think it was Freshfields off Fleet Street – and the room was full, packed. 'We want to do a deal.'

'I told them I'd come back. I went to see the Malaysians at their hotel but they wanted to do due diligence – six to eight weeks – and I knew Freddy didn't want to sell. I said: "I'm sorry, I can't give you that time."

'So I went back to Freshfields and said I'd do a deal. I brought in my lawyers.

I'd just gone down for the day, I didn't have a change of clothes or anything, and for three days we sat down and worked on the deal.'

It is tempting to picture Hall and Ashley negotiating the deal, discussing their retail pasts and futures, it's just Ashley was not there.

'When I met them all,' Hall says, 'I asked: "Why do you want to buy?" It was essential I knew what they were going to do. I met his team, I didn't meet him – he has a team going around doing his deals.

'His team told me they were going to use Newcastle United to brand Sports Direct in the Far East. I thought that was ideal – globalise Newcastle, which we hadn't done, though we tried. Basically that was it.'

This sounds a plausible explanation for Ashley's purchase, that Newcastle United would act as a form of shop window for Sports Direct. For clarification purposes, I asked Hall again if this was the reason. Hall says he, too, had repeated the question.

'He [Ashley] saw the Far East as a big part of his marketplace. They love football there, so the two went together. Newcastle were globalised and he had a brand. Newcastle were a global brand, big fanbase. He had a strategy.

'He decided, in a sense, that he wanted something to brand his goods, his business, in the Far East. He felt, or his team felt, that buying a good football team would get him a lot of publicity abroad. So the two made sense. He would globalise Newcastle United through his marketing and he would get a marketing tool/brand name – and he always bought brands, Newcastle was a brand name. So the two made sense.'

The fact that the deal was done so quickly meant the due diligence the Malaysians were preparing did not take place. It has long seemed an unusual oversight by Ashley, particularly as he later claimed the club he bought was in a rather worse financial position than first thought. But Hall was dismissive of this idea: 'He would have done due diligence in a week.

'He said he didn't want to do due diligence. "We're going to accept the club."

'[When] I left, I never knew the final accounts of the club because I wasn't there. I'd stepped down from the board, sort of semi-retired. So I don't know them totally, but when I was there, we had a £50m mortgage on the club and about £15m deficit on players, but the mortgage, you could leave it there.

'The only debt the club had was basically a £50m mortgage on the stadium. He knew, he knew, he just had to look at the accounts, they would tell him there was a mortgage on the stadium. There was nothing hidden. Everything was in the books. Nothing hidden at all.'

It is sometimes said Mike Ashley has never given an interview during his tenure as Newcastle United's owner. But he has, at least twice directly, and there have been other announcements on his behalf from the club.

On 21 October 2007, five months after buying Hall's shares, the *News of the World* published a joint interview in which Ashley and Paul Kemsley, then Tottenham's vice-president, friend and former work colleague of Ashley's, spoke to Rob Beasley.

Eleven weeks before he bought out Sir John Hall's 41 per cent of Newcastle United for £55m, Ashley netted £929m in cash by selling 43 per cent of Sports Direct when it was floated on the Stock Exchange.

In the City of London, Ashley had attracted a maverick tag, but there was little personal detail. It was said he had been a county-level squash player and had started his sports shop empire from a single store in Maidenhead, but there was only the beginning of a biographical outline.

Asked about the aura of secrecy surrounding him, Ashley said then: 'I have never been a recluse but I do wonder why anyone would go out of their way to court publicity. I was certainly happy that I managed to stay under the radar for so long. Why not?

'But when I floated Sports Direct on the stock market earlier this year I realised it wasn't just my company going public. I knew I would finally have to come up above the parapet too. So why not now do things I've always wanted to do? Like buying a football club.'

Ashley looked back to the deal in May. He said that he had been informed on a Saturday that Hall's shares were for sale and that 'by Monday I was able to tell him that I was very happy to purchase his shares at £1 each at a time when they were only trading at around 75p. I also told him that the money was already deposited with a lawyer and that everything could be completed in just 24 hours.'

Ashley then confirmed there had been 'no time to do the usual due diligence', and added: 'So I paid £140m for the club with the expectation that there was a debt of £70m. Actually it was around £100m so there was suddenly an extra £30m to find.

'But I just thought "Shut up about it." I'm a big boy and I didn't cry.

'To me the real issue was this: Was the debt bigger than I thought? Yes. Would it have changed my decision if I'd known the full extent of the debt? Not one iota.'

And his ambition at Newcastle United? 'I want to have fun and win some trophies.'

Around ten months later, Ashley gave another interview, this time to a new glossy club magazine publicised as *A New Mag For A New Era*. Sam Allardyce, the manager Ashley inherited, had been replaced by Kevin Keegan, the third coming.

In this interview, Ashley talked more about himself: 'People have to understand that I've always been a big football fan. Who was my team? England. I've been to every World Cup since Spain in 1982 and to every European Championships.'

Ashley described Newcastle United as 'one of the diamonds of the Premier League' but returned to the scuffed state of the club he bought in a rush. 'Financially the club was in a difficult position because I really do think it had over-extended itself.'

There were other comments of a similar nature and although matters quickly deteriorated with Keegan, leading to him to leave and win a case of constructive dismissal in which the club's conduct was described as 'profoundly unsatisfactory', once the club bottomed-out under Ashley – 2009's relegation – locally it began to be said that the club was at least financially stable.

It was also not forgotten that the Hall family and the Shepherds, Freddy and Bruce, had made money from Newcastle United. Freddy Shepherd's salary package for 2004 alone was £717,145. Douglas Hall's was £635,465.

The Hall family stake netted £55m. Freddie Shepherd's 28 per cent stake earned him £37.6m. Before those sales the Halls, through salaries, share sales and other routes are estimated to have received £36m from Newcastle United, the Shepherds around £8m.

There is still keen argument on Tyneside as to John Hall's involvement since he first began agitating against the previous McKeag family regime in the late 1980s.

One side says without Hall, Newcastle United would have folded and this debate would not be happening – and there are memories of the board Hall ousted and directors previous to that. Jackie Milburn showed the players' opinion of Newcastle's board in the 1950s and of the late 1970s Alan Kennedy says: 'After me they sold Irivng Nattrass to Middlesbrough for £365,000. Irving was a better player than me, a great player. They got nearly three-quarters of a million for the two of us. Unheard of. Where did the money go? I don't know. I'll just leave it there.'

The other side says the club became the Hall family's cash cow. How does Hall feel about this and the view that Ashley has been prudent by comparison?

'I think at times we took risks,' Hall says. 'In a sense it was all a calculated risk. There were times when you wanted a player but you didn't have the cash in the club, so you went to your sponsors. The Brewery did that, put money in. You wanted a player to win something.'

That ambition – 'to win something' – is remembered. The Hall-Shepherd board had faults but cold support for Newcastle was not one of them. On the day Newcastle broke the world record to sign Shearer, one director, Russell Jones, said: 'Perhaps people will realise now why we need a 75,000-seater stadium.'

It has fresh relevance as in 2014 the Newcastle United Supporters Trust discovered the land on Strawberry Place where the stadium could be expanded has been put up for sale by the Ashley regime. Ambitions have changed.

'I always wanted to see a team of Geordies because I felt there was sufficient talent here to get hold of and develop,' Hall says. 'My aim was to establish centres of excellence all around the region. I wanted an event where the player of the year was given something like the green jacket in golf. I wanted to lift the desire to play for Newcastle United.

'But you need managers who will play local players. You need a manager who will share that culture and you then give him time. It's an ethos.

'Nobody is interested in 11 Geordies anymore.'

And money?

'We're talking about business. I put money in, took the risks, you cannot have it both ways. Had I not taken the risks . . .

'This place [Wynyard Hall] became a guarantor for Newcastle United. When we wanted to borrow I had to put this up as collateral. We'd paid for this. So this was used to guarantee Newcastle United. I took money out [of the club] but that's the name of the game, capitalism.

'Let's go back. I did what I set out to do and I got the club to put shares on the marketplace – a million pounds worth of shares. I've got the leaflet here, remember that deal?

'Go and look at that, the share issue. What happened? The fans didn't buy 5 per cent. I had egg on my face. When I went into the boardroom after that, you should have heard what they said to me.

'My hands are clean. Yes, we got money out of the club. But we took the risks.'

MEANWHILE BACK IN DUNSTON, Kevin Keegan was on stage. Keegan was going though his career using a slideshow. There was a disappointing lack of Newcastle material but when some questions came from the floor, Keegan answered.

He said he had found Ashley 'OK' and switched to those who were around him. Keegan said that one, 'a former steward at Chelsea', had blocked his effort to sign Luka Modric. Keegan had persuaded the midfielder to visit Tyneside before signing for Tottenham.

Modric would have cost £18m, which cuts against the idea of Ashley prudence. This was the summer of 2008, Ashley was 14 or so months in.

Having appointed Keegan, someone who had left the club once before over the issue of control, Ashley gave Dennis Wise the job of director of football, which was immediately perceived as infringing upon Keegan. Then, instead of Modric, two little-known players arrived, Xisco for £5.5m from Deportivo La Coruna and Ignacio Gonzalez on loan from Valencia.

Keegan knew neither. James Milner was sold for £12m and if Ashley had a strategy it was difficult to determine. Keegan walked away and the next match brought the banner 'Cockney Mafia Out'.

From London, in came Joe Kinnear, who swore some 50 times at his first press conference. Ashley's popularity had nose-dived. He put the club up for sale. If Ashley had a calculated plan to exploit Newcastle on behalf of his retail business, this cannot have been part of it.

Nor did other behaviour suggest that. Ashley had made an impression as a kit-wearing fan-owner standing with the Newcastle support. He would be in the Strawberry pub just before home games kicked off when his natural position as owner said he should be in the boardroom.

He didn't want that. But now he had alienated Keegan and appointed Kinnear.

Results flatlined and Kinnear's health became an issue. Worn down by disillusion, Shay Given, after 12 years and 462 appearances, left for Manchester City in January. In February Kinnear, 62, fell ill. With eight games left, Ashley turned to Alan Shearer, who hoped to re-ignite Michael Owen. Wise left the building.

Newcastle were third-bottom with six wins. They won once more and, for the first time since 1989, since it all took off under Keegan and Hall, Newcastle United were relegated. It was on the last day of the season, at Villa Park, against a team containing Milner.

Owen had not scored for Shearer; Owen scored once in his last 17 Newcastle games. His agents instantly produced a brochure extolling his virtues as an athlete, ambassador and icon. He joined Manchester United.

Ashley had regrets but appointing Shearer, he said, was not one of them – 'the best decision I have made'. That was said in a club statement 48 hours after relegation but after one meeting Shearer was not spoken to again, and by August Chris Hughton was caretaker manager, then permanent manager.

Out of the chaos of that 2009 summer came a measure of stability in the Championship. Attendances did not plummet, many Premier League players remained and Newcastle were promoted. They also appointed Graham Carr as chief scout. Carr would become the de facto director of football, the man behind shrewd, cheap signings from France such as Cabaye, and was sitting beside Ashley at the Hawthorns the day in December 2010 when Newcastle lost 3-1. Two days later Hughton was sacked.

Newcastle were looking for their sixth manager in Ashley's three-and-a-half years. This is where Pardew came in.

Nationally, there was head-shaking. The external view was voiced by Alex Ferguson after Ashley had dismissed his first, Allardyce:

'When you analyse the situation up there, it is beyond belief. They have had two managers who have won World Cups – Jack Charlton and Ossie Ardiles – as players, four who have won the European Cups as players – Kevin Keegan, Kenny Dalglish, Ruud Gullit and Graeme Souness – and Sir Bobby Robson, who took England to the World Cup semi-finals. You would think one of them would have won something given the right time. I don't know what you can say about the situation up there but it is a strange club. I would say Newcastle are the most difficult club to manage in the game.'

IN DUNSTON the Keegan event ended abruptly, as if the lights had gone on at a school disco. His entrance had been that of a prophet, his exit was that of a performer, routine finished. No one was gulping for air.

But on the way out an hour later, there was a long queue. At the end of it, sitting in front of a formica desk, was Kevin Keegan. Men, and women, were bringing books, photographs, old programmes and other paraphernalia to be signed. Keegan was obliging happily. As Brian Clough said of Bob Paisley: 'Let's face it, this game's all about the fans. Not enough of our lot remember that. But Bob always did.'

Newcastle United's prime minister in exile signed and signed, whereas across the River Tyne the day before the real government was having a party.

It was Sports Direct day at St James' Park with the workforce bussed in from Nottingham and elsewhere and Mike Ashley himself in attendance. Steve Harmison and Graham Taylor were there. Flames lit the Milburn entrance. There were games upstairs and matches on the pitch, around which electronic hoardings projected corporate messages and one which declared: 'Mike Ashley's Sports Direct Army'.

That was not the chant three days later at Anfield. The away end was once again sold out. Despite being charged almost £50 to watch the final match of a season that had drifted close to futility, 2,800 still filed through Gates P and O to sing of their displeasure with Ashley and Pardew, to mock, with tedious repetition, Steven Gerrard, and to see Newcastle lose again.

Standing outside on Anfield Road before kick-off, we saw John Alder pass by. He was easy to recognize in his black suit and white shirt, his attire earning him the nickname 'The Undertaker' among Newcastle's regular travellers.

Alder, 63, had missed one Newcastle United game since 1973. As he and other fanatics would report, it was Watford away in 2006, the one time Newcastle won a penalty shoot-out. Alder missed the game because his mother was gravely ill.

Liverpool away would be Alder's last competitive Newcastle game. He was, as expected, at Oldham for the first pre-season friendly in July but two days later Alder and fellow fan Liam Sweeney, 28, were killed in the Malaysian airliner MH17 shot down over eastern Ukraine. Alder and Sweeney were on their way to Newcastle's friendlies in New Zealand. Footage from the wreckage showed Alder had books on Keegan and Clough in his bag.

The tragedy, which caused a generous, spontaneous response on Wearside, highlighted the scale of some fans' commitment and other fans' appreciation of that. Alder and Sweeney were part of the cultural bedrock of north-east football. Year after year they put money into their club; they did not take any out.

At Anfield they were part of an atmosphere in the away end was anything but harmonious. Pardew may derive some solace from the split. It was 50/50 with the younger element more anti-Pardew than those who had seen so much of this before. Maybe the latter recalled fifth-place in 2012 and Pardew being named Manager of the Year, or maybe they were just beaten.

There were other concerns, one of which is again about money.

In 1994 Liverpool were charging Newcastle fans £14; in 2004 it was £29; now it's £48.

This issue is not just Newcastle's support's, it affects the fans of all clubs with large travelling followings; because Newcastle fans are guaranteed to turn up in such numbers, Chelsea and Manchester United thought they could get away with charging £55 – and did – Man City £48, Tottenham £41 and Aston Villa £39.

The nearest games in the 2014/15 season apart from Sunderland will be at Hull, Burnley and Manchester. And they will be there, paying for it. If there is a constant down all the years at Newcastle United, it is the milking of devotion. The club's greatest strength becomes a weakness.

Happy Christmas 1974: Sunderland, second behind Manchester United in the old Second Division, prepare to meet York City. (Mirrorpix)

CHAPTER TEN
SUNDERLAND

22 JANUARY 2014. A midweek lunchtime at the Stadium of Light: usually the place is deserted bar a few staff coming and going from Black Cat House, the football club's administration block at the top of the massive car park. This has been Sunderland's home since leaving old, loved Roker Park in 1997. For nearly two centuries the wind whipping up from the River Wear swirled around Monkwearmouth colliery but now there is a 49,000-capacity stadium and it is the statue of Bob Stokoe running, arms out, hands up, into the breeze.

On this Wednesday lunchtime, Stokoe had company. There were thousands milling round the statue manouvering themselves into long queues waiting for the doors to open, rather than miners heading home after their shift.

These doors were on buses that keep arriving in the car park. Someone said there would be 130 of them, though it didn't look that many and when one o'clock came and went anxiety began to pass through the queues. There were 9,000 Sunderland fans desperate to get under way and there didn't seem to be enough buses.

But there were. Then the doors eased wide. There was no rush, no crush. The series of queues snaked in between the convoy. We got on bus 24; it left at 13.39. Only six hours and six minutes to kick-off.

This was the beginning of one of the best, and longest, days in Sunderland's modern times. No-one knew it then, as they stood waiting for the bus, but Sunderland would go to Old Trafford in the second leg of the semi-final of the League Cup, lose 2-1, and leave that stadium as finalists.

The score in the first leg a fortnight earlier had been 2-1 to Sunderland. It had been the latest instalment of a season that resembled crazy paving, which would lead to the club's first major Wembley final since the 1992 FA Cup, and to the brink of relegation.

The absence of cup semi-finals was one of the reasons why 9,000 tickets at £45 and up had been sold in a finger-click, another was that the club had supplied these buses free, a thank-you for what had gone on earlier in the season.

The sight of such a large red-and-white convoy departing Wearside for Manchester left an impression of what the club could be with success, or even excitement.

Sunderland, second-bottom of the league, were onto their third manager in under a year, and that could not be described as success – or excitement of the variety fans seek.

Gus Poyet had succeeded Paolo Di Canio in October and had taken charge of his first Sunderland game – a 4-0 defeat at Swansea – 94 days before Old Trafford. Poyet is Uruguayan and had no previous connection to Wearside, but he got under the skin of Sunderland quickly, and did not like all he saw there. He realised, though, the importance of this occasion to the people who buy tickets and the effect it could have on a set of players he was still getting to know.

The *Sunderland Echo* was sold outside the stadium, as were copies of 'The Final Whistle', the souvenir edition of the *Football Echo* that used to be printed on a Saturday night before the internet arrived and skewed local newspapers. During the 1930s those after-match *Football Echo* editions sold 70,000 copies across Sunderland and Co. Durham. The 1973 FA Cup final edition sold 95,000, the most ever, and here its front page was re-printed with its headline: 'They've Done It!'

As the bus left Wearside, all this history was putting people in the mood, as did an up-to-date quote from Poyet from his pre-match press conference: 'Celebration brings people together and then you feel for the club in a different way.'

It was simple but it was true. At clubs such as Manchester United the act of winning cemented bonds and created memories of days and nights spent together in jubilation.

This applied to the fans, players and staff and Poyet said: 'There's no better connection for a player and supporters than to win trophies. I would like my players to have that feeling. I want these players to remember this club from the inside.'

Some of Poyet's players would have 'that feeling' but what this night at Old Trafford reaffirmed was that the game is for supporters just as much as it is for players and managers. It is supporters' effort, their money, their noise that creates professional football.

Poyet grasped that. 'That 9,000 are going just confirms things for me,' he said. 'It confirms how big football is for this city and these fans.

'I'm feeling that every day here. They deserve something to cheer about. I am living in Sunderland and, because I can't cook, I go to restaurants all the time and I meet people every day and I know how much this club means to them. People talk about Wembley and how important it is to win this game and they don't want to know about the league. I'm the one bringing the league into the equation. They just want to go to Wembley.'

Having said that, when the bus pulled in to Wetherby services, barely an hour into the journey, it felt a very long way from Old Trafford, Wembley or any football atmosphere. The bus was full but it had gone quiet.

At 17.11, when the road sign read Sir Alex Ferguson Way, animation returned. Everyone skipped off, it was time for a pre-game pint.

We walked away from Old Trafford and slipped into the Railway Club on Chester Road. The colours inside were red, United red. The screens were broadcasting the latest news of United's signing of Juan Mata from Chelsea, who would land in a helicopter the next day at a cost of £37m.

David Moyes' programme notes referred to the future and 'preparation for the summer'.

Sunderland's team cost around the same as Mata. It contained three players on loan with the other eight signed by five different managers.

But Poyet had begun to mould something that looked like a team and Chelsea had been beaten in the last minute of extra-time in the quarter-final. There was a style emerging, an identity, and the fans were relishing it. Up among them, on tier two of the East Stand, kick-off brought nerves and a howl of noise that kept coming.

Then, eight minutes before half-time, United scored and the noise stopped.

The scorer was Jonny Evans, who had played for Sunderland as an on-loan teenager to great effect in two spells. In his first Evans played 18 league games and Sunderland lost one. Evans marked this goal in muted fashion.

The small consolation was that the aggregate score was 2-2. Sunderland were not behind. Stay like this and there would be extra-time, one goal and Sunderland were at Wembley.

It stayed that way, there was extra-time and as it ran to a close and a penalty shoot-out loomed, Phil Bardsley, formerly of United, decided to have one last blast. His shot, more a daisy-cutter than a blast, was straight at David De Gea and fans on tier two were in the process of formulating their disappointment when De Gea spilled the ball. It trickled over the line. Fans looked around at each other in shock. Then they erupted. Sunderland were 3-2 up.

The racket from the 9,000 burst all over Old Trafford. The yellow-coated stewards had a job stopping some Sunderland folk from falling from the steep seats. There was no time left. This was it. Sunderland were on their way to their first Cup final in 22 years. Then Javier Hernandez scored.

It was Old Trafford exploding now. Tension released, this was old-school United, never say die United. It was, as Roy Keane was prone to say, typical Sunderland.

Penalties. When Craig Gardner missed the target with the first of the ten, Wearside felt Keane's words again. There was no way they were going to win this. Then Steven Fletcher had his effort saved.

In between, however, Danny Welbeck, another who had been on loan at Sunderland, missed. But United took the lead through Darren Fletcher and even when Marcos Alonso swept the ball in, it felt too little too late. The long journey home beckoned.

But then Adnan Januzaj missed and Ki Sung-Yeung scored. Suddenly it was Sunderland 2-1 up. As the pressure to score intensified, Phil Jones missed and it only required Adam Johnson to drill the ball in and Sunderland were, now, at last, through. Johnson missed. On and on and on.

What next? A last United penalty of their five. Rafael da Silva needed to score to make it 2-2. Otherwise the visitors had finally won this endurance test. Rafael lacked conviction as he ran up and his low shot gave Sunderland goalkeeper Vito Mannone a chance. Mannone scrambled across to save and that was it. Mannone was the hero.

Of ten penalties in a shoot-out of immense drama, seven had not gone in. Sunderland won 2-1. The 9,000 went berserk.

As chorus after chorus of 'Oh, Vito Mannone' rang around the stadium, over in the United directors' box owner-chairman Ellis Short and club icon Jimmy Montgomery were beaming.

Montgomery knew what it was like to feel for the club in a different way, as Poyet had put it. Born in the town where he made a record 627 appearances for Sunderland, it was Montgomery to whom Bob Stokoe was running in 1973.

At 1.39 the next morning our bus pulled up outside the Stadium of Light, some 12 hours after we left. It felt more than half a day.

Stokoe was still there. On the base of his statue it says: 'I didn't bring the magic, it's always been here. I just came back to find it.'

VITO MANNONE LEFT HIS HOME near Milan not long after his 16th birthday and just a month after his father Michelangelo died of cancer. He could not speak English. He moved to London, to Arsenal.

Mannone had played at youth level in Italy for Atalanta and was signed by Arsenal for the future. However, Mannone found Jens Lehman, Manuel Almunia,

Lucasz Fabianski and Wojciech Szczesny in front of him at differing points and Mannone played 15 times in seven years at Arsenal. He signed for Sunderland in the summer of 2013, one of Di Canio's incoming group.

Mannone arrived as Simon Mignolet left for Liverpool. Mignolet had been Sunderland's player of the year and was part of a goalkeeping tradition that stretched back to Ned Doig at the very beginning of the club's Football League days. Doig won four league titles with Sunderland.

If the No. 9 is special at Newcastle and the No. 7 at Manchester United, the No. 1 matters on Wearside, though more quietly. Jimmy Montgomery is part of that and when Mannone was asked about it he mentioned his awareness of Craig Gordon, for whom Sunderland paid £9m in 2007, a British record then for a keeper.

Johnny Mapson was another. Mapson was a teenager when he won the FA Cup in 1937. He was at Roker Park for 17 years. Mapson was signed in haste after only two games for Reading because of what happened to another Sunderland goalkeeper, Jimmy Thorpe.

Thorpe worked in a Jarrow shipyard before joining Sunderland on his seventeenth birthday in 1930. He made his debut straightaway and by 1935 had established himself as Sunderland's number one.

Sunderland were to win the league in 1936 and Thorpe received a medal but it was awarded posthumously because he died that February three days after being kicked in the head in a game against Chelsea. Thorpe, a diabetic, had fallen into a coma after the injury and never recovered consciousness.

When thwarting a Chelsea attack by diving on the ball, three Chelsea players started kicking at Thorpe, as was legal then. The referee, a Mr Warr, waved play on and Thorpe stayed on the pitch. The game ended 3-3 having been 3-1 to Sunderland at the time of the incident and Warr needed a police escort from Roker.

Thorpe went home rather than to hospital. On the Monday, he collapsed. On the Wednesday he died. He was 22.

The Football League investigated and absolved Chelsea and referee Warr. They introduced a new rule: no longer was any player allowed to try to get the ball from a goalkeeper's grasp by using his feet. Barging was still allowed.

The rule-change was of no benefit to Thorpe's young wife May and their three year-old son Ronnie, or to his distraught parents. Thorpe's mother died within three months of her son.

Ronnie Thorpe grew up without his father and over 70 years on Ronnie's pain was still present as he brought out the scrapbooks in his house in Tunstall in Sunderland. He showed me a picture of himself, aged three, holding the league winner's medal awarded to his father.

'It's my mam I felt sorry for,' he said. 'She was told "You're young enough, get a job." There was some form of benefit for me till I was 16 and she got that to help bring me up.

'The club did nothing for us then. Only one man from the club showed any remorse, a Colonel Prior, there's a pub named after him in Sunderland. They hadn't sent a doctor to see my dad after the game or anything.

'Imagine if it happened today, there'd be a testimonial, this and that. There was none of that then because footballers were treated like cattle, lowest of the low even though there might have been 60,000 paying to watch them.

'The football authorities brought out a new rule, but because my Dad had been diagnosed with diabetes a few months before the Chelsea game, they tried to blame his death on that. That was their excuse. The diabetes didn't help him, I imagine, but then neither did getting kicked in the head.'

The Second World War and the passing of time meant that for decades Thorpe lay in Jarrow cemetery unregarded except by his family. When the Sunderland heroes of 1936 were lauded it was Raich Carter and Bobby Gurney.

Ronnie, meanwhile, followed his father into the shipyard, and had a trial for Sunderland as a centre-half.

'I remember I went on my bicycle to it. It was 'turn up and play' but I had that feeling, you know, that I never sort of fitted in.'

Modern Sunderland made good on previous neglect on the 70th anniversary of Jimmy Thorpe's death. The club impressed Ronnie with its kindness and generosity. His father's grave was restored and a new headstone mounted. Jimmy Thorpe is not forgotten.

VITO MANNONE HAD HIS 26TH BIRTHDAY at Wembley. He could do nothing about Manchester City's three goals, particularly the first two. Sunderland could have had Mapson and Montgomery alongside Mannone and still not stopped Yaya Toure's equaliser or Samir Nasri's bullet second.

Stokoe, Montgomery, 1973, was not equalled or surpassed.

Poyet had walked out alongside City's manager Manuel Pellegrini at the new Wembley. In 1973 Stokoe had walked out alongside Don Revie. The difference said much about the globalisation of English football and how it has affected the north-east. Poyet comes from Montevideo, Uruguay, Pellegrini from Santiago, Chile. The width of Argentina separates those two.

Stokoe grew up in a coalmining family in High Spen, Gateshead, Revie around 30 miles away in Middlesbrough. Poyet and Pellegrini probably got on better, though, because Stokoe and Revie had no northern brotherly love, they detested each other.

They had played against each other in the 1955 final, when Stokoe's Newcastle beat Revie's Man City 3-1. In 1972 Stokoe went public with accusations of corruption against Revie and Revie was damaged by them.

When Stokoe later described the scene in the Wembley tunnel in 1973, he said: 'I glanced across at the Leeds players and one of them mouthed obscenities towards me.

'As we walked out, Don Revie was next to me. He turned to me and said something along the lines of "Revenge is sweet, Stokoe". There were a few unnecessary expletives in his statement.

'I smiled nonchalantly at him and walked on, my hands behind my back as though I was out for a walk. I was wearing my tracksuit along with a mackintosh coat, as rain had been forecast and I am a practical man. I stuck my hat on my head, too. I didn't want to get a soaking. After all, this was Wembley.'

Stokoe's mac and trilby are in a glass case at the Stadium of Light.

Poyet had been asked if he was going to wear a hat. He said no and every decision he made that week felt justified by a first half he said went 'perfectly'.

Sunderland had alarmed City and impressed a wider audience on television by taking the lead through Fabio Borini, and by taking the game to opponents assembled at extraordinary cost, who had beaten West Ham 9-0 in their semi-final.

Judging by the correspondence from Manchester to Wearside the following week, also noted was the vivacity, colour and noise of Sunderland's thousands. Phil Bardsley, not an obvious well of sentimental thought, said afterwards: 'Going out for the warm-up was one of the most touching moments I've had in a long time. The roar was something special.'

Bardsley, like Poyet, like captain John O'Shea, hoped the display rather than the defeat would set the tone for the rest of the season. They were earnest.

As they spoke downstairs at Wembley, City players in sky-blue headphones sauntered by, and when the door opened where their team bus was parked a fan sang loudly: 'We are City from Maine Road.' It was Noel Gallagher.

Sunderland still had to go to City in the league and the table showed they were stuck in the relegation zone despite the praise for their League Cup effort. Everyone agreed, the next three home games were decisive. Sunderland drew the first 0-0 with

Crystal Palace and lost the next two, to West Ham and Everton. In between they lost at Norwich, Liverpool and Spurs and were knocked out of the FA Cup at Hull.

Just over a month after Wembley and the picture painted of a club reviving, Poyet studied the wreckage of a 1-0 defeat at home to Everton caused by a Wes Brown own goal. A fifth consecutive league defeat left Sunderland bottom of the Premier League, seven points off safety and Poyet sounded as he looked – beaten, puzzled, crestfallen.

He was standing in the narrow corridor beside the players' bar on the ground floor of the Stadium of Light. The bar door would open to unleash wafts of chatter that countered the lone-voice quiet outside. Poyet had stood here a few times already in his six months in post, but not as many as the reporters or the club staff asking and listening. It was intimate but not intimate.

Reporters asked about the future, immediate and beyond. The Man City trip was four days later, then Chelsea away.

The previous day, strangely, Poyet confirmed that two players, Bardsley and Jack Colback, would be leaving in the summer as contract negotiations had broken down. Both started against Everton and both would be considered essential – the right sort – if Sunderland were to bounce back from a relegation that had switched from a possibility to a seeming inevitability.

Now Poyet was pushed on his future, and in his lack of commitment to staying, there seemed to be a commitment to going.

'First of all,' Poyet said, 'it's difficult to talk now after a game because the feelings don't help to answer your questions.

'I think there's something wrong in the football club and it's not an excuse. I need to find that. If I don't find it, we've got a problem.'

Six words: something wrong in the football club. They went off like an alarm bell.

Twenty-four hours earlier, Poyet had spoken of the 'support' from the owner-chairman Ellis Short; now it appeared Poyet was publicly calling into question Short and the senior management's competence, as well as the squad's quality.

If so, this was not outrageous. After all, only nine days earlier Sunderland's failure to correctly register their Korean striker Ji-Dong Won the summer before had been revealed, and they had been fined by the Premier League.

This came after Sunderland had reportedly declined an offer of £5m for Ji from 2013 Champions League finalists Borussia Dortmund, an incomprehensible piece of information to Sunderland fans who saw Ji pull out of a free header in front of goal at Crystal Palace.

This in turn came a few months after the perplexing, short-lived appointment of Paolo Di Canio. There was a view, externally and perhaps internally, that there was a lack of football experience at the top of Sunderland. It seemed Poyet was saying so publicly.

Of the 'problem' Poyet referred to, he was asked if he knew what it was. Poyet could feel the wind blowing down the corridor, it was leading him in a certain direction, one which he half-wished to follow, one which he was half-battling against.

'No, I don't,' he said. 'I think I know what it is, but no, I don't. You know, you think "It's too many times, too many things".'

'I always say to myself: "What happened with Brucie [Steve Bruce] in the second year? What happened with Martin O'Neill? What happened with Di Canio? And what happens with me now?"'

'I don't want to get away from the responsibility because I am responsible. I am the first one. But who is going to be next? A, B, C – you can call him anything and the club will be in the same situation. I don't like it, it's not me. I need to find the solution and whatever it is, I need to put it there.'

Poyet would later point out that he was head coach as opposed to manager, insinuating a lack of authority.

There was no explosion in Poyet's tone. English is his second language but he understands it inside out. He was as calm as he could be in the circumstances, and he was not the first to be in these circumstances.

In the recent past Sunderland managers had questioned squad strength – notably Ricky Sbragia and O'Neill – and against Everton Poyet had just sent out a team which featured signings by Roy Keane, Bruce, O'Neill, Di Canio and himself. There had been an accumulation of players under a series of managers. It was constant revolution, not team-building.

This was put to Poyet, that others had tried and failed, good managers.

'That's what I mean,' he replied. 'I mean, it's sad because at the end of it, the one who goes is the manager. You try, you try, you try, you try but at the end the one who loses his job and looks bad is the manager. So I'm going to find it before I go.'

He laughed then, but the next question was serious, about whether he had 'the appetite' to find the solution required.

'I'm going to leave it a better club,' he said. 'I think we are a better club from the moment I got here. I think there is a better understanding of what our football is about, what we need to do.

'But it's not enough.'

In the space of six weeks, Sunderland had gone from the League Cup final at Wembley to this. They had scored three times since Wembley. Poyet maintained that the League Cup run 'helped', but it revealed something about his players.

'I think this team needs an electric shock.

'When last year, Paolo Di Canio got here, it was a shock. When I got here, we had a shock – we beat Newcastle and Man City and it was a big impact and a change of philosophy and way of working.

'Then we were so-so and we had a couple of results in December because Marcos [Alonso] was already with us and there were new players coming and the Cup was another shock that put us in a great situation. As soon as we didn't play anymore for that, it's back to basics. It's back to: Whatever you do, there is an own goal; whatever you do, there is a sending off.'

A radio reporter had just said to Poyet: 'At least you can rebuild', to which he now said: 'I don't want to rebuild. I didn't come to Sunderland to rebuild nothing, I want to be part of a process and to be something that gets better all the time.'

The conversation was such that the last question was about regret.

'No, never,' he said. 'No chance. I will never regret coming here.'

It felt like the end, the end of a period not long enough to be called an era.

With that, the corridor emptied, the huddle dispersed, and those who had been here before immediately recalled a day seven years earlier when Niall Quinn had stood in the same place.

Quinn spoke of 'a gremlin' in the club that day, 'something in the air'.

Sunderland had just lost 3-2 at home to Plymouth in the Championship. They lost the next game, too, at Southend. That left them bottom, 24th. Quinn's fronting of a recent takeover had seen him inherit the boardroom, the dugout and a squad that had been relegated from the Premier League with a record low 15 points. He was a worried man. Wearside had a few of them, its talking wounded.

TO MANY SUNDERLAND FANS, the Everton result was déjà vu. It was, as Poyet identified, about more than just a 1-0 loss on the pitch. Around the club there were bigger questions and no obvious answers.

It was akin to the last relegation, in 2006, when Sunderland won one home game, when Anthony Le Tallec was joint top scorer in the league with three, when Mick McCarthy's tenure came to an end, Kevin Ball stepped in as caretaker, when chairman Bob Murray had run out of steam. The club smelled of defeat.

In May 2006, though, the Quinn-led takeover was bubbling under and gradually materialised; eight years on, between Sunderland's defeat in the League Cup final and the Everton loss which took some back to 2006, Quinn sat in a hotel in Manchester and recalled that mood, and a season of rare and strange glory.

As these things do, the takeover began as a thought, in this case over lunch in London in February 2006.

Quinn had left Sunderland in 2002 after six years and over 200 games for the club. He was its centre-forward but more than that, he had developed into its spokesman, its champion. At one point fans had planned to stage a 'Saint Niall's Day' until he intervened.

After that loss to Plymouth the *Football Echo*'s headline was: 'Ain't Niall's Day'.

As his playing career approached its end, Quinn joined Peter Reid's staff at Sunderland. He departed when Reid's successor, Howard Wilkinson, arrived for his underwhelming six months. In 2006, Quinn was meeting chairman Murray in London.

'Bob invited me for lunch,' Quinn says. 'He wanted me to join the board of the club's Foundation. The club looked doomed but he wanted the Foundation to stay strong. The Foundation needed to be distanced from what was happening on the pitch.

'We met in London. During that lunch it became very obvious that Bob's energy had been sapped, all the work he'd done down the years had been forgotten. He was looking to move it on and had some interest from an American consortium. As the lunch went on I thought about how well Ireland was doing economically and about the possibility of me putting something together. Bob said his door was open. That's how it started.'

Quinn had recently relocated back to Ireland and started asking businessmen he knew there if they would be interested in joining a group that could take over Sunderland and restore it to the Premier League.

'The first two people I went to – Patsy Byrne and Jack Tierney – they put me in touch with the man who had helped J. P. McManus and John Magnier buy Manchester United – Denis Brosnan. The only time Denis could meet me was during the Cheltenham Festival and he, Jack, Patsy and myself met there.

'Denis told us to get a team together, he gave us a template. It was invaluable. I had a structure and now needed people. I had to explain to them that football might not be the safest bet. But Sean Mulryan came along, a massive influence. We built some momentum. Suddenly we were a viable alternative to the Americans.

'Between March and May we got a kitty of money, legal representation and set about trying to acquire what was a plc. Sunderland were on the Stock Exchange, subject to the Blue Book of Rules. We had to deal with the plc board as well as the football board. It was complicated. I was sitting up in bed at 4am reading about the pitfalls of takeovers.

'I rang David Dein, I tortured him. He was lovely. A director at Wolves very kindly told me about the mistakes he had made. That was so good of him. That was as good advice as any.

'Strangely enough, number one was: "Don't listen to the fans." That wasn't something I was going to say given I was trying to win them over. What he meant was: "Don't get sucked in".

'Eventually we met both Sunderland boards on a long day in London, in Covent Garden. They would allow the sale of the majority of the shares but not quite the 90 per cent we needed. But Bob allowed the takeover to take place in stages.'

This was July, the new season was a month away. Quinn, and the group known as Drumaville, were close to a formal acquisition, yet it was not done, the club had no manager – McCarthy having been dismissed in March – and there was an embargo on signing players, other than free transfers. Quinn was incoming chairman as well as de facto director of football. Soon he would be manager. It was messy.

Once the takeover process had the momentum Quinn spoke of, he had begun to sound out those who might become Sunderland's next manager. The first was someone who, like Quinn, had been at Arsenal before Sunderland, Steve Bould.

Almost 37, Bould had joined Sunderland in 1999. He played only 23 times before retiring through injury. He made an impact on the training ground at Whitburn, though.

'Before the takeover we approached Steve Bould,' Quinn says. 'When Steve came to Sunderland he made us more professional, he was as important as Kevin Phillips in those couple of years.

'The defence we now had needed shoring up and he knew 'the Arsenal Way'. Steve was the one early on, but he'd moved his family and had this coaching job at Arsenal.

'We were still trying to get the remaining shareholders to sell. Then we asked Bolton about Sam Allardyce, Bolton wouldn't give permission, and Martin O'Neill didn't feel it was appropriate as his wife was ill at the time. Then there was Roy and Roy, we felt, was going to happen. Then at the last minute he felt that it was going too quickly for him. So, after that Carlisle friendly, Roy wasn't coming.'

The Carlisle friendly referred to was on 29 July, the weekend before the season started. Quinn was in the dugout, he had veteran Bobby Saxton with him. There was no sign of a permanent manager but Kenny Cunningham, Robbie Elliott and Darren Ward arrived on free transfers.

Quinn was a reluctant chairman-manager who needed bodies. He had a conversation with Gary Speed about becoming player-coach: 'It was brief. Gary thanked me quickly, which gave me the impression that the Newcastle link would be difficult.'

The first game came – Coventry City away – live on TV. Daryl Murphy gave Sunderland a 52nd minute lead. It was sunny. Quinn was leaning on the Ricoh Arena dugout. Then with 20 minutes left Stern John equalised for Coventry and seven minutes later Gary McSheffrey scored the Sky Blue winner.

'Once Coventry equalised you could see a shroud of defeat falling around the players' shoulders,' Quinn says. 'Two or three games in, it was rampant. We realised then that these lads had been stained by the previous season.'

Wearside's atmosphere, lifted by Quinn's reappearance at the club, fogged over. One player asked to leave, informing Quinn that football in the north-east is too serious.

Three days later the new era had its first home game. Mikael Forrsell scored the only goal – for Birmingham City.

Three days after that Nick Chadwick scored Plymouth's late winner – prompting Quinn's 'gremlin' lament – and the fourth game of the season was at Southend. It was lost 3-1.

In early July, Quinn had spoken about the search for a new manager and said: 'I have to get a manager who really does stick his chest out and is passionate about driving this club back to where it should be and who the fans can connect with. What I can't have is someone who sees it as a stop-off point for another job. I need someone who wants the challenge of making Sunderland great again. I want to get everyone back on the magic carpet. I firmly believe I can reconnect the club to the people.'

Four defeats in, there were all sorts of jokes about that magic carpet. And it was to get worse. As Sunderland's season stop-started, three days after Southend there was another away game, this time at Bury in the League Cup.

Coincidentally Bury, in League Two, had started their season with four straight defeats and lay 92nd in the four divisions.

At least Sunderland had a new addition. Arnau Riera had been signed from Barcelona B, where he had been Lionel Messi's captain. Arnau was given his full debut at Bury.

'Arnau had played in a diamond with Lionel Messi and Cesc Fabregas,' Quinn says, puffing out his cheeks, 'so we were told.

'At Bury I was making my way from the boardroom to the dressing room to the dugout. I heard the whistle blow – I thought it was for kick-off – and as I got to the dugout, I saw Arnau walking towards us. I said to whoever was on the bench: 'Is there something up with him?'

'I think it was Sacko [Saxton] who said to me: "He's just been sent off."

Arnau's debut lasted three minutes. Bury beat Sunderland 2-0. Tired, drained, Quinn was close to tears afterwards. He had hoped to bring back Kevin Phillips to the Stadium of Light but that afternoon, Phillips joined Championship rivals West Brom and West Brom's next match was at Sunderland.

Quinn had to get to Manchester Airport that night for an early flight to London the next morning. Another meeting. Five games, five defeats. No magic carpet.

'The Bury chairman offered me a lift to the airport. He said he'd do it if we gave him our half of the gate.'

Watching from afar was Keane. So, too, was Michael Kennedy, the solicitor who represented both Quinn and Keane, even during the Republic of Ireland's Saipan debacle four years earlier, when Keane walked out on the World Cup and Quinn supported manager McCarthy.

Keane had then lacerated Quinn in an autobiography, calling him a coward, while Quinn was not shy in his criticism of Keane. It was hard to imagine them working together anywhere, never mind at Quinn's beloved Sunderland.

But Keane had also referred to 'big Quinny', hinting at a different relationship, and in his autobiography Keane had also spoken of: 'My own split personality.'

As that implied, Keane was hard to know: like another future manager of Sunderland, O'Neill, Keane could be both distanced and warm, sometimes in the same sentence. Keane attracted admiration for his principle, which he would demonstrate one unforgettable day at Barnsley; yet a year later, after three straight defeats, he would talk of acting. '"Fake it to make it," as they say. I was doing that yesterday.'

Soon Keane would be the face of ticket campaigns at Sunderland; simultaneously the glass in the window of the manager's office door changed from transparent to opaque.

And in 2006 Keane and Quinn had met again. The meeting was arranged by the Drumaville group and took place at Mulryan's house. Mulryan was a prominent Irish businessman.

Quinn has been asked many times about this reunion with Keane and on this day says simply: 'We'd made up in Sean Mulryan's house and agreed to be professional. We agreed the club was a sleeping giant and we might get it out of its slumber. We wouldn't interfere in each other's roles and we both stuck to the bargain. There are certain things I would do differently but it was a great time, a great experience.'

The men would never be pally, but nor were they antagonistic at Sunderland. There was a personal and professional separation, they spoke when necessary. There was 'a trust in the air' as Quinn has put it, albeit temporary.

And on Day One, for the cameras, there were handshakes and smiles and an acknowledgement from Keane that at times in the past he had 'crossed the line'. Keane was 35 and in his first managerial post. He was, and he stressed it: 'A manager, not a coach.'

But before Day One, there was a match on the pitch: West Brom, Kevin Phillips.

Following the Bury tremor, Quinn says: 'Michael Kennedy rang and said Roy might be ready. We'd already met in Ireland. He said he'd come up to watch the West Brom game. It was a Bank Holiday Monday. We'd lost the first four and were bottom but the players were magnificent. Roy came up for that game and sat in the crowd. The next day we sat down and spoke again.'

Sunderland won 2-0. There were 24,000 there. It was the second time in 17 months Sunderland had won at home.

Quinn left the dugout after that – 'sacked after a win', as he would say – and Keane took over. The overall club takeover was complete and Sunderland could buy players again. In the three days of the transfer window remaining, Sunderland bought six.

'We bought six players in that window – Stan Varga, Ross Wallace, Graham Kavanagh, David Connolly, Liam Miller and Dwight Yorke. Six players, six agents. It was chaos. My big mate Aidy in Seaham, he rang me at about midnight and asked me if there were any more players coming. I always remember him saying: "It's like when me whippet had pups".'

'But it worked, it livened the dressing room. As a club it showed we meant business. We then won Roy's first two games in charge, at Derby and Leeds, and had 35,000 for Roy's first home game, against Leicester.

'We drew and it was a little flat. Afterwards, Roy's assistant Tony Loughlin – really good lad – Bobby Saxton and myself were sitting talking. Tony said: "Draws are no good in this league."'

'Bobby turned to him and said: "Tony, there'll be a time when you get a draw and you'll kiss the ground. You've got to understand the importance of getting a draw."'

'Three months later, Burnley away, David Connolly scores an equaliser in the ninetieth minute and Tony runs onto the pitch and gets down on his knees. Sacko said to me: "Hey, look at him." That was a good memory. Bobby Saxton deserves credit for that season. To have grey hair around you in that situation was important.'

In the space of a fortnight, Sunderland had jumped from bottom to 14th.

There was then a dip. On Boxing Day over 40,000 saw Leeds beaten 2-0 at the Stadium of Light but Sunderland lost at home to Preston four days later and were 12th in the Championship, 16 points behind leaders Birmingham, managed by Steve Bruce.

While losing to Preston, Sunderland had agreed to sign defender Johnny Evans on loan. Between 1 January and 14 April Sunderland played 17 Championship games and won 14. The other three were drawn.

In February, at home to Derby, Miller scored a 90th minute winner to take Sunderland to within six points of Birmingham. There were 36,000 at the game, the club had rediscovered itself.

On the way out an old man skipped through the gates, a sight as memorable as any that season or any other. Keane was in his element; still, no one knew what would happen a fortnight later.

'We had just beaten West Brom away, won five of six, we were up to fourth and beginning to believe,' Quinn says. 'The board had made an effort again in January. We got Jonny Evans from Man United, Anthony Stokes from Arsenal.

'We were at Barnsley and took so many fans Barnsley moved their season-ticket holders.

'Pre-match, we're in the boardroom. I was called over. Roy had sent three players home – Stokes, Marton Fulop, Toby Hysen. They'd been late for the bus.

'They'd travelled down to the hotel but he sent them home again. I was thinking about how I'd explain the buying of Fulop and Stokes – especially Stokes because we'd had to fight off Celtic and Charlton for him – and he's sent them home. But Dwight Yorke was magnificent. I remember the fans singing 'Keano' that day.

'In the car park afterwards, I was on my own. The barrier got stuck and I got out. In the car behind me was Roy. Normally we spoke on a Sunday morning. He rolled down the window and I said: "Well done."

'He just said: "We needed a bit of discipline." The barrier went up and he shot off. I think that was his best day at the club.

'We still had a lot of work to do. But we got a late goal at Stoke next time and we were on a run. That was my golden time as Sunderland chairman.'

There would be twists – a 3-1 defeat at Colchester – but when Carlos Edwards scored an 80th minute winner in front of 44,448 in the last home game of the season, Sunderland had taken control of their future. A victory at Luton, already relegated, on the last day, would ensure promotion. Sunderland won 5-0. Birmingham lost at Preston. Sunderland had won the Championship.

'When we beat Burnley, when Carlos Edwards got the winner, there were 44,000 there,' Quinn says. 'It felt like the club was back where it belonged. Look at the team who played against Bury and the one who played against Burnley: two players played in both.

'We went down to Luton to try to win the title and I was informed that I had black trousers on with my blue suit. I didn't quite have the shoes on the wrong feet, but we'd been celebrating. It was great justification. People had said we were mad.'

Leeds United came bottom that season having been deducted ten points for entering administration. Leeds slipped into the third division, a fact Keane mentioned in his response to promotion.

'God knows what would have happened if Niall hadn't come into things: maybe Sunderland would have been slugging it out with Leeds instead of preparing for the Premiership,' Keane said.

'Niall has had a vital role to play. The club was on its knees, there's no getting away from that. For one reason or another, the heart of the club had been ripped out over the last few years. It wasn't just because of the way the team had been playing, off the field stuff didn't help either. The supporters were definitely disillusioned, but they always had a respect for Niall because of the way he was as a player and the way he conducted himself with his testimonial and all of that. When Niall came in, it got one or two people back on the good side of the club. That feelgood factor was always going to be vital.'

The unlikely reunion of Niall Quinn and Roy Keane – allied to money – had rescued Sunderland from Leeds United's fate: three years in League One. But Keane did not want to celebrate with an open-top bus.

'Roy, rightly, said we'd not have a parade around the town, we had to make a different kind of statement,' Quinn says. 'We went on a spending spree, if that's the right term. Roy was vociferous about bringing Craig Gordon to the club to do what Peter Shilton and Peter Schmeichel had done at his clubs. And Craig Gordon was great that first season.'

Three months after promotion, Sunderland bought Gordon from Hearts for £9m, the most a British club had paid for a goalkeeper.

It broke Sunderland's record too, for Tore André Flo from Rangers.

That was in 2002 as Reid looked for a Quinn-a-like striker. Flo made his debut in the Sunderland-Manchester United game post-Saipan in which Keane was sent off for elbowing Jason McAteer. After that game Quinn and Alex Ferguson exchanged words in Reid's office. Flo had scored; no-one noticed. He moved to Siena.

In the summer of 2007, with Gordon, Michael Chopra (£5m), Kenwyne Jones (£6m), Kieran Richardson (£5m), Danny Higginbotham (£3m) and Greg Halford (£3m) among others, Quinn understandably felt: 'We'd upped the ante.

'The board had put more money in. Then we went back to Luton, in the League Cup, with all these new players, about £40m-worth. Luton had been relegated, placed in administration and been docked points. We'd beaten them 5-0 three months earlier. They beat us 3-0. Greg Halford got sent off. *That* is football.'

It was one detail of a difficult season.

Although Keane was weekly box office, as predicted, his desire to rid Sunderland of the 'yo-yo' tag was under threat. 'Typical Sunderland,' he would say when one good result was followed by a bad one.

Sunderland survived that first season after promotion, finishing 15th, three points above relegated Reading. But there were larger concerns, as Quinn recalls: 'We'd given ourselves a three-year plan to get into the Premier League. We got up in Year One.

'But the Irish economy started sliding off the side of the earth. It was all rushed, so 18 months in, that's why Ellis Short came in.'

The Drumaville businessmen had bought Sunderland for around £10m – taking on £40m debt – and now Short, a Dallas-born banker living in London, upped his share to 30 per cent in 2008, eventually buying the others out in May 2009. The estimated fee was £22m.

Quinn and Short had first met at the Ryder Cup at the K-Club near Dublin in 2006. Short had been living in England for several years by then and had been bitten by 'the football bug' according to Quinn. Born in 1960, there were few other facts known about Short, though reporters were once advised that describing Short as a billionaire was more accurate than describing him as a millionaire.

Short's presence as sole owner and over-riding power on the board changed things, inevitably. Part of the change affected Short and Keane. In Keane's third season at Sunderland, the team were ninth in the Premier League on 25 October, the day they beat Newcastle at home for the first time in 28 years.

One month and five losses later, Sunderland were 18th and Short and Keane's relationship had stretched to snapping point. A few days later it snapped. During that spell, Keane grew a beard that drew considerably more comment than Alan

Kennedy's three decades earlier. Keane's last game, his one hundredth as Sunderland manager, was a 4-1 home defeat by Bolton.

Keane disputed the exact nature of his departure and brought legal action. Sunderland asked coach Ricky Sbragia to step up.

Sbragia's first game was at Old Trafford; Sunderland lost 1-0 in the 90th minute. They won the next two matches and Sbragia became Keane's permanent successor. Enough was done to keep Sunderland in the Premier League – two points above relegated Newcastle – but Sbragia saw faults and said so out loud. He would not be in post beyond the end of the season.

'Once Ricky kept us up it became obvious in the last few games that he wasn't enjoying it,' Quinn says. 'We were leading Spurs 1-0 at home and they equalised in the last minute. We'd have gone tenth with a win. Ricky criticised the players and they responded badly. We lost the next four. It became hard work. We got through it.'

When it came to Sbragia's successor, Quinn says: 'We'd always had Steve Bruce on the list.

'Maybe some would say we'd delusions of grandeur but we had good feedback from Louis van Gaal. I spoke to him personally a couple of times on the phone at home. One time his wife answered and told me: "Keep working on him, I want to go to England." That was adventurous but Ellis was all set to back it if it came off.

'That was after Ricky. Roberto Mancini's people got in touch with us at that time, too. He'd been having English lessons. It was interesting. We opted for Steve and he got us a top-ten finish. He understood basic things like needing goalscorers – we had Danny Welbeck for a while.

'But it faded for Steve, he left November-time. All the August window we had chased Kevin Kuranyi at Schalke. I flew to see Schalke and I met Felix Magath there. I always felt he was someone Sunderland could go to, to try to kick on. A couple of years later he ended up at Fulham. I left a card but he never called. I met him twice and thought: "This fella has something."'

CONNOR WICKHAM HAD BEEN IN LONDON that weekend of the 2014 League Cup final. He was there with Leeds where he was on loan, playing in a Championship match at QPR. He had earlier been on loan at Sheffield Wednesday and having joined Sunderland at 18, he was yet to make an impact nearly three years later.

Wickham was reported to have been a £10m teenager when he was bought from Ipswich but the fee was closer to £2m plus another £2m plus another £2m, all dependent on achievement. Given what happened when Wickham was recalled from Leeds, Sunderland may have had to pay out.

Wickham had been reasonable in the defeat against Everton and Poyet kept him in for the match at City. When City went 1-0 ahead in just two minutes, Sunderland's future as a Championship club looked assured.

Critics thought that was Wickham's level, but in the second half Wickham scored his first Sunderland league goal in two seasons. Suddenly he looked a different player and when his second came six minutes later the team bottom of the Premier League were leading the team destined to win it.

Then Nasri equalised in the 88th minute. Poyet's team had not done enough, surely.

It was Stamford Bridge next. Again Sunderland fell behind early, to Samuel Eto'o. But Wickham scored again and when Borini struck home the winner, Sunderland were only three points from salvation and it was Cardiff at home next. Wickham scored for the third game running and when Seb Larsson scored the only goal at Old Trafford a week later, the Wearsiders were out of the relegation zone.

It stayed that way, in fact it got better, Sunderland finished 14th. Before Manchester City they had lost five in a row; after City they won four in a row. From bust to boom.

In TV and Premier League place money, Sunderland earned £71.7m, up £28m from the season before. The season ended in a red glow, almost 46,000 seeing the last home game of the season, against Swansea.

Poyet had said the team required 'a miracle' after subsiding 5-1 at Tottenham in April. A month later the miracle had appeared.

He was willing to go along with that for a while but he also said: 'Can I go on like this for another seven months? No. I don't want to die. I don't want a heart attack.'

This was said for effect, though Poyet had been ill enough to visit hospital in Newcastle once in his seven months.

And then there were those six words: something wrong in the football club. The assumption was that Poyet was here to stay, but he was not making it. Had West Ham sacked Sam Allardyce, Poyet might have gone there. West Ham chose not to and on 28 May 2014 Poyet signed a contract until 2016.

'Stability is absolutely key to long-term and sustained success for any football club,' he said. 'This new contract gives both the club and me that stability.'

The sighs in the Sunderland boardroom must have been long and deep. Bruce had been dismissed in late November 2011. Had Poyet departed, the club would have been seeking a fifth manager in 30 months.

Poyet had been appointed in October 2013 following the rupture of Di Canio's few months on Wearside. This was a peculiar episode in the history of the club and not just because of the politics embodied by an extravagant Italian. There was his manner with the players, as expressed at his previous club Swindon Town, and there was the fact he succeeded Martin O'Neill. It did not feel like transition, it felt like a lurch.

In January 2013, a year and six weeks since he followed Bruce, O'Neill took Sunderland to Wigan and won 3-2 to move to 11th in the league.

O'Neill was getting his feet under the table and while the form earlier in the season had been in and out, the victory at Wigan made it five wins from eight. O'Neill, however, remained realistic about his squad, something he had expressed to Short at the end of the previous season.

The Irishman had been that odd thing growing up in rural Co. Derry, a Sunderland fan. O'Neill did not know just who Charlie Hurley was, he knew why he mattered. It had been hoped for years locally that one day O'Neill would manage Sunderland, to the extent that when he did join the *Echo* re-printed the headline of 1973 above a picture of O'Neill: 'They've Done It!'

At O'Neill's first game, against Blackburn, a guttural, terrace roar came up from the ground, one of the most memorable moments at the Stadium of Light. Having won two of their previous 14 matches, Sunderland won seven of the next ten. It was the O'Neill effect, or as Poyet might say, the shock effect.

It did not last, the season petered out and O'Neill could note that on loan Nicklas Bendtner was top scorer with eight. The board listened and bought Steven Fletcher from Wolves and Adam Johnson from Man City at a cost of more than £20m.

Fletcher scored twice at Wigan in that win that left Sunderland 11th, but he scored only once in the next eight games during which the team chiselled out a meagre three points.

Tension within the club was kept from public view. It was exposed after a 1-0 defeat to eventual champions Manchester United. In his programme notes for that game, Short had written: 'Right now, it is important for us all to be on the same side and get behind the team. Not being together will not help us to get results.'

Chairmen have to say this. O'Neill was sacked that night. The speed with which Di Canio came in said that he was already in the background.

There was turmoil in certain Wearside quarters. The Durham miners who have a banner on the stairs above reception at the Stadium of Light were angry.

If it is an exaggeration to say Sunderland and the north-east is leftist, it is left-ish. It could be coincidence that in the 1966 World Cup the USSR played four times at Roker Park and won all four games, though the club noticed and wrote about it. The Red Flag is a Sunderland anthem, if not for political reasons. The club had just appointed a man with a Benito Mussolini tattoo.

It is worth saying again that a fanbase has a variety of views and there were those who thought O'Neill and his team were sliding to relegation. They were pleased with a change, any change. That Di Canio's managerial experience consisted of two seasons with Swindon in League Two and League One appeared to be a secondary consideration.

But then everything was obscured when in Di Canio's second match, Sunderland went to St James' Park and won 3-0. It was a surprise – a shock – and rarely can so much have been read into one 90 minutes.

At 1-0 Newcastle's Papiss Cisse had a legitimate equaliser ruled offside. That would have altered the course of the game and the aftermath – the punched horse and the acclamation of Di Canio – but the goal was disallowed, Sunderland won on their rivals' turf and cool analysis was not called off the bench.

In their next away game Sunderland lost 6-1 at Aston Villa. Few mentioned that when they stayed up. No one made a T-shirt of that.

And it was the season to stay up as the new TV deal proved in May 2014. Sunderland's income from that stream alone was up £28.2m.

Perhaps a combination of relief and gratitude saw Di Canio and the club's new director of football Roberto Di Fanti sign 14 players across a range of fees, ages and talent.

'I prefer the word "refurbishment" rather than "revolution",' Di Fanti said. 'Our chairman said: "Listen, what I want is the big clubs to come here to Sunderland, to play at the Stadium of Light, and be scared of losing." In the past sometimes it didn't happen.'

On the new season's opening day 44,000 turned up to see Fulham win 1-0. Di Canio had four new signings in the team and another came off the bench. In his programme notes at this game, Short began: 'Last season was certainly not what we expected. It was emotionally gruelling for all of us.'

When Sunderland had one point from four games, it was gruelling again and then they lost 3-0 at West Brom, where the first goal was scored by Stephane Sessegnon. He had been sold by Sunderland 19 days earlier.

Sessegnon has a role in Sunderland's modern history but the story at the Hawthorns was about Di Canio. This was part of the problem. After the match, rather than seeing his players in the dressing room to discuss why they had one point from 15, he went over towards the travelling fans and made chin-up gestures. It smacked of modern celebrity, of indulgence.

By the time he got back to the dressing room, the mood inside had changed. The players were disgruntled with what they saw as petty discipline – the banning of ketchup and phones, the enforced silences as a show of professionalism – and made their thoughts known to the board. Di Canio was removed. The team had won one match under him in the new season. It was against Milton Keynes in the first round of the League Cup.

SUNDERLAND'S PROGRESS TO WEMBLEY was a great rush for supporters and players as well as Gus Poyet. But they still have not won that competition and the renewed focus on 1973 revealed it to be an oasis, one dating back to 1937.

The under-achievement is prolonged and, given the scale of latent support, can be mystifying. Sometimes people just shake their heads, at other times the attempts at explanation centre on wrong-headed priorities or poor recruitment or senseless sales.

The players of 1955, for example, can still become agitated when they recall how they were going for the Double in March of that year. They were second in the First Division and through to the FA Cup semi-final. A decision was taken within the club to prioritise the Cup, such was its standing. Sunderland lost the semi 1-0 to Manchester City and ended up fourth in the league.

The Roker Park match programme in those days carried the line on its cover: 'Only club which has never played in any other than the First Division'.

It had to be removed when Sunderland were relegated in 1958. It took six years to recover but when they went down again in 1970, the memories of 1937 were dusty. Only one season in the 1970s was spent in the First Division and it got worse in 1987 when Sunderland were relegated to the Third Division.

The Gateshead man who persuaded Kevin Keegan to go to Southampton, Lawrie McMenemy, had been hired at some expense. Wearside had seen the Keegan uplift on Tyneside and McMenemy said he was the man to take Sunderland out of the Second Division. The joke was that he did, just in the wrong direction.

Bob Stokoe was called back towards the end but Sunderland went down in a play-off against Gillingham.

The club's financial position was comparable to Middlesbrough's a year earlier when Ayresome Park had been padlocked. Sunderland narrowly avoided that same photograph.

Bob Murray's chairmanship had started, as had the search for a site for a possible new ground. But the club were still up and down, rattling around the second division, forgetting to register Dominic Matteo on loan and escaping a points deduction.

Sunderland didn't reach the Premier League until 1997. It was the year the club became a plc, valued at £47m, it was the year they left Roker Park. Everton were beaten 3-0 in the last league game. Chris Waddle was very good that day.

Peter Reid had been hurried through the door two years earlier in yet another late dash to avoid relegation. He kept Sunderland from the third division and took them to the Premier League. It was up and down and there was the Wembley play-off final 4-4 epic with Charlton in 1998. Sunderland lost 7-6 on penalties but from that loss emerged a stronger team.

It came up the next season. Reid bought conservatively but wisely and made a team from more than the sum of its parts. In January 2001 Sunderland moved second in the Premier League by winning 2-0 at West Ham. Reid had acquired the spine – Thomas Sorensen, Stan Varga, Gavin McCann and Kevin Phillips – for £1.9m.

Phillips cost £325,000 from Watford a year after Alan Shearer cost Newcastle £15m.

Expectations on Phillips were zero. He scored 90 goals in his first three Sunderland seasons, 30 in his first season in the Premier League.

Phillips formed a partnership with Quinn that made Sunderland competitive in the top flight for the first time in a generation. After victory at West Ham, had they beaten Manchester United at home a fortnight later, Sunderland would have been top of the Premier League.

The ground was full, the noise returned. In 1987 Sunderland's average crowd was 14,000, in 1997 it was 21,000 as Roker diminished. Now it was 45,000. There were back-to-back seventh-place finishes. Out of very little when he walked into Roker Park, Reid made Sunderland formidable in the Stadium of Light. He made them relevant, important again, and while he also made mistakes, without Peter Reid it is uncertain where Sunderland would have gone.

The shock, to use a word, is that within two years Reid was gone and so were Sunderland. They went down in 2003 with a record low 19 points. Having come back up under Mick McCarthy, it was a record they beat three years later – 15 points.

Which is where Quinn came back in.

Sunderland got back to the Premier League and have stayed there since. For all the flux at board level and in the manager's office, the whirring turnover in players, that seven-season stay is success in terms of the club's modern history. Gus Poyet's short reign has already brought a cup final, a miracle and a sense of renewal. If he finds the solution to the something that's wrong, Sunderland's future could be bright.

Monkey power: Hartlepool United mascot, H'Angus, whips up the faithful before the Division Three play-off semi-final against neighbours, Darlington. (Getty Images)

C H A P T E R E L E V E N

HARTLEPOOL UNITED

THE BANNER ALONG THE MILLHOUSE STAND terrace declared: 'Poolie Til I Die'. The flag in the away end stated: 'Sardines on tour.'

Monday 21 April 2014: Hartlepool United versus Morecambe, Monkeys v Shrimps, 19th versus 18th in League Two, but this was no meaningless end-of-season carry-on in the Football League's basement. The local paper began its back-page match preview thus: 'Hartlepool United have 13 days to save the club's Football League life.'

It could have sounded like overstatement from the *Hartlepool Mail,* but 'Pools' were two points above League Two's automatic relegation places and, 48 hours earlier, had lost 3-0 at Burton Albion. It was a sixth consecutive defeat and a performance so poor the manager Colin Cooper could barely speak afterwards.

As defeat followed defeat, and three became four became five, anxiety had grown within Victoria Park. After Burton, if there was panic, it was understandable.

Two years earlier Hartlepool were ninth in the division above. The club had been in League One for eight of the previous nine seasons and had developed a reputation that differed from the old one of penury and struggle.

Pools had finished comfortably mid-table in League One in 2012 so to come second-bottom in 2013 was a shock. It was one that reverberated through the next season and here Hartlepool were on the brink of a two-year collapse and an exit from the League they joined in 1921 as members of the original Third Division North.

The club had plunged before. It took them from 1921 to 1968 to win promotion – with a team organised by a young Brian Clough before he left for Derby – but the altitude of the Third Division affected Hartlepool. They were immediately relegated and the next season finished second-bottom of the Fourth Division. Today that would lead automatically to another relegation; then it led to Hartlepool's latest re-election plea.

Crowds dropped then and they had dropped again. Against Mansfield a month before Morecambe, the attendance dipped beneath 3,000. The club felt itself in jeopardy. It reacted by reducing tickets to £5 for the Morecambe game.

At the geographic extremities of the Football League, represented by places such as Hartlepool and Morecambe, there is always an emphasis on the enhanced visibility of being part of 'the 92' and what it does for identity. Hartlepool United's original crest had been a running deer – the hart in Hartlepool. It had been changed to incorporate a phrase, 'the town's club'.

But it is a two-way relationship: a town cannot say how much it values having a Football League club then not support it. In January 2013 Morecambe let fans in for free for one game so desperate were they to stimulate interest and now Hartlepool United, not for the first time, were asking the town to come back.

'I don't think a fiver gets you a lot these days, certainly when it comes to football,' Cooper said in his programme notes.

The offer worked. Nearly 5,000 turned up, a season high.

But those who did so were questioning why when Morecambe took the lead after 24 minutes and when Pools then had Simon Walton sent off. Losing 1-0, down to ten men and with the next match a 780-mile round trip to Plymouth, Hartlepool United looked bewildered. This did not seem a team capable of saving a club.

The lads on the Millhouse terrace were agitated. Walton's dismissal had occurred directly in front of them and it was a bad decision. But from their sense of injustice and scratchy noise came a spark. Fans were roused and the feeling spread all around the low-level stands. The aggressive encouragement, rising in volume, rattled Morecambe.

Cooper had to reorganise and sent on Jack Compton four minutes later. It was not a popular substitution: Compton had not scored since October. But he caught the swell of anger and tore at Morecambe. Six minutes later he volleyed in an equaliser that had Victoria Park bouncing.

Suddenly it felt as if Pools had 12 men. Marlon Harewood, 34 and a long way from the Premier League, was transformed. He was urging on the fans urging him on. Hartlepool had a mutual feeling and Morecambe were falling back.

Cooper made another change, bringing on Jack Barmby, the 19-year-old son of Nick. On loan from Manchester United, Jack Barmby had been given 4/10 in one paper for his brief appearance at Burton, where his failure to acknowledge the depressed travelling support had been noted.

Barmby was joining a beaten team then; here he was joining a team believing in itself for the first time in over a month.

Within two minutes of his introduction, Barmby collected a rebound from

Morecambe's keeper. A less gifted player would have snatched at the ball and had a shot. Barmby didn't. He dummied to shoot, then took another touch. It was one of those split-second moments in matches that linger. It felt like there was enough time to ask Barmby what he thought he was doing. But he knew. He had floored Morecambe and slid the ball in. Poise amid the noise.

Hartlepool were 2-1 up and the old Victoria Ground, hit by a Zeppelin raid in 1916 and by another German bomb in 1942, scene of so much drab failure and uncertainty, was rocking with joy. For a moment the club may even have forgotten that reparations claim the German government declined.

Hartlepool held on, safety was reached.

'One of the best half-an-hour's excitement you will ever see at the Vic,' said Tuesday's *Mail*, and inevitably there were lines about Cooper's gamble: a pair of Jacks.

Cooper played for Middlesbrough and Nottingham Forest and twice for England. He played against Brazil in the game at Wembley when Juninho scored. He had seen much in the game but was appointed Pools manager the previous summer following relegation and had been dragged downwards. After Burton he had asked his players for 'an unselfish act'. Now he was on the pitch being hugged by chief executive Russ Green. Players were either on their knees or punching the air. They were running to the terraces to join the celebrations there.

'It meant something,' Cooper said.

The scale of relief made this special. Days when fans back-slap each other out of Victoria Park are rare. This was an afternoon when, the club hopes, bonds were revived. Even as savage seagulls swooped in, the ground emptied to smiles.

Ten days later Russ Green was still cheered and spoke of the south-west inspiration.

'We made the game £5 a ticket,' he says. 'Part of it was an appeal to the town, part of it was that we had been to Portsmouth a few weeks earlier and it was like going to Wembley. They beat us 1-0 but it was their fans who won that game. The same could be said about Morecambe, our players could feel our fans and we won.

'It made us safe and it made us feel positive about the future. What came through against Morecambe again was just what the club means to the town.'

It was an occasion and a contest that refuted the need for Premier League 'B' teams. In midfield Hartlepool had a 17-year-old, Bradley Walker, who had been called up to train with England Under-18s. Walker won the Football League's Apprentice of the Year award. The previous year Pools' Luke James had won the same award. Hartlepool are growing their own, though Green was aware of local leagues in peril.

'I'm gutted,' he says about the loss of two local leagues, 'those are our grassroots. Football has become quick-fix and the professional clubs are helping to kill them.

'Why not let boys play for their local teams? At Academy level it becomes a bit of a selfish game. That's understandable, you're playing for yourself to make it; you're not playing with your mates. We have Development Centres but boys are allowed to come and go. There's a lot to be said for them keeping roots in local teams.'

The commercialising and professionalising of boys' childhoods is a common concern. But clubs must search, and sell. Hartlepool sold 20 year-old Jack Baldwin to Peterborough United during the season for £500,000. Pools hope they have struck a balance and have a new initiative aimed at the difficult 16-19 age group.

'Eight of our squad of 21 have come through the ranks, all local lads,' Green says, 'and we're starting a shadow squad next season for 16-year-olds and up. It's a 'second-chance saloon' – though it will be called Hartlepool United Elite Academy – but that's what it is, a second chance for 16–19 year-olds. They'll get education and a trade if they don't make it.'

Such plans could be put into practice after safety was assured, another reminder of what Football League status means in places dismissed as 'branch line towns'.

Hartlepool, the town, had been a target for *The Economist* months earlier and the club cannot be considered successful by Manchester United standards, but Hartlepool United have just had their most prosperous two decades. That, in part, is due to Football League status, as profile is what attracted the quiet oil company behind the club to first invest.

'I think the town is picking up a bit,' says Green, a Yorkshireman. 'There's new offshore work, there's been a resurgence in rig refitting and in that sector, there've been grants. *The Economist* thing was shocking. This is a forward-thinking town, you'd be surprised. It's not a deadbeat town, not at all.'

Green's defiance is admirable, yet Hartlepool is frequently cited among the worst three towns for UK unemployment and the club first felt a local economic bite not long after its formation in 1908 as an amalgamation between Hartlepool and West Hartlepool – hence 'Pools'. During a shipyard strike in 1911 the drop in turnstile income accounted for three-quarters of that season's debt. This is the club where they cherish the story of signing a Workington player, John Foreman, for '£10 and a box of kippers'.

Green has estimated before that the 'real' unemployment figure in Hartlepool is 'at least 20 per cent'. That was in 2011, not long after the club had studied decreasing attendances and offered a breakthrough '£100 season ticket'. It was a recognition of reality.

'We brought in an incentivised scheme,' Green says. 'A season ticket was £395. If we sold 3,000 you got it for £200; if we sold 3,500 you got it for £150. But if we reached the magical figure of 4,000, you'd get it for £100.

'One, it would generate income in the ground, and two, bring the atmosphere back. We did kids' tickets for £50, which is pretty good, £2 a game. Initially there was a surge and we got to 2,600. But it was sticking a bit. So we made the decision then to guarantee it for £150. It went crazy and we sold 5,900.'

Three years on the club was still offering reductions and the £5 ticket for Morecambe proved their worth.

'It's the secondary spend in the ground that goes up,' Green says. 'Our catering went up, our bar-takings went up, retail went up 500 per cent and it's still up.

'On the last day of the season we did the same £5 for Exeter City. It's a big thank-you. It's also for Exeter fans, travel costs a lot and there are tough times everywhere, not just in the north-east.'

Gestures must be subsidised. There was a time not so long ago when Hartlepool United simply could not have afforded this. In January 1993 they reached the fourth round of the FA Cup, a round they have never been past, but three days before Pools travelled to Sheffield United, they were wound up at the High Court in London.

After much scrambling, a local businessman of the old school, Harold Hornsey, stepped in. Hornsey started in the shipyard and worked his way up to own a clutch of hardware stores. He was known for his work ethic. In 1994 I interviewed then-manager David McCreery at the Vic and Hornsey stopped to talk. He had a brush in his hands, having been sweeping the terraces.

A Hartlepool man, Hornsey saved the club. But four-and-a-half years on from his takeover, it remained a shillings and pence job. An Aberdeen-based businessman, who had lived in Newcastle, Ken Hodcroft, heard that Hornsey might accept help. In September 1997, Increased Oil Recovery (IOR) Limited bought Hartlepool United. Hornsey was made chief executive.

A year later Peter Beardsley was playing in Pools stripes and by 2003 Hartlepool were a League One club. They reached the play-offs twice and the second time faced Sheffield Wednesday in the final at Cardiff. With eight minutes to go, Hartlepool led 2-1, only to concede an equaliser and lose in extra-time.

This was wild success in comparison to the 90 years before. It would not have been achieved without IOR's backing, nor would the day in 2013 have come when Hartlepool beat Notts County 2-1 and their scorers were Peter Hartley and James Poole.

IOR bought Hartlepool United because, Hodcroft says in the club's official history: 'At the time IOR was quite aggressive in the North Sea in the oil business. We wanted to raise our profile.' Hartlepool's MP was Peter Mandelson, whose profile in 1997 was distinct. Mandelson is 'president' of the club.

Alongside Hodcroft at IOR – or in the background – is a wealthy Norwegian businessman called Berge Gerdt Larsen.

It's said that Larsen's physical involvement entails a once-a-year visit to Victoria Park to play a match with staff, but Norwegians started appearing on the teamsheet soon after IOR's involvement and the shirt sponsors when club mascot H'Angus The Monkey stood for mayor – and won – were DNO. Det Norske Oljeselskap is the 'Norwegian Oil Company'.

In the club's centenary, 2008, the away kit was sponsored by Larsen Oil and Gas.

Without Hodcroft and Larsen, Green says: 'I dread to think where Hartlepool would be – look at Halifax Town or Stockport County.'

Green estimates that IOR fund the club to the tune of '£1–1.5m a year – every year', which is expensive profile.

'Running a football club is a good ice-breaker in business,' Green explains. 'There are boardrooms in Angola, Dubai, other places, with Hartlepool United shirts on the wall. That's because of IOR. It's been a loyal company.

'It got involved on the PR side, my remit now is to make the club break even, or even make a profit. Times are tough in the world but they're still getting something out of it.'

Hartlepool United: oiling the wheels of global trade, selling tickets for a fiver.

So many fans: Gateshead's best day for half a century, beating Grimsby Town at the International Stadium to reach the 2014 Conference play-off final against Cambridge United at Wembley. (Getty Images)

CHAPTER TWELVE

GATESHEAD

GATESHEAD HAD NEVER SEEN ANYTHING LIKE IT. Late February 1953, and for the first time in Gateshead FC's history, they had a place in the quarter-finals of the FA Cup. The opposition were Bolton Wanderers, Nat Lofthouse's formidable forehead and all. Gateshead had beaten Crewe Alexandra, Bradford City – Liverpool – Hull City and Plymouth Argyle to get to this stage and the run had inspired spectator interest in a club that, like its predecessor South Shields, had often struggled to overcome local indifference in the shadows of Newcastle United and Sunderland.

Now they were queuing around the block. Gateshead Town Hall became the distribution point for precious cup tickets and the queue stretched into and through nearby streets. It was a long line, one that contained many women and prams, as husbands were at work. At first it was orderly. But the appetite and anxiety grew and the queue broke. There was a surge and a young woman was crushed. It was not fatal, but she lost a foot.

On the day of the game Redheugh Park was sold out. Almost 18,000 saw Lofthouse score, a header. Gateshead lost 1-0.

Bobby Cairns, who played that day for Gateshead, was killed later that decade in an accident at West Sleekburn pit.

The achievement was in a Third Division North club getting to the last eight at a time when the FA Cup was often valued higher than the league title, and when there was nothing else, no League Cup, no Europe.

So Christopher Wood was proud of his team. He lived on the new Leam Lane estate and his wife Joan had joined the queue on his behalf that day at the Town Hall. They had a son called Graham who also followed Gateshead, but there was only one ticket.

In 2014, 61 years later, Graham Wood couldn't remember whether that was because they could not afford two tickets or because it was one per person. He did not mind. Two years after that Bolton game, Gateshead drew Tottenham in the

FA Cup third round and he was at Redheugh Park for that, along with more than 18,000.

Besides, Wood now had another ticket, this time for Wembley, and his smile was wide. Graham Wood had gone from Gateshead boy-fan to Gateshead owner-chairman.

There may have been around 56 years between his first game and his takeover of a club once again in financial trouble, but Wood had fulfilled the fan's dream: the professionals' shouts from the training pitch at the International Stadium were the sound of the difference he has made.

It was mid-May 2014 and Gateshead were five days away from the Conference play-off final at Wembley thanks in no small part to Wood's annual investment of £500,000 in his hometown club. They were five days away from righting a wrong that he also witnessed up close: Gateshead's spurious expulsion from the Football League in 1960.

'Our last crowd [in the Football League], I remember it well, was 2,366,' Wood says without recourse to notes or books. It was the recollection of a real supporter.

'It was a home game against Walsall, who'd won the league. I think there might have been some regret that the town didn't give the club the support it could have done. Throughout the course of that season we'd struggled and crowds had dipped below 2,000 at times.'

Even so, it is possible to see Gateshead's exit from the league as a sporting and economic injustice. Season 1959/60 was the second season of the new Third and Fourth Divisions, a national reorganisation having replaced regional Third Division North and Third Division South. There were new travel considerations.

The bottom four clubs in Division Four had to apply for re-election. In the previous system, it was the bottom two clubs from North and South. When in Third Division North, Gateshead had only once needed to apply for re-election – in 1937.

In the new Fourth Division's first season Gateshead came fifth-bottom, so no need to re-apply, but in season two they slipped to third-bottom, though they still finished above Oldham Athletic and Hartlepool United. Southport, who had been bottom in the inaugural Fourth Division and second-bottom of the last Third Division North, were again in need of re-election.

On paper Southport's case was much weaker than Gateshead's but there was also history that said that few clubs ever failed to get re-elected. That is why it was such a jolt when Gateshead were voted out.

'There was no build-up to it, no expectation,' Wood says. 'People were so confident Gateshead would get back in.

'In those days football was a closed shop and if you applied for re-election you were automatically going to get back in because of the old pals' act. There was a lot of criticism of that throughout non-league football. Some very deserving clubs just could not get into this closed shop.

'We broke that trend. There was a lot of regret then.

'The team that did get in, Peterborough United, they really did deserve it. They were getting huge crowds in the Midland League. Lovely stadium. They deserved it, but the team they replaced should not have been Gateshead.

'It was a combination of things, geography played a part, and we were never the best supported of clubs. In those days clubs shared gate money, so there was a financial implication. The counter argument to geography is that Hartlepools re-applied and not for the first time. They did get marginally larger crowds. Maybe that tipped the balance.

'Maybe Southport should have gone before. That was their third application in a row.'

Gateshead's home, Redheugh Park, was a run-down stadium with a dog track around it built on a piece of land known locally as Clay Hole. Travelling rivals did not consider it an attraction, less so when leading director David Absalom decided there would no longer be free alcohol available to visiting officials. The contrast between Redheugh Park and where the historic vote was taken, London's Café Royal, is unlikely to have gone unnoticed.

The effect upon Gateshead was immediate and traumatic. They had to play somewhere and became founder members of the Northern Counties League. At the same time they staged friendlies with Scottish clubs in the hope it would boost their application to join the Scottish Football League. It had 18 clubs in its First Division and 19 in its Second. Every Saturday, a Scottish club was available.

'We were trying to prove that we could hold our own in Scotland and we would have,' Wood says. 'If that had happened, we'd have been much better off. The Scottish League wouldn't have it, neither Celtic nor Rangers would have it and they'd a lot of influence. Ironically it's them who want to come to England now.'

Gateshead were in a spiral of decline that began to accelerate. When the Northern Counties League folded, they joined the new Northern Premier League in 1968; two years later they had to apply for re-election and were refused. Excursions into the Wearside League and the Midland Counties League followed. In May 1968 not even the arrival of the great George Hardwick could save the club. An England international who had played with such distinction for Middlesbrough that his statue stands outside the Riverside stadium today, Hardwick had been manager of the Netherlands national team - with Faas Wilkes in it – and PSV Eindhoven as well as Sunderland. After taking the Gateshead job Hardwick discovered the club "couldn't afford to heat the water for the showers" and had to "borrow a set of socks from Darlington." Hardwick said he "cringed with embarrassment". He lasted nearly two years, which is a tribute to him.

In 1971 the club moved to what was called Gateshead Youth Stadium. In 1972 Redheugh Park was demolished. In 1973 Gateshead FC went into liquidation.

To say that the story since has been one of a phoenix rising, of redemption and re-acceptance, would be misleading. For three years 'Gateshead United' gave it a go and it was not until the 1990s when local journalist John Gibson, with the economic support of Cameron Hall Developments, caused a revival. Bryan Robson's brothers, Gary and Justin, both joined Gateshead.

But the funding ended in 2003 and Gateshead were within an hour of folding again. Men such as Gibson and manager Derek Bell, with the notable assistance of Paul Gascoigne and Alan Shearer, helped raise funds to keep Gateshead going.

Graham Wood was watching from afar. His family – he is a third-generation boiler-maker – had left Gateshead in 1961 and Graham had become a successful businessman in Sheffield, then in America. In the late 1980s his boiler-making firm had been invited to sponsor Sunderland by Bob Murray and Wood, a Sunderland fan as well as Gateshead, joined the board at Roker Park.

He left for America in 1995, returned to London three years later and: 'When I heard that Cameron Hall had withdrawn their support from Gateshead, I contacted John Gibson. I asked if I could help, and then it goes on and on.'

Wood moved back to the north-east. 'I've got about 98 per cent of shares, there's a couple of hundred small shareholders. It's cost me about half a million a year for the past four years – we turned professional – about a million before that. If that income wasn't there, Gateshead would probably be in the Northern League, maybe a league above.'

Instead they were planning for Wembley. Under Wood and manager Ian Bogie, Gateshead moved from Unibond League to Conference North to Conference Premier.

In September 2013, with just four points from the opening six games, Wood appointed Gary Mills as manager. Aged 18, Mills had played in the 1980 European Cup final for Nottingham Forest against Hamburg in place of the injured Trevor Francis; of greater relevance, in 2013 Mills had taken York City from the Conference back into the Football League after eight seasons away.

Mills led Gateshead from 19th in the Conference to third. He introduced a patient, passing style while revealing some managerial tics that suggested he was once under the influence of Brian Clough. He took his squad to see the film *12 Years A Slave* and, when he could, Mills would take them to a favourite pub in the Midlands on away trips.

But as Gateshead climbed the table and gathered praise for their technique, attendances remained stubbornly low. There were 502 present at the International Stadium when Hyde United were the first visitors of 2014 and even when Gateshead were cementing their top-five play-off position in April with a 5-0 victory over Tamworth, the attendance was just 705. Those who do go regularly call themselves 'Heed Army'.

The stadium is regarded as part of the problem, though of course the proximity of Newcastle United and – Gateshead officials will tell you – the televising of Newcastle games in Gateshead pubs, are significant factors in small crowds.

The International Stadium grew out of the Youth Stadium thanks to Brendan Foster among others, who staged the Gateshead Games in 1974. Foster broke the world record for 3,000 metres at the stadium. But for football fans, the location on the Felling bypass, away from central Gateshead, is distant and unappealing.

Then there is the track around the pitch provoking the common comment that this is not a football ground, an opinion buttressed in season 2012/13 when the playing surface deteriorated in the wet winter to the extent that Gateshead were forced to play 'home' games at York City, Blyth Spartans, Carlisle United and one in Boston, Lincolnshire. The final home game of the season was at Middlesbrough's Riverside stadium. There had been no fewer seven home games at Hartlepool United's Victoria Park, Hartlepool perhaps remembering 1960.

Gateshead did well to keep going. They could have done with a morale-boosting game at St James' Park or the Stadium of Light, or both, but got neither.

'Hartlepool were brilliant, they've got to have a special place in Gateshead's history,' says club encyclopedia Jeff Bowron.

But on Sunday 4 May, with Grimsby Town the visitors in the play-off semi-final second leg, stated misgivings were forgotten as 8,144 turned up to see Gateshead win 3-1. It was a record crowd. The nomads were back home and it felt like home. Among them was local MP Ian Mearns, not in corporate hospitality but in among fans, frequently noisily. Mearns is that rarity: an MP whose connection to football is not a political stunt.

'It was wonderful,' Wood says of the occasion, 'something I'd dreamt about since 1960.'

The club has plans drawn for a new ground in the centre of town but after this experience Wood says: 'I'm beginning to think: "Why? Why do we need to move?"

'There are things we could do to make it better. There's this myth that's developed that it's not a football stadium, it is actually not just a football stadium and it has developed in the seven years I've been here. When I first got here the corporate facility accommodated 12 people, we'd try to squeeze in 14. We had 223 in for the Grimsby game. There's a roof over the far side now, 7,400 seats under-cover, the biggest ground in non-league football, would be one of the biggest in League Two.'

Defeating Grimsby left Gateshead just 90 minutes against Cambridge United from League Two, 90 minutes from reversing 1960. Gateshead were at Wembley in the Conference play-off final.

There were nine local players in the side that won against Grimsby and more on the bench. James Marwood scored a superb goal. Marwood is son of Brian, from Seaham, who played for England.

For Wearsider James Curtis progress to Wembley meant he would be breaking club history with his 505th appearance on the day he had been due to get married. A two-day wedding postponement would be worth it if Gateshead were to go back into the Football League. It was all anyone could talk about, 1960 and all that.

'In those days it was probably more prestigious to be in the Football League,' Wood says. 'Today the Premiership has changed everyone's perspective. In those days the crowds were more evenly spread.

'But it's still prestigious, very prestigious. I was talking to some people in Gateshead Council the other day and they really do think it would mean an awful lot to the town. I think Gateshead is getting more its own identity now. It used to be if you were away from the area you'd say you came from Newcastle, but you say Gateshead today.'

Gateshead lost. They are still non-league and 1960 itches still.

It was 2-1 to Cambridge. The collateral agony came from the origins of the winning scorer, Ryan Donaldson, who joined Cambridge from Gateshead and whose father Ian played for Gateshead.

Ryan, from across the Tyne, interrupted his celebrations to say: 'I wouldn't have picked to have scored against Gateshead. But I'll be a fan next year and I'll keep everything crossed that they can do it.'

How does it feel to be 92nd? – David Frost trains with Darlington's players at Feethams in 1973. (Mirrorpix)

CHAPTER THIRTEEN

DARLINGTON

'LIFE'S LIFE,' SAID RALPH BRAND, gazing soulfully into the distance on one of those yellowy nicotine-stained 1970s mornings. Brand was sitting on the wooden pews in Darlington's main stand at their ground, Feethams, which must have looked new when it opened in 1883.

Brand, a Scot who played for Rangers, Manchester City and Sunderland, had just been appointed Darlington manager, the club's fifth in two years. He was musing philosophically because he had been asked about sex, women, footballers, and the night before a game. Normally an inquisitor would be informed to go somewhere quickly for speaking to a manager in such a way, but it was Brand's first dugout job and he was unsure of his future given recent turnover. Plus, the question came not from a local-paper sports reporter, the question came from David Frost.

In 1973 David Frost was already famous and on the way to becoming The Man Who Interviewed The World. Four years before pinning down Richard Nixon, Frost took his LWT weekly documentary, *The Frost Report*, to Darlington to pin down Ralph Brand and what it was like 'to be 92nd', to live among the mulch at the bottom of the Football League.

There was a pause from Brand before he elaborated on 'nature's needs', and the pause was matched by the hush in the Pease Suite in Darlington's Dolphin centre.

Joseph Pease was one remarkable man, a railway pioneer on the Stockton and Darlington line and an MP who, as a Quaker, refused to pledge an oath of allegiance to Parliament or take off his hat when entering the House of Commons. Pease died shortly before Feethams was built, and what he would have made of professional football is debateable. He might not have been overly impressed that Darlington's nickname became 'The Quakers'.

Thirty years on from *The Frost Report* a group of mainly middle-aged men paid £2.50 each to fill the Pease Suite in the centre of town to watch a rare re-showing of Frost's week with the Quakers.

Frost had died six weeks earlier and his death prompted memories of a largely forgotten Darlington adventure from 1973 spent with Brand, his forlorn players and a pugnacious chairman named George.

There was a ripple of rueful laughter when George Tait was introduced to the 2013 audience as a 'new eccentric chairman called George'. George Reynolds would arrive decades after George Tait, indelibly.

The Pease Suite's silence was reverential as Frost, straightforwardly and without condescension, unfurled his time at Feethams. It was February 1973 and Darlington were bottom of the old Fourth Division. As Frost said: '92nd'.

The Frost Report took in the eight days between a 5-0 defeat at Chester and a 3-3 home draw with Cambridge. The footage captured a different era, one of non-stop smoking and a player's wife working as a garage receptionist to boost income. The chairman was seen getting into his Jag as Darlington's teenage goalkeeper Phil Owers stood on a snowy pavement waiting for the No 1. bus.

The journey to Chester took over ten hours there and back and Darlington's three travelling supporters were seen overtaking the team bus in their Vauxhall Viva.

Some of this life and work appeared miserable more than funny and long after Frost's cameras had departed Feethams, Darlington were still 92nd, in need of re-election, and Ralph Brand was their former manager. This man who played in the same Scotland team as Denis Law and Jim Baxter was probably relieved to have been dismissed by George Tait.

Darlington got their re-election in 1973 and again in 1975, and 1979 and 1980. But once the re-election law was changed in 1987, Darlington fell out of the Football League two years later.

Having been formed in 1883, Darlington joined the new Third Division North in 1921. They won it four years later and spent season 1925/26 in the company of Chelsea, Middlesbrough and South Shields in Division Two, finishing above Nottingham Forest.

The following season brought relegation and Darlington's next promotion would not come round until 1966. That was a one-season-only experience and by the time Frost landed from his other world, Darlington were back among the company they had traditionally kept.

Brand was one of 11 managers in the 1970s but there was no change in Darlington's Fourth Division status and in 1982 Sunderland and Southampton staged friendlies at Feethams to raise the £50,000 then needed to keep the Quakers afloat.

Then in 1983 Cyril Knowles, an England international who started at Middlesbrough before winning medals and fame with Tottenham – 'Nice One Cyril'

– was appointed.

Within two years Darlington were promoted again and they stayed up. Knowles had brought something different. But when they were relegated back to the Fourth Division in 1987, Knowles was sacked. The folly of that decision was emphasised two years later when Darlington were in a familiar position – 92nd.

Knowles went to rivals Hartlepool, where they named a stand after him. He died aged 47 in 1991.

A 35-year-old Geordie, Brian Little, was the manager in place when Darlington fell into non-league football. Little had come in towards the end and his remit was the future. The elegant former Aston Villa and England midfielder, who retired at 26 through injury, had been coaching at Middlesbrough.

Under Little Darlington returned to the League immediately and then won the Fourth Division in their first season back. If that was good news, the bad was that Little's work alerted Leicester City, who offered him their manager's job in 1991.

Relegation back to the fourth tier followed but with Jim Platt and David Hodgson in charge the Quakers came fifth in 1995/96. They had a combination of 20-year-old Robbie Blake and 36-year-old Gary Bannister up front and beat Hereford in the play-off semi-final. On 25 May 1996 Darlington were at Wembley.

Over 40,000 saw them lose 1-0 to Plymouth. And just as the players in Ralph Brand's day wondered where the fans were, Darlington's of 1996 must have wondered where they came from to be at Wembley. Although the team improved, and although Feethams was still a charming if slightly jaded ground, a walk around the boundary of Feethams owners, Darlington Cricket Club, the average attendance that season was 2,400.

Darlington came 18th, 19th and 11th in the next three seasons. Then one day a local man called George Reynolds went out to buy a new car and was told there was a football club he could purchase instead.

And so it began. George Reynolds was the surreal chairman's surreal chairman. He was 63-ish in May 1999 and had just sold part of his Co. Durham chipboard business to an American conglomerate for £41m. Later it would be said the figure was £32m.

But that was not the half of it; once Reynolds started to run through his life, that was barely a hundredth of it. If people wanted to inject colour into the black-and-white world of Darlington, it was as if Salvador Dali had just knocked on the door.

After his conversation at the Vauxhall dealership, Reynolds attended the home game against Brentford at the end of April. A Marco Gabbiadini goal secured a 2-2 draw and Darlington would end the season 11th. Things had been worse.

Reynolds had been recognised. He was asked for his autograph and left flattered. Soon he would be the subject of supporters' happy chants. As he went home Reynolds thought to himself: 'I had always been interested in football and had an executive box at the Stadium of Light. But could I own a football club? My only playing days had been in goal in Kirkham Prison in Lancashire, and I was never very good.'

The Quakers were about to have the most voluble chairman in Britain. Even discovering that the club's rumoured debts of £3m turned out to be £5.2m did not put off Reynolds. He paid it off, then announced that the plan for a club which attracted 2,514 fans to see Brentford was a 25,000 all-seater stadium in another part of town.

I went to see him three months later. George Reynolds was to be found at George Reynolds UK on the George Reynolds Industrial Estate. He wasn't wearing shoes, which is how he started off in life.

Born into poverty in 1930s Sunderland, this was a Dock Street boy who spent the years from eight to 16 in an orphanage that doubled as a workhouse. Reynolds left it illiterate; he fell into crime and acquired a Mr Softee ice-cream van in order to smuggle gelignite for his other profession, breaking into safes.

He spent four years in prison in the 1960s for that and other misdemeanours but, crucially, Reynolds learned to read and write in jail and, with a small fortune from selling contraband, he did what those in that situation seek to do: buy legitimate businesses and, hopefully, legitimacy. Reynolds succeeded, up to a point.

He reeled off three role models that day: Richard Branson, Brian Clough and Norman Stanley Fletcher.

'It was learning to read and write that made me dangerous, very dangerous,' he said. 'Prison was good for me. It rehabilitated me, I spent a lot of time in the library.

'I've been through it all. I'm not proud of what I've done but I'm not ashamed either. I may have used a crowbar to steal but I'm not like the plcs or the people in the City – they use a pen. I've been locked up for a lot less than what some of them do.'

The pertinence of that opinion of plcs and city crime was to grow as Britain changed, football changed, and as Darlington changed. It was all to go wrong and in acrimonious fashion for Reynolds and Darlington. Declared figures did not add up, the authorities began to investigate. By 2005 Reynolds was back in prison for defrauding the Inland Revenue of £400,000.

But in that first season, Darlington came fourth and met rivals Hartlepool in the play-off semi-finals. Darlington won. In May 2000 they were back at Wembley. They lost to Peterborough.

The new stadium was under construction. It was called the Reynolds Arena and in the summer of 2003, Darlington moved in. Six months later, with debts estimated at £20m, the club were in administration.

The £16m stadium on Neasham Road became the white elephant many said it would be. Somehow, under various owners and various chairmen, the club kept going. Under manager Dave Penney, in 2008 they reached the play-offs again. This time they lost to Rochdale.

But the next season brought another administration, Penney left, and on 8 May 2010 Darlington FC played their last match in the Football League. It was at home to Dagenham & Redbridge in front of 2,720 in a 27,000 capacity stadium. Darlington lost 2-0. They had finished 18 points from safety.

Under Brian Little 20 years earlier Darlington had bounced back, but not this time. In the second season in the Conference, they came 22nd, 114th in the English football pyramid.

They had come back from the dead to see out the season. On the morning of 18 January 2012 the administrator Harvey Madden announced to the small remaining staff that the club ceased to exist. Twenty minutes later two fans from the Darlington Football Club Rescue Group swerved into the car park in a Peugeot 308 listening to Mott the Hoople and handed over a bag. Shaun Campbell and Doug Embleton had brought enough money to reverse liquidation and see the club through the next fortnight. Someone cared.

The sign on the glass doors of what was now the Northern Echo Arena read: 'Apologies to our loyal customers. Our Sunday carvery has been placed on hold.'

It was a bit worse than that. Darlington FC, as a legal entity, as a going concern, was not on hold, it was no more. A new club, Darlington 1883, was formed but the Football Association took a harsh view of this. Instead of the assumed relegation to Conference North level, the FA relegated Darlington 1883 four divisions to the Northern League. And they no longer had a ground – the Arena was not theirs and Feethams had been sold.

Oh, to be 92nd seeking re-election.

✦

DARLINGTON 1883 won the Northern League in their first season and were promoted to the Evostik Northern Premier League's First Division North. They were based at Bishop Auckland's ground, which is not in Darlington. A former Sunderland player, Martin Gray, became manager.

But the finances continued to trouble. A Leeds United fan and businessman called Martin Jesper was asked to help out. Jesper applied an accountant's logic.

'The club had failed, it couldn't fund itself in the Arena,' Jesper says. 'A rescue group was formed. I was approached by someone advising those trying to buy the club. I looked, said my bit – that it wasn't sustainable in the Arena – and walked away. Around September 2012 I got a call saying the fans had raised money, bought the club but needed help. There was an interim board, everyone was volunteering.'

He was speaking in April 2014, still there, still volunteering. Darlington 1883's second season in Bishop Auckland was coming to an end and they lost a play-off to clinch a second promotion, which would have added momentum. As it is, the new club have agreed a ground-share back in Darlington with Darlington Rugby Club at Blackwell Meadows, but the news is not all good.

Without a transfer windfall three months earlier, Jesper says: 'I don't think the club would be here now. We got £75,000 from Fulham for Dan Burn in January. Honestly, had that money not come, I don't think we'd be talking now. People did not understand how precarious the situation was. We're talking days.'

He remains concerned by turnover, also by fatigue. Darlington's football club has had a draining effect upon its fanbase.

'So many supporters and local businesses had been burnt over the years trying to bail out the club, it ended up relying on the core 200 or so,' Jesper says. 'The economy in Darlington was stable in past times because of the mix of industries, but there are a lot of people on the breadline there now.'

The 'phoenix' club, Darlington 1883, is fan-owned and like others of the same structure operates in a different way from the traditional hierarchical boardroom. There are 221 fan shareholders. Democracy is welcome but money is again Darlington's issue.

'My concern is how far fan ownership can take us, because the reality is we're squeezing money from a disheartened economy,' Jesper says. 'And this is not an easy sell. We had to sort out the legacy debt first. It becomes very hard work because you have to keep going back to the fans, the same fans.

'It might be that you get to Northern Premier League level and you have to look at another model. Or you say: "Darlington will always be at this level." The potential is there to be as big as York City, or Gateshead, who are funded in a more traditional, benefactor way.'

David Frost uncovered a ramshackle club in 1973, but it played at a football stadium and was in the Football League. As for Ralph Brand, he's driving a taxi in Edinburgh. George Reynolds is back. He opened a pie shop in Durham.

And the stadium which brought down Darlington Football Club, the Quakers, is occupied by a different entity playing a different game and doing it well. Mowden Rugby Club is booming.

It's up there, Bishop Auckland.' Schoolteacher Warren Bradley, the only man to play for England as an amateur and professional in the same season, gives his pupils a geography lesson. Bradley played for Bishop Auckland before joining Manchester United in the wake of the Munich air crash. (Mirrorpix)

CHAPTER FOURTEEN

THE NORTHERN LEAGUE

SPRING-BLOSSOM SUNSHINE poured through the stained-glass windows of Elvet Methodist Church in the cobbled centre of old Durham. It cast a pinky glow on the football programmes laid with care beneath, blessing them. Rarely have Billingham Synthonia and Bedlington Terriers looked so pure.

The church held a congregation, a choir and a Sunday morning sermon warning of 'a world involved in the misuse of money' and the perils of searching for 'cheap grace'. Hymn 682 was sung. It contains the line: 'Shame our wanton, selfish gladness.'

These are simply not phrases heard in football, in north-east England or anywhere else.

But there were football men on Old Elvet, there for a service of thanksgiving. It was for the Northern League.

Formed 125 years earlier, to the week, in a room at the Three Tuns hotel, then across the road, the Northern League is the second-oldest football league in the world. Only the Football League is older. The Northern League is proud of its history and status.

Beginning on 7 September 1889 with ten clubs, the Northern League grew in numbers and success. Newcastle East End, and West, first played in the Northern League, as did Sunderland and Sunderland Albion, Ironopolis (Middlesbrough) and Middlesbrough FC itself. For two seasons, Sheffield United were Northern Leaguers.

When their first teams left for the Football League, in 1902 Middlesbrough, Newcastle United and Sunderland all fielded 'A' teams in the League, their reserves. Today they might be called 'B' teams. They finished first, second and third and in 1906 the Northern League decided it would be entirely amateur.

That status did not prevent 'expenses' being paid, which partly explained why an amateur club such as Bishop Auckland could afford to have some famous names on their books over the decades.

The Northern League supplied 24 winners of the FA Amateur Cup in days when the final would see 100,000 pack Wembley Stadium, and on ten occasions 'Bishops' were the victorious representatives. This is the club that gave the world Bob Paisley in 1939 and, in 1958, Manchester United three players after the Munich air crash – Bob Hardisty, Warren Bradley and Derek Lewin.

All three were England amateur internationals. Bradley would go on to play for England as a professional and gave his caps to Bishops during one of their later economic crises.

Crowds came to be measured in hundreds rather than thousands but there were still players of the highest calibre involved. Another who made the move from Northern League to England is Chris Waddle, who played for Tow Law before signing for Newcastle United in 1980.

Blyth Spartans were a Northern League club when they reached the fifth round of the FA Cup in 1978. They defeated Chesterfield, managed by Arthur Cox, and Stoke City, who had Howard Kendall in the team, before meeting Wrexham. Wrexham, about to become Third Division champions, were held to a draw and for the replay, Spartans switched the game to St James' Park, Newcastle. Over 42,000 went to see Spartans lose narrowly.

The Northern League's chairman Mike Amos could tell a thousand such tales from the League's back catalogue, including the one about Seamus O'Connell (Bishop Auckland and Crook Town) who scored a hat-trick against Manchester United on his debut for Chelsea in 1954 and lost 6-5.

Amos also likes the story of O'Connell strolling naked through a London society party prompting a posh lady to observe: 'Hung like that, you should trot.'

There is something about Bedlington's Dean Gibb being sent off in a penalty shoot-out that appeals, too.

Appropriately, at Elvet Methodist when Amos stood at the lectern, he refrained from re-telling these particular chapters of Northern League history. A fanatic, Amos chairs, organises and champions; as such he understands organised religion.

After the service there were pies and Bovril in the room behind the pulpit and later the same day there would be ale in the Crown Posada on Newcastle's Quayside. Amos recalled how after interviewing Bob Paisley at his house in Liverpool, Paisley drove him back to Lime Street station in his slippers.

Paisley, Amos reckons, has a claim on being the Northern League's greatest export. Paisley played for Bishop Auckland in the 1930s, his final match being against Willington at Roker Park in a Co. Durham cup final in 1939. After which he was formally signed by Liverpool.

'But then,' Amos says, 'there's Jack Greenwell.'

Greenwell has less fame than Paisley, probably correctly. But Paisley never played for or managed Barcelona. Greenwell did – for eight years.

Like Paisley the son of a Durham miner, Greenwell was born in Crook in 1884. He joined Crook Town as a midfielder but guested for neighbours West Auckland when they went to Turin in 1909 and won the Lipton Trophy – 'the first World Cup'. Ticer Thomas was also there, grandfather of Dave Thomas of Burnley, QPR and England. Today when West Auckland arrive at opponents' grounds in Northern League Division One, the sign on the front of their bus states: 'Winners of the World Cup'.

Three years later Greenwell, somehow, made the transfer from Crook Town to Barcelona and he invited his former club over for a tour. Crook Town beat Barcelona 4-2.

Greenwell played 88 times for Barca and then in 1917 became the club's manager. He stayed in the job for six years and invited Crook Town back. Crook won again, which is why at their Millfield ground out in the rolling Durham countryside there is a pennant and a trophy from FC Barcelona dating back to 1922.

After leaving Barcelona, Greenwell joined city rivals Espanol and led them to seventh in the inaugural La Liga championship in 1928. They won the Copa del Rey a year later. The miner's son from Crook also managed Valencia; he then fled Spain during the civil war and pitched up in Peru managing their national team. A unique life ended in Bogota, Colombia, where Greenwell was in charge of Santa Fe.

As Amos says: 'Unbelievable. It makes you realise that the world was a lot smaller 100 years ago than we think. But in an age when communication and transport were basic, Jack Greenwell was something special. His life was incredible, almost literally.'

Greenwell's Crook Town are still going. They finished season 2013/14 15th in Division One.

Today the Northern League has 45 clubs in two divisions covering Alnwick Town in the north, Guisborough Town in the south and Penrith and Whitehaven over in the west. The players are semi-professional in terms of practice if not wage, five promotions away from the Football League. Spennymoor Town are the most recent champions and have been promoted to the Evo-Stik First Division North for 2014/15.

The glory days of mass attendances are long gone – most clubs are happy with 150 paying £5 or so – but the league survives and its 125th year has given all a boost.

Amos is particularly chuffed that they found Charles Craven, the young engineer living in Darlington who started it all in 1889. Some genealogical detective work unearthed Craven's grave in St John's churchyard in Felbridge, Surrey.

'The whole anniversary season went tremendously well in that everything we planned, happened,' Amos says. 'Thanks to the wonders of technology we found the grave of our founder Charles Craven, and his family. His grandson Bob Rogers was in Hong Kong and he came over. That was brilliant. He was so excited, he didn't know anything about Charles Craven and he was so pleased that we had taken the trouble to find him.

'We had the ceremony in Felbridge and that coincided with Tow Law's 3,000th game, the 125th anniversary dinner and match. Bob came to it all. At the 125th anniversary match he bought 40 tankards for the players, all of this at his own expense. It was so gratifying.

'And to round it off we had the League Cup final at St James' Park. Had West Auckland won the FA Vase final at Wembley that would have been the cherry on top, but right from the exhibition at the National Football Museum in Manchester at the start, it all came off.'

The FA Vase has given the Northern League a greater profile, Whitley Bay winning a hat-trick of Wembley finals from 2009. Dunston and Spennymoor have won it since. West Auckland were beaten in the 2014 final, not long after Sunderland lost at Wembley and the week before Gateshead were beaten there.

West Auckland have their historic consolation, 'the World Cup'. In fact they won the Turin tournament twice, beating Juventus in the second final. It's why West have two stars on their jersey.

'We're not complacent,' Amos says. 'There's more awareness of the Northern League, we like to think. And there's a different emphasis – clubs are becoming community clubs with junior teams and kids' teams, 20 years ago there was hardly any of that. Some clubs are struggling of course and they're hanging on with pride. But we're not in a bad place at all.'

IT IS GOOD FRIDAY, and it is a good, sunlit Friday morning. At 10.50, outside a basic football ground on the edge of the Meadow Well Estate, scene of riots in 1991 that brought national attention to this part of Tyneside, there is a queue to pay £4. Queues are not a common occurrence at this entrance hut. North Shields are playing West Allotment Celtic in Northern League Division Two, six flights below the Football League – six. The attendance is 1,312.

The queue is still there when kick-off comes, not just because locals wish to see North Shields confirm their promotion and celebrate winning the Division Two title; the queue contains football fans from far and wide because this is the beginning of the Northern League's Easter Ground Hop.

The Ground Hop is the non-league follower's Easter pilgrimage: kicking off at North Shields on Friday morning, ending at Newton Aycliffe on Monday night with nine venues in between, it is a test of endurance that most people, including many football fans, would find incomprehensible.

It is a Northern League original. Initiated in 1992, the first Groundhopper extravaganza began in Peterlee and the happy experiment lasted until 1996, since when other leagues around the country have adopted the idea.

This is the Northern League's 125th anniversary re-run. There are 11 games in all with staggered kick-offs; the mood is convivial. Grounds can be ticked off one by one and there are a few men here – it is almost exclusively male – who look as if they like to tick off lists.

'Mad as a box of frogs,' is a remark you hear about some of the combatants, which would have been more appropriate were we in Spennymoor – they used to have to clear the pitch every spring, adjacent as it was to a frog's pond.

Over 100 pilgrims have signed up in advance to spend all day Friday, Saturday, Sunday and Bank Holiday Monday watching Northern League football, ferried to and fro on a bus that looks as if it saw action in Peterlee in 1992.

There are a lot of carrier bags, but then a snatch of conversation at Ashington versus Crook Town is, in a tone of disbelief: 'So you don't collect programmes?' Those bags are necessary.

There are rare match programmes to buy at each ground – at North Shields, where they were sold out before kick-off, an entrepreneurial type is hawking one 'signed by the teams' for £20. There is also some stardust. Malcolm Macdonald, president of North Shields, is in the crowd, while the club's manager is Graham Fenton, the Blackburn Rovers Geordie who invaded Newcastle dreams in 1996.

There are badges. 'I got two Blyth Spartans,' says a Birmingham voice. He may or may not be responsible for the Facebook page 'Non League Bins'.

Another turns up at North Shields in bare feet. He is wearing a '92 club' top. That shows he has already been to all the grounds in the Premier League and Football League. Now for the Northern League.

Three hours later those bare feet are at Whitley Bay versus Newcastle Benfield, but then the sun is strong on the coast. By 7pm, though, once the groundhopper trail had moved north to Ashington, temperatures had plummeted and you could see your breath, Mr. 92 has on a pair of sandals.

But he has seen three games, all good and competitive, and all well-attended. He has heard north-eastern vernacular but also accents from the South, the Midlands and 'the Germans' who have driven here to bear witness to Ground Hop weekend. In the Ashington clubhouse they see signed, framed England shirts from Bobby and Jackie Charlton, Ashington's most cherished boys.

And at Ashington there is another sight, unforgettable in its own way and probably the highlight of Day One, perhaps of the whole Groundhopper four days.

Midway through a game that finished Ashington 7 Crook Town 3, there is an interloper at Gate 5 at Woodhorn Lane. It skips in, whirls around, then takes its place alongside supporters leaning on the white perimeter fence. Some treat this with nonchalance, as if it's not for the first time.

It is a horse, a white horse with a brown face, just having a look.

Up there, there's often a horse.

ACKNOWLEDGMENTS

There are many people I've spoken to directly while researching this book and all have given their time freely. My thanks go to Mike Amos, Stan Anderson, Faustino Asprilla, John Barnwell, Michael Bolam, Prof. David Byrne, Vince Carrick, Andy Clay, Ian Coates, Alysha Cook, Chris Goulding, Russ Green, Stephen James, Martin Jesper, Sir John Hall, Aitor Karanka, Vic Keeble, Howard Kendall, Alan Kennedy, Grant Leadbitter, Dr Bill Lancaster, Rob Lee, Steve McClaren, Michael McGill, Keith Morris, Mike Mulligan, Denis Murphy, Northumbria Police, Graham Paisley, Dave Parnaby, Niall Quinn, Tony Richardson, Claire Robinson, John Topping, Graham Wood.

My thanks also go to the press offices at the clubs in the area, both today and over the years: at Gateshead, Jeff Bowron, at Hartlepool United, Mark Simpson; at Middlesbrough FC Graham Bell is due particular gratitude, Michael McGeary and Dave Allan; at Newcastle United, and at Sunderland to Louise Wanless and Rob Mason.

Staff at Newcastle Central Library, the Tyne & Wear Archive at the Discovery Museum and at Sunderland's Winter Gardens have all been very helpful.

Reporting colleagues are also due much gratitude, either directly over the last several months or down the years. Steve Brown, Paul Fraser, John Gibson, Philip Tallentire and Simon Turnbull have each been of great help in the course of research and, in particular, Martin Hardy and Andy Richardson.

In the north-east over the years I am in debt to Simon Bird, Bob Cass, George Caulkin, Carl Liddle, Gary Oliver, Paul Tully, Tim Rich, John Richardson and Colin Young. Apologies for any omissions.

Nationally I have too many colleagues to mention but, again, thank you. A long time ago at The Observer, Tony McGrath and sports editors, Simon Kelner and Alan Hubbard gave me a chance. Several others followed, latterly Neil Robinson and Lee Clayton. Malachy Logan and The Irish Times merit a special mention for a long association and the commissioning of a series of articles on Sunderland in 2006 which led indirectly to this book. Thank you to James Corbett at deCoubertin Books for publishing it and Sabahat Muhammad, Thomas Regan and Ian Allen for their roles in production.

So many books, newspapers, magazines and programmes have been read and consulted and every one has been valuable in some way.

Last, but obviously not least, my thanks go to all my family. For your tolerance.

BIBLIOGRAPHY

Allardyce, Sam "Big Sam" Headline Publishing 2015
Anderson, Stan 'Captain of the North' (SportsBooks, 2010)
Appleton, Arthur 'Hotbed of Soccer' (Sportsmans Book Club, 1960)

Bell, Colin 'Reluctant Hero' (Mainstream Publishing, 2006)
Bellamy, Craig 'Goodfella' (Sport Media, 2013)
Benyon, Hudson, Sadler 'A Tale of Two Industries' (Open University Press, 1991)
Bolam, Mike 'The Newcastle Miscellany' (Vision Sports Publishing, 2007)
Burn, Gordon 'Best and Edwards' (Faber & Faber 2006)
Busby, Matt 'Soccer at the Top' (Weidenfeld and Nicholson Ltd, 1973)

Candlish, Alan 'Ha'Way/Howay The Lads' (SportsBooks, 2006)
Carrick, McGill, Scott 'History of Wallsend Boys Club'
Cassidy, Denis 'Newcastle United, The Day The Promises Had To Stop' (Amberley Publishing, 2010)
Chapman, Herbert 'On Football' (Robert Blatchford Publishing, 2007)
Charlton, Bobby 'My England Years' (Headline, 2008)
Charlton, Bobby 'My Life In Football' (Headline, 2009)
Charlton, Bobby 'Bobby Charlton's Book of Soccer' (Cassell & Co, 1960)
Charlton, Jack 'The Autobiography' (Corgi Books, 1996)
Clarke, Ged 'Newcastle United, Fifty Years of Hurt' (Mainstream Publishing, 2006)
Clough, Brian 'The Autobiography' (Corgi Books, 1994)
Colls & Lancaster 'Geordies, Roots of Regionalism' (Edinburgh University Press, 1992)
Conn, David 'The Beautiful Game' (Yellow Jersey Press, 2004)
Cox, Jack 'Don Davies – An Old International' (Sportsmans Book Club, 1962)

BIBLIOGRAPHY

Dalglish, Kenny 'My Liverpool Home' (Hodder & Stoughton, 2010)
Dunphy, Eamon 'A Strange Kind of Glory' (William Heinemann, 1961)

Eastham, George 'Determined To Win' (Sportsmans Book Club, 1964)
Everton, The Encyclopedia (deCoubertin Books, 2012)

Ferguson, Alex 'Managing My Life' (Hodder & Stoughton, 1999)
Ford, Trevor 'I Lead The Attack' (Stanley Paul, 1957)
Freese, Barbara 'Coal, A Human History' (Arrow Books, 2006)

Gibson, John 'Kevin Keegan, Portrait of a Superstar' (Comet Books, 1984)
Gibson, John 'Soccer's Golden Nursery' (Pelham Books, 1970)
Gibson, John 'Spirit of Tyneside' (John Donald, 1990)
Ginola, David 'Le Magnifique' (Collins Willow, 2000)
Griffiths, Bill 'Pitmatic, The Talk of the Northeast Coalfield' (Northumbria University Press, 2007)

Hamilton, Duncan 'The Footballer Who Could Fly' (Century, 2012)
Hardwick, George "Gentleman George" Juniper Publishing 2001
Hardy, Martin "Touching Distance" DeCoubertin 2015
Harrison, Paul 'Northern And Proud, The Biography of Bob Stokoe' (Know The Score Books, 2009)
Hartlepool United, 'The Official History' (2008)
Hermiston, Roger 'Clough & Revie' (Mainstream Publishing, 2011)
Hopcraft, Arthur 'The Football Man' (Sportspages, 1988)
Hutchinson, Roger 'The Toon' (Mainstream Publishing, 1997)
Hunt, Brian 'Northern Goalfields Revisited' (2000)
Hurst, Geoff '1966 And All That' (Headline, 2001)

Inglis, Simon 'Football Grounds of Great Britain' (Collins Willow, 1991)

Joannou & Candlish 'Pioneers of the North' (Breedon Books, 2009)

Keane, Roy 'The Autobiography' (Penguin, 2002)
Keegan, Kevin 'My Autobiography' (Little, Brown, 1997)
Kendall, Howard 'Love Affairs & Marriage, My Life In Football' (deCoubertin Books Ltd, 2013)

Kennedy, Alan 'Kennedy's Way' (Mainstream Publishing, 2004)
Kennedy, Ray 'Ray of Hope' (Penguin, 1993)
Kuper, Simon & Szymanski, Stefan 'Soccernomics' (HarperSport, 2014)

Lee, Rob 'Come In Number 37' (Collins Willow, 2000)
Liverpool, The Encyclopedia (deCoubertin Books, 2013)

McIlroy, Jimmy 'Right Inside Soccer' (Sportsmans Book Club, 1961)
McKinstry, Leo 'Jack & Bobby' (CollinsWillow, 2002)
Maddren, Willie 'Extra Time' (Willie Maddren MND Fund, 1998)
Matthews, Stanley 'The Way It Was' (Headline Publishing, 2000)
Milburn, Jackie 'Golden Goals' (The Soccer Book Club, 1957)
Mortensen, Stanley 'Football Is My Game' (Sampson Low, Marston & Co, 1949)

Nett, Will 'My Only Boro' (Sixth Element Publishing, 2011)
Neville, Gary 'Red, My Autobiography (Bantam Press, 2011)

O'Farrell, Frank 'All Change at Old Trafford' (2011)
Orwell, George 'Inside The Whale' (Penguin Books, 1957)

Paisley, Bob, 'An Autobiography' (Arthur Barker Ltd, 1983)
Paisley, Family 'The Real Bob Paisley' (Sport Media, 2007)
Palmer, Myles 'Arsene Wenger The Professor' (Virgin Books Ltd, 2005)
'Park Drive Book of Football' (Pelham Books, 1969)
Pearson, Harry 'The Far Corner' (Little, Brown 1994)
Potts, Margaret & Thomas, Dave 'Harry Potts, Margaret's Story' (SportsBooks Ltd, 2006)

Revie, Don 'Soccer's Happy Wanderer' (Museum Press, 1955)

Quinn, Niall 'The Autobiography' (Headline, 2002)

Reynolds, George 'Cracked It!' (John Blake Publishing, 2003)
Robson, Bobby 'An Englishman Abroad' (Macmillan, 1998)
Robson, Bobby 'My Kind of Toon' (Hodder & Stoughton, 2008)
Rothmans, 'Book of Football Records' (Headline, 1998)

BIBLIOGRAPHY

Seed, Jimmy 'The Jimmy Seed Story' (Phoenix House, 1958)
Shackleton, Len 'Clown Prince of Soccer' (Nicholas Kaye Ltd, 1955)
Shankly, Bill 'My Story' (Sport Media, 2011)
Shearer, Alan 'My Story So Far' (Hodder & Stoughton, 1998)
Sinclair, Neil 'Sunderland: City and People Since 1945' (Breedon Books, 2004)
Smith, Bruce 'Arsenal Fact File' (Virgin Publishing, 2000)
Smith, Jim 'It's Only A game' (Andre Deutsch Ltd, 2000)
Sunderland AFC, 'The Official History' (Leighton, 1999)
Sunderland AFC, 'All The Lads (2000)

Ternent, Stan 'Stan The Man' (John Blake Publishing, 2004)

Varley, Nick 'Golden Boy' (Aurum Press, 1997)

Whittaker, Tom "Arsenal Story" Sporting Handbooks 1957
Wilson, Jonathan 'Nobody Ever Says Thank You' (Orion, 2011)

NEWSPAPERS

Daily Express
Daily Mail
Daily Mirror
Daily Telegraph
Evening Chronicle, Newcastle
Evening Gazette, Middlesbrough
The Guardian
Hartlepool Mail
The Independent
Independent on Sunday
The Irish Times
The Journal
Leicester Mercury
Liverpool Echo
News of the World
Northern Echo
North Mail
The Observer

Sunday Sun
The Sun
Sunday Mirror
Sunday Times
The Times

FANZINES

A Love Supreme (Sunderland)
Ex (West Ham United)
Fly Me To The Moon (Middlesbrough)
The Mag (Newcastle United)
True Faith (Newcastle United)

INDEX

INDEX

C

D

E

F

G

H

I

J

K

L